The Value of Homelessness

DIFFERENCE INCORPORATED

Roderick A. Ferguson and Grace Kyungwon Hong, Series Editors

The Value of Homelessness

MANAGING SURPLUS LIFE
IN THE UNITED STATES

Craig Willse

Difference Incorporated

University of Minnesota Press

Minneapolis

London

Portions of chapter 4 were previously published in " 'Universal Data Elements,' or The Biopolitical Life of Homeless Populations," *Surveillance and Society* 5, no. 4 (2008): 227–51. Portions of chapter 5 were previously published in "Neo-liberal Biopolitics and the Invention of Chronic Homelessness," *Economy and Society* 39, no. 2 (2010): 155–84.

Published by the University of Minnesota Press
111 Third Avenue South, Suite 290
Minneapolis, MN 55401-2520
http://www.upress.umn.edu

Library of Congress Cataloging-in-Publication Data
Willse, Craig.
   The value of homelessness : managing surplus life in the United States / Craig Willse.
   (Difference incorporated)
   Includes bibliographical references and index.
   ISBN 978-0-8166-9347-4 (hc)
   ISBN 978-0-8166-9348-1 (pb)
 1. Homelessness—United States. 2. Homeless persons—United States.
3. Housing policy—United States. 4. United States—Economic conditions—
2009– 5. United States—Social conditions—1980– I. Title.
   HV4505.W54 2015
   362.5'920973—dc23

                                                          2014046945

Printed in the United States of America on acid-free paper

The University of Minnesota is an equal-opportunity educator and employer.

21 20 19 18 17 16 15   10 9 8 7 6 5 4 3 2 1

Contents

Acknowledgments

THIS BOOK WOULD NOT HAVE BEEN POSSIBLE WITHOUT THE INTEL-lectual, emotional, and material support of so many people. The project was born in communities of housing service providers, activists, and organizers. I thank the friends and allies I made in those work settings for their camaraderie and commitment to housing justice. I especially thank the tenants and program residents I worked with when I was a case manager and organizer for all the ways they pushed back and reframed my sense of what I should be doing.

Formal research for this project began as part of my doctoral work at the City University of New York (CUNY) Graduate Center. I thank Patricia Clough for her dedicated mentorship and the countless hours of conversation that run through the pages that follow. For the ways she challenged my thinking, and offered me the space and time to answer those challenges in my own ways, I am forever grateful. From my time at CUNY I am thankful as well for the guidance and support of Neil Smith, whose own work deeply informs the present project and without which it would be difficult to think about housing in the terms we do today. Stanley Aronowitz and Barbara Katz Rothman also offered inspiring models of politics and scholarship along the way. At the University of Minnesota Press, I thank Richard Morrison for his enthusiasm and shepherding and the fun and thought-provoking conversations as the book developed. I feel very lucky to have worked on this project together. I am thankful to Jason Weidemann for patiently and expertly guiding me to the finish line, and to Doug Armato, Anne Carter, Rachel Moeller, and Erin Warholm-Wohlenhaus for their support and labor. Many thanks to Michael Bohrer-Clancy and Tatiana Holway for their thoughtful and thorough copyediting. I thank series editors Roderick Ferguson and Grace Hong for their humbling faith in my work, for their generosity of time and energy, and for the models they provide of thoughtful, politically committed scholarship and mentorship. Conversations with Grace challenged and inspired me beyond this book and I look forward to how they will shape my future work. The book also benefited from a residency with the Center for Ideas and Society at University of California–Riverside, and I thank the faculty who hosted me and provided feedback: Amalia Cabezas, Jodi Kim, Dylan Rodriguez, and Andrea Smith. I presented the project as it developed at the University of Washington Queer Worlds Symposium, Seattle University School of Law, Center for Ideas and Society, University of California–Riverside, and CUNY Workshop on Methods, and I appreciate the work of the conveners and engagement of the participants.

Greg Goldberg, Soniya Munshi, and Dean Spade have been my best friends in the academy, and I am glad for their contributions to my thinking but even more so for their company. Collaborations with Dean have profoundly shaped my intellectual and political trajectories, to the extent that the trajectories themselves have grown from our friendship; for this I am endlessly happy and appreciative. I am grateful as well for the support of my parents, Jeri and Dave Willse, and my siblings, Keith, Matthew, and Katie. "Home" has been given meaning by my extended queer family, especially Calvin Burnap, Lis Goldschmidt, Colby Lenz, KayCee Wimbish, and Dean, Rania, Katrina, Riley, and Kale Spade. Colby helped me both get into and out of the nonprofit industrial complex and has kept my housing politics growing and evolving.

So many other people have made my academic and political worlds rich and meaningful over the years of work on this book, and I thank all of you, especially John Andrews, Ted Baab, Morgan Bassichis, Brandon Bozek, Corrin Buchanan, Jeff Bussolini, Jordan Camp, Angélica Cházaro, Wendy Cheng, Emily Drabinski, Kate Drabinski, Lisa Duggan, Elizabeth Falcon, Jordan Flaherty, Travis Foster, Joshua Freker, Pooja Gehi, Preston Gover, Ismalia Gutierrez, Rebecca de Guzman, Ben Haber, Eva Hageman, Christina Hanhardt, Emma Heaney, Christina Heatherton, Lucas Hilderbrand, Matt Hooley, Lynn Horridge, Josh Howard, Ren-yo Hwang, Priya Kandaswamy, Brian Kaneda, Alec Karakatsanis, J. Kēhaulani Kauanui, Kerwin Kaye, David Kazanjian, Devon Knowles, Cayden Lovejoy and family, Lauren Jade Martin, Torin Monahan, Ananya Mukherjea, Mary Mullen, José Muñoz, Mimi Nguyen, Kaitlin Noss, Owen O'Connor and Sparrow Wimbish, Jackie Orr, Jackie Oster, Allison Palmer, Roy Pérez, David Proterra, Jasbir Puar, Durward Rackleff, Tareq Radi and family, Chandan Reddy, Jeanne Reilly and

Audra Willse, Emily Roysdon, Catherine Sameh, Rachel Schiff, Lucas Shapiro, Anne Simmons, Nikhil Singh, Sonja Sivesind, Erin Small, Sam Solomon, Eric Stanley, Zak Stutman, David Suarez, Emily Thuma, Zora Tucker, and Joe Ugoretz; my colleagues at George Mason, especially Denise Albanese, Johanna Bockman, Dina Copelman, Ben Cowan, Noura Erakat, Bassam Haddad, Roger Lancaster, Alison Lansberg, Tony Samara, and Paul Smith; and the past and present members of Fuck the Mayor Collective, Super 8/Revolting in Pink, the Los Angeles Liberation School, the Coalition for Nonprofit Housing and Economic Development Learning Circle on Gentrification and Resistance, the Sylvia Rivera Law Project, and George Mason University Students Against Israeli Apartheid.

Housing and Other Monsters

The ghost or the apparition is one form by which something
lost, or barely visible, or seemingly not there to our supposedly
well-trained eyes, makes itself known or apparent to us, in its
own way, of course. The way of the ghost is haunting, and
haunting is a very particular way of knowing what has happened
or is happening. Being haunted draws us affectively, sometimes
against our will and always a bit magically, into the structure
of feeling of a reality we come to experience, not as cold
knowledge, but as a transformative recognition.
—Avery Gordon, *Ghostly Matters*

An important step in getting rid of monsters is to stop thinking
of them as monsters.
—*The Housing Monster*

WHAT IS A HOUSE? WHAT IS A HOME?
We know a home is not just a house. Meaning, memory, ritual, the
production of domesticity and its relationships to gender, sexuality, ethnicity, family, labor, the nation—all this makes a home and is made by
a home. The home is an active symbolic, a space for living inside. A home
is nonetheless embedded in the built form of the house and its neighborhood, both of which exert structural force, another affective materiality
that enmeshes with the symbolic. The grid of rooms within a house, the
grid of houses along a street, the facilitation and restriction of movement through those grids—all this, too, must be kept in mind.

I want to show how this house and this home, these congealments
of forces that mold and modulate bodies, individuals, and collectivities,
are situated as well in a larger technical system for sorting and managing
populations. A shorthand term for this system could be "housing." As a
system, housing is bigger than any one house or home. At the same time,
housing is produced in part through all those specific and real houses and
homes, and constituted as well by geography, capital investments and

withdrawals, social policy, and legal frameworks. A house or a home is an extraction from this technical system called "housing," an actualization of the political, economic, and social forces that swirl around inside the system. A house is not only a building, and it is not only a place where meaning is made and constrained. As this book shows, a house is a technology for the organization and distribution of life, health, illness, and death. "The housing monster": a house is a thing that makes live and lets die.[1]

And so we can ask, what is homelessness, to live without a home?

To be without a house, to be homeless, is not only to be not-housed, to be in nothing, outside housing. Quite the opposite. It is to be very much caught inside this monster that distributes life chances and death likelihoods. This is a system in which everyone is caught, including those of us who are housed. To live without a house, or without the guarantee of continued access to a house, is to be made especially vulnerable in this system of housing, to be exposed to the worst of its violence. This violent exposure is a condition we can describe as "housing insecurity." To live subject to housing insecurity is also to endure the making insecure of health and life that accompanies a lack of safe and stable housing.

The systemic nature of housing insecurity is masked by the objectifying work of the term "the homeless." When we speak of "the homeless," we mobilize a pathological category that directs attention to an individual, as if living without housing is a personal experience rather than a social phenomenon.[2] Instead, we might talk in terms of "housing deprivation." This phrase expresses that living without housing is systemically produced and must be understood as the active taking away of shelter, as the social making of house-less lives. "Homelessness" is a productive deprivation. Housing insecurity and housing deprivation mark out some populations for the probability of enduring a life without housing, denied the safety and health that a home helps secure. Housing draws from already existing racial subordinations and entrenches and intensifies the death-making effects of those racisms, and so this "some populations" is neither arbitrary nor accidental. Ruth Wilson Gilmore describes racism as "the state-sanctioned or extralegal production and exploitation of group-differentiated vulnerability to premature death."[3] As we will see, housing operates through systems of racialized subordination, to make and remake racism in these terms of likelihood that some will live and others will die.

If we most often think of housing in terms of the present—the answer to the question, "Where do you live?"—and if sociocultural approaches to space and place ask us to think of the presence of the past, then thinking of systems of housing insecurity and housing deprivation, of a house as a technology that makes live and lets die, turns attention to the future. The house generates inside and outside of it possibilities for life and experiences of near death. Housing insecurity and housing deprivation draw some futures close—shortened life spans, illness, suffering—and foreclose the likelihood of other possible futures. "Homelessness," far from signifying lack, is a crowded house, full of so much death and disease that there is hardly room enough for what should be a great excess of social and political shame.

In the summer of 1998, one year out of college, with few connections and little sense of direction, I moved to Los Angeles. I worked at a number of jobs I more or less fell into—first in a bagel shop, which I left after a short while, and then at a café. I enjoyed my job at the café, especially the solo opening shifts. I would spend those quiet mornings getting the shop ready for the day, pausing in my prep tasks as members of the twelve-step groups that met at the nearby Metropolitan Community Church wandered in. Those early morning patrons would leave half-smoked cigarettes hanging from the edge of an outdoor table and grab steaming cups of black coffee to take back to their meetings. I worked at the café until it went out of business a few months later, at which point I took on a variety of temp jobs, including one stint as a balloon handler in a parade through Beverly Hills. The parade took place on the Friday after Thanksgiving to kick off one of the biggest shopping days of the year. Short on volunteers, the event coordinators resorted to hiring participants through temp agencies to join the little kids costumed in giant shopping bags. Accompanying the shopping bag children and us hourly waged balloon handlers, local families inched slowly down the parade route in convertible Cadillacs, waving gauzily at the scant crowds on the sidewalks.

Absent any real sense of what I could or should do for work post-college, my life may have continued down this aimless streamer- and shopper-lined path if I were not suddenly hired for a job I had interviewed for a few months earlier. The job involved providing direct supervision to the residents of a transitional living program. Transitional living programs are what they sound like, a transition from one thing to another—generally, from an unhoused or unstable living situation into an independently maintained private home. Transitional living programs differ from both shelters (which are meant to provide emergency, short-term housing) and supportive housing (designed as long-term housing for people who, due to physical or psychiatric disability, are deemed incapable of maintaining their own housing).

The transitional living program that hired me provided shelter and case management services for people aged eighteen to twenty-two, targeting in particular housing-deprived youth who identified as lesbian, gay, bisexual, queer, or transgender. Residents could stay in the program for a total of eighteen months, presumably enough time to prepare for living on their own. I had found the job posting on a bulletin board at the LGBT community center that ran the program. I didn't have any social service experience, or much knowledge of homelessness, but in the year before coming to California, while living in New York City, I was involved in a variety of queer activist projects connected to broader issues of social, economic, and racial justice. In these settings, I began to learn about issues of housing and homelessness, and their connection to gentrification, racial profiling, and then-mayor Rudolph Giuliani's "quality of life" crackdowns.[4] At one meeting of activists, we discussed an organizing campaign launched by a group of people living in city-run shelters. I remember that I didn't understand how homeless people could possibly initiate community-organizing efforts, and in my mind I pictured a Hollywood-derived gathering beneath a highway overpass, men standing with open palms around a metal barrel glowing with fire.

After a two-day training for new hires, which focused on program rules and conflict resolution, I started a part-time mix of on-call shifts. I usually worked in the evenings (coming in around four o'clock, leaving around midnight) or during the graveyard hours overnight. Providing direct supervision was the lowest-paid position in the program. Despite management proclamations to the contrary, it was also the least esteemed. Though we had by far the most contact with the residents and were most frequently required to diffuse the volatile confrontations that

4

can take place in close living quarters, the bulk of the direct supervision in the "house," as it was called, was performed by people like me—inexperienced in social work and often quite young. White people did not make up the majority of house staff, though we may have been the most represented racial group. Like me, many of my coworkers arrived at the house motivated by a desire to work in a queer environment. We were looking for friends, dates, and connections to some larger community.

Caseworkers, program managers, and staff therapists worked on the other side of a locked door, the "office" side. Those from the office side visited the house throughout the day to track down errant residents or check on staff and were available by pager during evening, overnight, and weekend shifts. When I started my job, only one staff member on the office side was not white, although a second person of color was promoted over from the house during my time there.

Like the quiet mornings at the café, quiet late evenings, spent checking off chores and chatting with residents as they prepared for bed, were my favorite times in the house. I also enjoyed hanging out in the living room with residents in the afternoon. They would play over and over again the same VHS recordings of Ricki Lake and Maury Povich talk shows, shouting at the screen and parodying their favorite parts. I generally found the residents likeable and interesting and funny. I think they found me serious and perhaps a bit severe, or at least that is how I felt about myself. I put great effort into maintaining professional boundaries, politely but firmly diverting any conversation about my personal life toward other topics and reminding residents frequently of our different roles in that setting.[5]

Over the next year and a half, I went through a pretty quick series of promotions, moving from on-call, part-time house staff (the entry-point into the organization for almost all employees) to a permanent position, and then to the most desirable permanent house position—Monday through Friday, nine to five. I attribute my relative success in the environment to a combination of white privilege, interest in the work, desire to learn more about social services, and willingness to enforce rules, including those with which I did not agree. I stayed in my coveted house position for around six months. During that time I helped get a coworker fired for having sex with a resident. I also evicted a resident who returned to the house visibly doped up, in violation of the zero-tolerance drug policy. I stood over him as he stuffed his various belongings into an oversized duffel bag. He protested by blasting a Jay-Z song, "Hard Knock Life," that featured a loop from the musical *Annie.* Back home at my own apartment, I ended that night as I did many, exhausted, crying, too wired to sleep. Eventually, I was promoted to a case manager position, and I found myself out of the house, on the office side.

The house provided a vital sanctuary for the LGBTQ youth living there. It was a place to be among peers, relatively protected from the public and police harassment and the violence many of them, especially the gender nonconforming youth, faced outside. Without romanticizing, I would say that it seems true that the residents enjoyed building senses of self in relation to one another, even if they often related through fights and fall-outs.

Nonetheless, I came to question the official agency narrative about the youth: that they had become homeless because of their sexual and gender identities. It wasn't that their LGBTQ statuses and experiences played no role in their coming to live without shelter, but it was far from the whole story, and there was by no means a one-to-one correspondence between being queer and/or trans and being homeless.[6] The image presented to local government officials or potential funders was of young persons who were ejected from their family home upon coming out.[7] While certainly some of the residents had experienced just that, I observed that this was not the common trajectory. Much more common were lives of poverty. Most residents were black or Latina/o, and many were first- or second-generation immigrants. Most of the youth seemed to have faced at least as much violence in schools as in their homes, and many had been pushed out before earning diplomas.[8] Many of the youth had dead parents or parents in the prison system. Most of them had grown up in some ad-hoc combination of extended family homes and state foster care. Many, in fact, entered the shelter system directly from "aging-out" of foster care. Given this complex mix of factors, it seemed to me that not all LGBTQ youth were at equal risk of becoming homeless, and that the organization's narrative erased the ways in which risk is socially, economically, and racially stratified. I began to believe that saying the residents were homeless "because they were gay" was not enough. Their experiences were better understood by looking at the complicated ways that gender and sexual marginalization interact with schooling, state foster care, immigration law, and criminal punishment.[9]

It increasingly seemed to me that the official narrative of "LGBT homeless youth" was not only inaccurate, but politically suspect. This sense solidified in early 2000, when two propositions came up on the California ballots. Also known as the Juvenile Crime Initiative, Proposition 21, which passed into law, loosened the requirements by which a youth could be designated as being associated with a gang, increased punishment for "gang-related" activities, and allowed for increased surveillance of alleged gang members and their associates. Proposition 22, or the Knight Initiative, would add to existing marriage law the following text: "Only marriage between a man and a woman is valid and recognized in California." This proposition passed as well.[10]

In the months leading up to voting, many California social justice organizations launched counter-campaigns.[11] Though the missions of most did not specifically address queer and trans concerns, their campaigns sought to mobilize voters against both propositions. The LGBT services center that hosted our transitional living program decided to take a position only against Prop. 22, the "gay marriage ban." From my perspective, Prop. 21 would much more directly and negatively impact the residents of the house, who were already subject to regular police harassment and whose participation in criminalized survival economies placed them at disproportionate risk of imprisonment.[12] Given their economic positions, they would not reap the rewards of marriage—they had no property or private health benefits to share.[13] In this moment I saw how demarcating the homelessness of these youth as "LGBT homelessness" had very real political consequences for what battles could and would be fought with them in mind. This was a productive moment, not simply describing a reality but making a kind of knowledge that would circulate in powerful and powerfully constraining ways. Narrating their homelessness as "gay" made commonsense a political battle for what were legitimized as gay rights. The organization's failure to interrogate the social, racial, and economic bases of the residents' housing needs cut off political alliances along lines other than sexual identity.[14] In refusing to mobilize against Prop. 21, my employer missed a key opportunity to challenge the criminalization of youth by the punishment system, a system that with great immediacy and violence shaped the housing trajectories of our residents.[15]

Thus, I took from my experiences at the transitional living program a number of initial insights about the politics of social services and housing. I realized that programs like my own did not simply respond to housing needs, but were active forces in shaping the larger political terrain in which housing programs exist. I also realized that housing politics lay not just in the allocation of resources, or even the forging and refusing of alliances. The politics lay in the very conceptualization of the problem. The concept of "LGBT youth homelessness" set limits on what needs would be addressed and what issues—such as protection from imprisonment and police harassment—would be considered irrelevant and outside the proper scope of (white) gay politics.[16] Almost a decade later, the political consequences of the conceptualization of housing needs would wind up being the central concern of my research.

I left that job to return to New York and continued in the line of work as a hybrid caseworker/community organizer with residents of hotels and rooming houses (commonly called "SROs," for "single room occupancy").[17] Some of these SROs were private buildings trying to drive out residents and convert to upscale tourist hotels or luxury condos.[18] Others were publicly funded nonprofits that provided housing as well as health and social services for designated special-needs homeless populations. In my capacity as a tenant organizer, I often battled with nonprofit housing providers, including well-meaning social workers who enforced misguided and shortsighted policies that actually jeopardized rather than secured their clients' housing, as I had done in Los Angeles. I also participated in campaigns for the housing rights of people living with HIV/AIDS and became involved in the broader tenant rights and homeless advocacy movements in New York.[19] About a year into that job, I quit along with a coworker in protest of what we saw as institutional barriers to doing effective organizing. For the next two years, I continued organizing through a group I started with that coworker, and we concentrated our efforts on assisting residents of buildings in Harlem. We worked especially in a set of brownstones that, after having functioned as rooming houses for decades, had recently been thrown into legal limbo after a federally funded program poured millions of dollars into the pockets of slumlords, who flipped and abandoned the properties.[20] We worked largely in the housing court system, helping tenants start lawsuits for repairs and fight eviction cases. I would describe New York City Housing Court as a very broken system, except that it excelled at its actual purpose: to destabilize and destroy the lives of poor tenants and to protect the wealth and immunity of landlords and developers.

During this time, I began graduate school. As I dove into my studies, I was burnt out on my organizing work, overwhelmed by the enormity of the needs we were trying to address, and exhausted from the emotional toll of fighting what felt like a losing battle against the violent forces of gentrification. I initially took my research in new directions, and then my dissertation project on biopsychiatric technologies morphed into a project on the governance of homeless populations. (The words of Avery Gordon come to mind again: "Being haunted draws us affectively, sometimes against our will and always a bit magically, into the structure of feeling of a reality we come to experience, not as cold knowledge, but as a transformative recognition.")[21] Clearly, I had more thinking about this to do. My years in social services and housing justice movements left me with simple if confounding questions: Why, despite a proliferation of housing services, programs, and professional advocates, does housing remain beyond reach for so many people? How can we make sense of the fact that the size of the homeless population has expanded alongside the spread of housing services? The frustrations I experienced while I encountered the seemingly endless barriers to assisting people secure safe, stable housing were not unique to my worksites or cities. My experiences as house staff, caseworker, and tenant organizer were shaped by many preceding years of policy, discourse, and practice. My research necessitated digging into those histories to make sense of the contemporary landscape of housing insecurity and deprivation. The present project is an attempt to map that landscape.

Surplus Life and Its Diagrams

As the anticapitalist writing and publishing collective Prole.info describe it, the housing monster is a system in which we all live, and for most of us, that living is a constant and destabilizing struggle.[22] But as a system of insecurity and deprivation, housing manages our lives in such a way as to disaggregate our common experiences, individualize our challenges, and pit us in competitive, hostile fights with one another—for security, for an apartment or home loan, for control of a block or a neighborhood. This individualization of experience cuts us off from one another, casting us into the privatized realm of domestic space and its exclusions.

One indicator of this alienation is the incredible distance almost all of us who are housed feel from "the homeless." This is a deeply felt distance that contradicts the intimate, proximate spaces we often share with people living without shelter: we cross paths, with averted eyes or baleful stares, on public transportation, on sidewalks, in doorways, in ATM vestibules, at public libraries, on church steps, in parks. The affective illusion of separateness is made tenable by endless popular, media, and academic accounts that render people living without shelter denizens of a secret and shadowy underworld.[23] But housing deprivation is not a hidden problem that must be "brought into the light." It is housed populations who are hiding. We shudder and shirk, we turn away.

This distancing, a kind of social abandonment, renders "the homeless" an uncompelling topic for research. When discussing my work, I often encounter an assumption that we already know everything there is to know about this problem. What's to research? There is something deeply disturbing about this face-value status assigned to homelessness. I think it derives from a notion that homeless people themselves are obvious and easy to know. This is not simply the personal shortsightedness of those of us who are housed. It is a key effect of decades of homeless management that have flattened people living without shelter into case histories devoid of complex personhood. So within this uninterested resistance to my research topic is a belief that there is nothing much to know about homeless people themselves.

This affective, and even intellectual, detachment occurs not just despite temporarily shared public space, but despite deep and structuring social, political, and economic interimplication. Of course in many ways, this interimplication describes most everything in an interdependent globalized context. But I mean something more specific here. The production of mass homelessness is the immediate condition of possibility for neoliberal life in the United States. I say immediate because there are of course historical antecedents of conquest and slavery that in their afterlives continue to make the United States exist. In some ways, as I will show, homelessness is the modern incarnation of those afterlives. But it is also specific. Housing deprivation is produced to make literal room for the speculative urban consumer economies of neoliberal capital. As the following chapters show, homelessness is not a state with an essence. It is an effect of shifting racial, economic, social, and political formations. In the late nineteenth- and early twentieth-century United States, "the homeless" traveled with demands of agricultural economies, timed to growing seasons. In the suburbanizing, industrializing mid-twentieth-century United States, "the homeless" were held in place in the new container spaces of urban skid rows. In that moment, to travel became hobo rebellion, no longer in service of the economy, but in rejection of it.

But not soon after homelessness was locked down in skid rows, the beginnings of a postindustrial consumer economy came again to take that land and that space. And so homelessness was scattered, but detached from labor cycles for which other labor forces, especially the "undocumented migrant," came to be organized. This round of dispossession makes today's cities possible in an immediate way. For all of us who live housed, our lives depend on the existence of homelessness. This is not just about the city dweller's consumption of fake loft condominiums or five-dollar coffees; those activities are easy enough to opt out of, which is both as important and ultimately ineffective as tossing some coins in a paper cup. What I am describing here, and what this book documents, is a circumscription of life itself in this stage of capital, a speculative consumptive life that makes homelessness and makes us as well. To be housed is to be disciplined into ways of living and being that allow for forms of security and protection afforded within a neoliberal economy. This is an economy that extracts value from the abandonment of entire populations of people. The book that follows examines how social science and social work are the key technical mechanisms not only through which this abandonment takes place but through which it is coded as a form of help; rescued into abandonment becomes the mode of housing insecurity today. And so in fact those of us who live with housing could not be more bound to those who do not. This book is an attempt to repair those bonds and bring about a better understanding of our shared circumstances.

To do so, the book undoes the obvious beginning of the conversation, "the homeless." The putatively generic category of "homeless" actually signifies something very specific. Homelessness is not just a material state. It is a cultural artifact, a political-economic effect of racial capital's urban disorganizations. While many people experience forms of housing insecurity and deprivation, not every person living without shelter "counts," quite literally, as homeless. The category of homeless carries with it capital excess and turmoil, anti-black racism, the everydayness of police occupation, and the transformation of urban space into consumption enclaves. Thus, for example, today's migrant farm worker population, comprised primarily of highly exploited undocumented workers, is not the target of policies to "end homelessness."[24] Those policies have very specific ideas of housing deprivation in mind, and very specific aims. The ultimate aims, I argue, are not a social end to housing insecurity, but an economic management of its continuation through the production and circulation of those ideas and aims.

To describe the ways in which those made to embody and live the category of "homeless" become socially and economically productive, I use the term "surplus life." This category, as chapter 1 elaborates, is meant to bring together Karl Marx's formulation of surplus labor with Michel Foucault's framework of biopower, or an analysis of the political technologies of managing life itself. Marx describes surplus labor as those who could work but are kept out of work, in order to maintain high competition for low-wage jobs.[25] But today's mass unsheltered populations have been so marginalized from social life as to be beyond recuperation into labor. They are a corollary to (and often overlap with) the surplus labor that, Ruth Wilson Gilmore argues, contemporary prison regimes take out of circulation from labor markets.[26] Homeless populations can be thought of as those who slip through the nets of incarceration and remain behind to be managed as homeless. Their management, I argue, serves not only to reduce their impact on urban consumer economies, by getting them out of the way and off the streets. Rather, the management is an industry itself, a part of knowledge and service economies. These economies transform these living remainders into economically useful matter, matter to be managed, as surplus life reinvested not as labor but as "the homeless."

One non-profit service organization will serve as a quick illustration of what I mean here. A few years ago, I received a postcard in the mail from the Doe Fund, a New York City homeless services agency, which administers housing programs for unsheltered and formerly incarcerated populations. In partnership with Business Improvement Districts throughout the city, the Doe Fund also runs a sort of private workfare program in which they employ clients to perform basic street-cleaning and maintenance.[27] This "job-training" program is called "Ready, Willing & Able." Client participants wear bright blue jumpers emblazoned with the name of the program and organization as they empty trash cans and sweep sidewalks.

The postcard that arrived in my mailbox, a solicitation for contributions, included the following text:

> Thanks to the support of neighbors like you, the "men in blue" are an essential presence in the lives of millions of residents.
>
> Instantly recognizable in their signature bright-blue uniforms, they work each day to improve our communities and transform and rebuild their own lives. Having spent years homeless or incarcerated, the work they do within our neighborhoods enables them to advance towards better futures as independent, contributing members of society.
>
> With your support, we can ensure that more lives are made productive, and that our streets remain vibrant, clean, and safe.[28]

I had seen the Doe Fund's worker-clients around New York for years, and often marveled with disgust at the branding of the agency directly on the bodies of the workers—the so-called men in blue. The postcard's text regurgitates a quite familiar pathologization in the usual terms of personal responsibility derived from the war on the poor, this time with a humanitarian sheen of nonprofit intervention. But the postcard signals more than this.

According to its own literature, Ready, Willing & Able is "based on the belief that change requires a hand up, not a hand out."[29] Participation in the program helps clients "develop a strong work ethic and improve their ability to work in teams, solve problems, relate well to peers, and take supervision. Working thirty-five hours a week, trainees develop a positive attitude and become reliable workers—and they contribute to a cleaner, safer, and more vibrant New York City."[30] For their contribution to the cleanliness, safety, and vibrancy of the city, participants are paid between $7.40 and $8.15 an hour.

The Doe Fund's annual reports do not detail its organizational expenses, but because the Doe Fund is a tax-exempt nonprofit organization, that information is publicly available through the IRS. According to the Doe Fund's 2012 IRS Form 990, in 2011 (the most recent available record) the organization's founder and president, George McDonald, was paid a salary and additional compensation of $543,462. The Doe Fund also employs McDonald's wife, Harriet Karr-McDonald, as chief development officer, the position that oversees fundraising efforts, for which she received a salary and additional compensation of $287,092. To keep track of all this money, the position of chief financial officer is filled by the couple's son, John McDonald, who earned $208,708 for his services in 2011. Form 990 also reports that the Doe Fund rents office space from a building owned by the McDonalds. The total paid for rent and electricity in 2011 was $169,992. Thus, with all salaries and rent, in 2011 the McDonald family received $1,209,254 in compensation from the Doe Fund.

Based only on his salary and compensation for 2011, George McDonald's wage works out to about $10,450 every week, as opposed to the $285.25 earned in a week by Ready, Willing & Able's highest paid participants. The disparity points to the economic function that population management serves in a neoliberal economy. While participants in Ready, Willing & Able earn a small pittance for their labor of making New York City streets cleaner, their larger value is in their mere existence as a population in need of governance. In this way, housing deprivation itself is put to work for the economy, and not just the individuals subject to it. For the Doe Fund, an available homeless population translated into over $42 million in fundraising revenue in fiscal year 2012.[31] For the city of New York, the Doe Fund's management of this population has translated into three million bags of collected trash.[32]

In 2008, George McDonald was awarded the William E. Simon Prize for Lifetime Achievement in Social Entrepreneurship from the Manhattan Institute, a conservative policy think tank that describes itself as an important force in shaping American political culture and developing ideas that foster economic choice and individual responsibility. We have supported and publicized research on our era's most challenging public policy issues: taxes, health care, energy, the legal system, policing, crime, homeland security, urban life, education, race, culture, and many others. Our work has won new respect for market-oriented policies and helped make reform a reality.[33]

The William E. Simon Prize carries a cash reward of $100,000 paid to the individual being honored. That a neoliberal antigovernment agency like the Manhattan Institute would recognize the work of a social service agency is not a contradiction, but rather the most honest expression of exactly the alignments that this book explores. It points to how capital invests in caring for the homeless as a practice of its own self-preservation.

To make sense of the Doe Fund and its role in the social and economic life of New York demands analysis of the methods of homeless management. In particular, this book attends to methods of research that produce the homeless as a category and methods of social service that attach that category to governance structures and capitalist economies. The project takes on the social scientific discourse of homelessness not to learn "facts about the homeless," but to get a sense of how homelessness is molded and made. It addresses as well the tools and techniques being mobilized to produce and support that discourse, including health assessments used to measure life expectancies, database systems for storing, sharing, and calculating shelter population dynamics, and ethics protocols for research involving unsheltered populations. I argue that the shift to neoliberal capital and governance, along with concomitant shifts in quantitative scientific authority, "post-racial" media and policy discourse, and the professionalization of social services away from social movement bases, all account for a reorganization of homelessness today. This reorganization has increasingly emphasized population-level management, sometimes drawing from and sometimes actually subverting individual-level management techniques.

Attention to how homeless management happens requires a methodological infidelity to disarticulate presumed relationships between individuals and housing. The present project draws from a poststructuralist interrogation of categories of knowledge to generate a productive method that includes but also moves beyond deconstruction and critique. Such a methodology can be conceptualized, following the work of Gilles Deleuze and Félix Guattari, in terms of the diagram. The diagram both describes an abstract model for organizing concrete power relations *and* captures that model through political-intellectual inquiry. Regarding the former, the diagram explains the persistence of what sociologists might call "structure," but without imputing permanence or transcendence. Rather, the diagram is an accumulated effect of myriad and micro exchanges of force relations. As Deleuze describes it, a diagram "is neither the subject of history, nor does it survey history."[34] Rather, the diagram instigates an interplay of forces that draw together and make possible, producing concrete, material effects, or "assemblages." Deleuze also describes the diagram as an "abstract machine," meaning that it brings abstractions into material effect. The diagram thus can be thought of in terms of assembling, producing, piloting, interpreting, arranging: the abstract machine is an operational mode of power available to governance that produces governance. Finally, the diagram is not given; as Deleuze observes, "the diagram is highly unstable or fluid, continually churning up matter and functions in a way likely to create change."[35] Nonetheless, in its repetitions, the diagram becomes so forceful as to perhaps appear immutable, particularly when encountered in daily life at a human scale, as an institution, or "society."

The panopticon is perhaps the best known example of a diagram in this sense. As described by Michel Foucault, the panopticon is both a literal organization of space and a model for how to organize and produce subjectivities in relation to systems of domination and control. Famously, the panopticon teaches the prisoners to watch themselves under threat of an always potential and ready-to-be realized surveillance.[36] A specific prison, or schoolhouse, in addition to being a concrete assemblage, is an abstract machine that gives us panopticism. Panopticism is not a transcendental ideal, but a model produced through its articulations.

This is the first aspect of what we mean by diagram. Regarding its second sense, the diagram is not only a model *for* power, but also a model *of* power. Diagrams offer an unexpected and unusual way to access operations of power, describe them, and map them. As Eugene Thacker writes,

> The diagram provides a cross-section, a transversal (similar to the transverse cross-sections used on frozen cadavers in digital anatomy). Diagrams cut across separate organs and organ systems, they cut across institutions, governments, social classes, technical paradigms, and cultural forms. The resultant view is very different from the anthropomorphic body politic, though still familiar, if only in a dizzying way.[37]

To analyze diagrammatically is to disrespect accepted boundaries and the knowledge formations that guide us along those edges. To diagram is to make unacceptable cuts, revealing unexpected proximities and relations.

My evocation of the diagram is meant to allow us to consider the existence of something forceful at a scale that is greater than individual sites of homeless service provision and that links those sites together. As a diagram of surplus life, the present project captures an abstract level of knowing and managing homelessness, the operations of power that shape and instruct more midlevel and micro governabilities of homelessness. The goal of analyzing in diagrammatic terms is not to find "the" diagram of homeless management or "the" diagram of neoliberal governance, but to follow specific diagrams, or contractions, and to think of an abstract machine articulating across them. In mapping this diagram, we move against the grain. Rather than start with the statistical chart, or a homeless person, or even the shelter or sidewalk setting, I want to cut through the corpse of homeless management, slicing through capital, urban infrastructure, social science, and social service to find something other than the story social services and sciences have been telling us.

I employ the method of the diagram because the diagram is fundamentally ambivalent, both a description of power and a model for power. The indistinguishability is fundamental. It reminds us that knowledge production is part of the operations of power, that no knowledge formation is innocent. Power formations inevitably shape what we can see of them and how we see them. But these resultant knowledge formations also expose power, map it out so we can anticipate and interrupt its operations. The back and forth between these two senses of the diagram is constant and rapid, sometimes so fast it is simultaneous. This is temporarily useful in the pressure it applies to the existing diagram and the ways of understanding that see the diagram from its own perspective, that do not grasp its confusing or confounding operations. But it is also only temporarily useful because homeless governance will shift again—because it shifts always—so we need more resources. And finally, while its partial perspective is useful, the diagram is never a full account. This means other forms of power and resistance take place outside its bounds. By sticking too literally to a diagram, we miss that. And so we must remember the diagram is tactical. Here, I want to reveal latent levels of governance that have gone for the most part unremarked upon in academic work on homelessness; thus, my focus is on the role of social science and social service in governing housing insecurity. This means I do not engage other circumstances, such as social movements; nor do I write about "homeless people." Instead, I write about the systems that produce and manage them. This is an effort toward recognizing a monster to get rid of it.

In building a diagram of surplus life, this project assembles material from a range of sources selected to give a rich sense of how a discourse and management of homelessness has emerged and changed. These sources include government documents (policy reports, program evaluations, and congressional records), professional literature (program reports of nonprofit organizations), social scientific literature, and mass media. This material constitutes an archive that has helped situate my research questions in historical context. Along those lines, I have also relied on secondary historical accounts of urban development, the welfare state, and the social and political technologies that respond to unsheltered populations. Furthermore, over the course of several years, I conducted face-to-face interviews with people involved in some aspect of homeless management—program directors, service providers, and advocates/activists. These interview subjects came from sites in New York City, Philadelphia, Los Angeles, San Francisco, and Seattle—cities chosen for their concentration of homeless services, variance in policy and administration, and documentation in existing literature. I conducted these interviews both one-on-one and in groups. I met with a few informants several times.

In these meetings, I worked from a loose set of questions that sought to get at each informant's expertise about various aspects of homeless management. Though I went into interviews with these questions, the interviews were open-ended, meaning that informants put their insights and experiences into their own words, rather than selecting from an established set of responses. The meetings generally would shift at some point from formal interview to conversation, and I would begin to offer feedback and my own thoughts in addition to asking questions. I would share my preliminary and developing analyses and ask the informants to comment. In this way, the gathering of data and the analysis of it were not distinct processes; rather, the "data," or responses, were shaped actively by me, and my analysis was in turn actively shaped by my informants, who corroborated, corrected, and challenged my thinking as it was unfolding in relation to our conversation. I am not sure how different this might be from what happens in most open-ended interviews, or in participant-observation research, but I imagine I was somewhat unique among trained sociologists in how much of my own thoughts-in-formation I shared.

Finally, and related to this approach to interviews, I had several occasions during the course of my research to present my work to groups that included individuals involved in the homeless services industry. While these were not interviews, in the discussions that followed these presentations, I gained important feedback that profoundly challenged and shaped my thinking.

OUTLINE OF THE BOOK

To begin the process of disassembling "homelessness" from housing insecurity and deprivation, chapter 1 proposes a theoretical framework in which to situate the contemporary techno-conceptual organization of homelessness. Specifically, it identifies how the health and well-being of individuals and populations become constituted as objects of knowledge and intervention. The work of Michel Foucault on the place of life in politics—what he describes as biopower—offers a jumping-off point. In looking at biopower alongside the emergence and consolidation of neoliberal technologies of governance, chapter 1 argues that in the transition from a Fordist-Keynesian welfare state to post-welfare governance arrangements, the relationships of health to economy are being reconfigured. Put bluntly, I argue that in the post-welfare context, the growth of an economy is no longer strictly seen as dependent upon the growth and well-being of a national population. The mode through which the transition to post–social welfare homeless management takes place involves a shift from an imagination of social problems to one of governance problems best solved through rational and routinized applications of techno-science. In such a context, social welfare programs become economic enterprises, part of rather than a challenge to the postindustrial service economies to which knowledge production is central. These programs take as their object surplus life, which must be understood through the intertwined histories of race/racism and property relations and in terms of the ways of the co-constitution of race and property distribute life chances and premature death.

Chapter 2 then considers the role of social science in knowing and managing social disorder. If, as this book argues, homeless management is a form of knowledge production, then formal sites for making and distributing knowledge are key to the governance of housing insecurity. This chapter considers the historical emergence of social science as a technology for producing racial knowledge projects in relation to managing the sometimes conflicting demands of state-building and capital expansion. I argue that not only has social science played a central role in producing knowledge about housing-deprived populations, but that the study of homelessness has in turn served a discipline-building function for sociology, a site to test out and perfect new methodological techniques. Looking at a recent ethnography in the sociology of homelessness, as well as debates around it, I consider how a discourse of poverty and its heteronormative constructions of black masculinity underwrite contemporary narratives of homelessness. This serves to erase the production of housing insecurity, granting it, and its racialized distributions, a naturalized or de facto status. In producing this story about "homeless people," sociology ultimately produces an image of itself over and against its homeless subjects, organizing what I term the "rightness/whiteness" of sociological methods and ethics.

The book then moves to consider the on-the-ground forms that homeless management takes in the United States. It does so by looking at the role of the federal government in organizing conceptions of and responses to housing insecurity. Chapter 3 presents linked accounts of two histories: changes in forms of housing insecurity and deprivation, and changes in governance strategies for managing them. Starting with the first instance of federal involvement in the 1930s, the chapter moves on to the emergence in the 1970s of what historians call the "new homeless," which, I argue, is a consolidation of housing deprivation as an independent and permanent feature of the national population, one explained in terms of the racialized impact of neoliberalism more than simply changes in labor. The chapter then considers the return of the federal government to issues of housing insecurity and deprivation, this time in the mid-1980s, in response to the challenges of managing this permanent and growing population. I argue that this renewed federal involvement introduces the techno-science of governance problems into the homeless services industry. As the chapter shows, "governance problems" concern the proper and efficient allocation of resources. In its returned involvement, the federal government does not directly manage the surplus populations produced by neoliberal capital, but acts through "metagovernance," or the governance of governance, to reorganize how subnational government and nonprofit agencies do so.

The next two chapters consider two case studies of programs initiated by the federal government. Chapter 4 examines the development of federal data-collection standards through the Department of Housing and Urban Development's Homeless Management Information Systems program, or HMIS. I argue that the primary use of the "universal data elements" gathered through the HMIS program is the production of a population for regulating nonprofit agencies, rather than individuals. In other words, the HMIS program organizes the population as a mechanism *for* governance. The impact on clients is an indirect one of techno-conceptual organization in which individuals are not targeted, but are nonetheless caught up. Chapter 5, the second case study, investigates the emergence of "chronic homelessness" as a privileged target of governance. I situate the arrival of federal chronic homelessness initiatives in a history of progressive social service provision termed "Housing First." Housing First models have challenged long-standing protocols in homeless service provision that demanded sobriety and pharmaceutical psychiatric treatment as preconditions for entering housing programs. The chapter shows that Housing First models gain traction when the economic costs of chronically homeless populations register as an academic and political concern. Thus, governance models of managing population costs unexpectedly align with the agenda of progressive housing providers to shelter the most vulnerable and least served. While the immediate effects of chronic homelessness programs have been key to the survival of those they house, I present this case as a cautionary tale regarding short-term individual-level positive outcomes.

In the conclusion, I revisit the role of social sciences in managing housing insecurity, considering discourses of ethics and "the good." Looking at contemporary media accounts of housing insecurity reveals that notions of deserving and undeserving continue to circulate alongside governance regimes that distribute life chances and death likelihoods at population levels. I argue against a too-instrumental model of the role of academic inquiry in challenging violence and inequality, one that rests too assuredly on a notion of doing good. Rather, a "bad" social science that disrupts accepted frameworks may offer ways of reconceptualizing housing needs in a constantly insecure environment.

The ultimate aim of the present book is to shift academic attention from "the homeless" toward the apparatuses that produce and distribute housing insecurity and deprivation. Thus, this is a book about the constitution of homelessness as a problem to be managed. In this story, social services and social sciences become central characters. Social service and social science are usually imagined to be a *response* to social problems, mitigating or documenting, for example, the effects of a private housing market on populations living without shelter. But far from simply responding after the fact to homelessness, social services and science are active forces in shaping both understandings of homelessness and the actual material experiences of living without shelter. *The Value of Homelessness* charts the production of knowledge about homelessness and the development of governmental interventions to manage mass unsheltered populations. In so doing, it moves from asking, "Who are the homeless?" to asking, "How does homelessness become something to be known and managed?" That "how" will be interrogated in the chapters that follow, and what will emerge is that "the homeless," far from being the starting point for governance, are its retroactive effect.

ONE

Surplus Life, or Race and Death in Neoliberal Times

WHAT DOES IT MEAN TO SAY THAT A HOUSE IS A TECHNOLOGY THAT makes live and lets die? The disastrous impact of housing insecurity and deprivation on health and life chances is well documented. In 2005, the New York City Department of Health and Mental Hygiene and the Department of Homeless Services jointly issued a report entitled *The Health of Homeless Adults in New York City*. The report draws from data collected between January 2001 and December 2003 at two kinds of homeless shelters, single-adult shelters and family shelters. Comparing this shelter population data to data about the general adult population, the study draws a number of alarming, if not surprising, conclusions.[1] Death rates among those who stayed in the adult shelter system were twice as high as those of the general population of New York City, and adults who stayed in the family shelter system had death rates 1.5 times higher. During the time of the study, 3.6 percent of all New York City tuberculosis cases were among the shelter populations studied, making the rate of TB diagnosis eleven times higher than in the general population. Users of the adult shelter system were twice as likely to have HIV compared with the general New York City population.[2] The rate of *new* HIV cases among the shelter population was over sixteen times the rate for the general adult population. This means that whereas in the general adult population there would be seventy-five new cases of HIV for every 100,000 adults, for the shelter population, there would be 1,241 new cases for every 100,000 adults.[3]

In *Dying without Dignity: Homeless Deaths in Los Angeles County: 2000–2007*, the Los Angeles Coalition to End Hunger and Homelessness found that during the 7.5 years of their study, there were 2,815 homeless deaths in Los Angeles County.[4] If that figure alone is not sufficiently alarming, the study authors also note that "the average age of death was

48.1 years, falling far short of the 77.2 year life expectancy of the average American." The study furthermore argues:

> The 2,815 homeless people in our study were expected to live 211,878 years based on the average life expectancy of their gender and ethnicity. They only survived 135,528 of those expected years. In other words, their lives were cut short by 76,350 years. On average a homeless person's life is 36% shorter than a housed person's life. For homeless Latina females, their lives were 49% shorter than expected.[5]

The report concludes with an appendix titled "In Memory Of" which compiles the names of those whose deaths generated the numbers in the study. Arranged in three columns, the list of names goes on for twelve and a half pages.

Finally, a study conducted by the National Coalition for the Homeless, *Hate, Violence, and Death on Main Street USA,* evidences how the systemic violence of housing deprivation further exposes people living without shelter to direct, individualized abuse and attack. Summarizing data from 2007, the report found that at least 160 homeless persons in the United States suffered violent attacks in 2007; twenty-eight died from those attacks. Those deaths represent an increase of 40 percent compared to lethal attacks on unsheltered persons the year before.[6] The report contains narrative descriptions of all twenty-eight deaths, such as this one: "Felix Najero, a 49-year-old homeless man, was set on fire outside of Bethany Christian Church where he rested for the night. The fire burned seventy-five percent of Najero's body, spreading across his face, chest, and stomach. Najero died four days later in New York-Presbyterian/Weill Cornell Medical Center."[7] The report also discusses the phenomenon of perpetrators video-recording their attacks. These recordings, known as "bumbashing" or "bum fight" videos, are subsequently distributed and sold on the web and as DVDs.[8]

These and similar reports bring into violent relief how housing insecurity and housing deprivation make people sick and make people die. The studies also underscore that insecurity and deprivation roll out along entrenched lines of gender, sexual, and racial difference, overexposing already marginalized and subordinated populations to these violent harms. But not only this. They also remind us that death and illness have become the curious objects of methodological inquiry. In

Surplus Life, or Race and Death in Neoliberal Times

other words, while pulling apart the sutures that bind housing to life, health, illness, and death, we must also ask about the production and circulation of *studies* of illness and death. The documentation of these harms presupposes and reconsolidates the ways that life, health, illness, and death have been taken on as concerns for knowledge production and for political management. This chapter builds a framework for considering these claims and for thinking about how life, health, illness, and death become things to be known and managed. It also demonstrates the ways in which knowledge production and governance become useful in a context of neoliberal economic restructuring. Studies of homelessness and the forms of illness and death housing deprivation bring forth set that illness and death into circuits of knowledge and capital.

BIOPOWER AND RACE

Michel Foucault proposed the concept of *biopower* to analyze the relationships of knowledge production to the governance of life. According to Foucault, biopower is "what brought life and its mechanisms into the explicit realm of calculations and made knowledge-power an agent of transformation of human life."[9] While many might classify Foucault's work as theory, I draw out a methodological approach to understanding techno-conceptual formations, providing an "analytics of power." In other words, as Mariana Valverde points out, biopower does not describe an essence or a thing, but rather serves to organize for analysis divergent and diversely related techniques centered on the politicization of biological life.[10] Paul Rabinow and Nikolas Rose agree, writing that "the concept of 'biopower' serves to bring into view a field comprised of more or less rationalized attempts to intervene upon the vital characteristics of human existence."[11] Hence, less than a theoretical account of a type of power, biopower provides an analytic frame for understanding the making of "life itself," including unsheltered life, into an object of knowledge and governance.

The politicization of human life operates through a multitude of technologies that Foucault groups into two trajectories, or what he calls "poles." The first is an *anatomopolitics* that takes up the body of the individual subject and its arrangement and relations in space.[12] Often Foucault and others refer to this simply as "discipline" or "disciplinary

25

power." The army barracks, the workshop, the school, the prison, and the family can all be understood as disciplinary enclosures, or, in the sociological sense, institutions. The function of a disciplinary enclosure is to align the body and mind of the subject with norms of behavior and thought. This includes norms for relating with other subjects organized through the enclosure. Enclosures also mark out some subjects as abnormal.[13] Foucault described the aims of anatomopolitics in terms of the production of "docile bodies" or "the parallel increase of [the body's] usefulness and its docility."[14] Docility does not describe weakness or passivity, but rather the augmentation of both a subject's capacity to think and act and its capacity to submit to political and social norms. "A body is docile that may be subjected, used, transformed and improved."[15] The soldier is perhaps the most obvious example of this; the factory laborer would be another. In the case of homelessness, as chapter 3 will show, "docility" has manifested as performance of work ethics, addiction and mental health work, and imagining oneself as a subject to be improved toward housing.

Foucault names the second pole or trajectory of the politicization of biological life *biopolitics*.[16] Whereas anatomopolitics concerns the individual subject and his or her relations in space with other individuals, biopolitics concerns the regulation of the population, or human species. "Biopolitics deals with the population, with the population as a political problem, as a problem that is at once scientific and political, as a biological problem and as power's problem."[17] Biopolitical technologies describe tactics, techniques, and practices that address individuals en masse, meaning that individuals, rather than being direct objects of rule, become component parts of a larger body. At this massifying scale, biopolitical technologies seek to understand and to regulate the overall "mechanics of life" including "propagation, births and mortality, the level of health, life expectancy and longevity" as well as "all the conditions that can cause these to vary."[18] Biopolitical technologies concerned with these life processes include demographic sciences of birth and death rates, population planning, public health initiatives, and health and life insurance.

Together, disciplinary and biopolitical technologies bring biological objects and processes into political calculation; disciplinary technologies do so by addressing the animal body of the individualized subject, whereas biopolitical technologies do so by addressing the species body of the total population. Foucault argues that through these technologies, animal life in individual and species form becomes constitutive of the force field of modern power relations. He famously writes, "For millennia, man remained what he was for Aristotle: a living animal with the additional capacity for a political existence; modern man is an animal whose politics places his existence as a living being into question."[19]

To illustrate this special place of life in modern politics, Foucault contrasts modern regimes of biopower with the classical regime. Foucault argues that the new power over life is representative of a basic shift from a classical power of *deduction,* a power to take or seize, to a modern power of *production.* Modern power strives "to incite, reinforce, control, monitor, optimize, and organize the forces under it: a power bent on generating forces, making them grow, and ordering them."[20] This is not to say that in the modern world things are never seized, or never put to death. Far from it, as I discuss below. Rather, Foucault means to argue that technologies of governance demonstrate a tendency toward fostering and promoting productive forces and the conditions that allow for their multiplication.[21] Life, in such a context, is not given or taken, but allowed for: "One might say that the ancient right to *take* life or *let* live was replaced by a power to *foster* life or *disallow* it to the point of death."[22]

Thus, technologies of biopower aim to know life in order to optimize it and foster its growth. But Foucault also argues that when life enters the political realm, not all life is deemed worthy of investment. Rather, some life, or some parts of a population, is considered a drain on the life of the overall population. This life threatens to introduce inferiority or weakness that will diminish a population's capacity to grow and thrive. So in addition to technologies that multiply and promote life, we have the development of technologies that identify parts of the population that are "unworthy," that drain life. Foucault argues that modern governance eliminates this weak, sapping life. Biopolitical governance enacts these eliminations either directly through killing or more slowly through social abandonment. Foucault refers to these processes of elimination as "state racism." Society directs state racism "against itself, against its own elements and its own products. This is the internal racism of permanent purification."[23] State racism describes an analysis of biological capacities for living, thriving, and proliferating, and death is the technique used to manage, by cutting out, those elements of the population or species evaluated as harmful to biopolitical life; state racism produces "the break between what must live and what must die."[24] This, then, is the ironic intention of Foucault's declaration that "society must be defended": it is a self-murderous defense.

Valverde describes technologies that incite life and those that end it as the "two faces of biopolitical power."[25] The death produced by state racism is not the same as the seizure of life that characterizes a classical regime; state racism is not antithetical to biopower. Rather, the death of state racism is a biopowerful death, which is to say it is productive, because it allows the overall life of a population, or "the human race," to extend and prosper. Foucault writes, "I think that, broadly speaking, racism justifies the death-function in the economy of biopower by appealing to the principle that the death of others makes one biologically stronger insofar as one is a member of a race or a population, insofar as one is an element in a unitary living plurality."[26] If the deaths of state racism are productive, they are also not anomalous. All regimes of biopower deploy technologies for the evaluation of life in order to make cuts into a population, separating out that life which is a drain on the life of the overall human species. In fact, Foucault writes that the modern state is necessarily racist, as state racism is what "allows biopower to work."[27]

The concept of state racism helps account for the persistence of death—and mass death at that—in regimes of biopower directed toward multiplying and expanding life. State racism points to how death becomes a productive cutting out that allows life to live on. In the lecture on state racism, Foucault stresses that the "racism" to which it refers is not the same thing as ideological or cultural racism, and the "races" it concerns are not strictly coterminous with a cultural taxonomy of racial categories. "Race," here, should be read as "human race." Those targeted by state racism are any part of a population deemed biologically, socially, or economically unfit. While projects of state racism would include all kinds of ethnoracial wars and cleansing, state racism describes the production of any category targeted for elimination—so for example, in U.S., British, and German eugenics, those marked as mentally or physically disabled.[28] Nonetheless, those writing after Foucault have emphasized that the line between projects of state racism and other forms of racism is not so sharp. Patricia Ticineto Clough argues that "the projection of hate and fear onto a population that makes it into a mythical adversary, may come to function as a support of evaluations of populations, marking some for death and others for life."[29] In other words, cultural or ideological racisms may bolster projects of economic investment in some populations and social withdrawal from others; state racism and cultural or ideological racism are not mutually exclusive. Furthermore, state racist projects of making cuts into an overall population will of course line up with other projects of racial subordination, which have coded entire peoples as unproductive and unnecessary. To the extent that U.S. (and more broadly, Western or European) technologies of race have produced race as biological categories, those categories fold easily into all biopolitical projects of killing off.

We could push Foucault further though, perhaps against the grain of his work, and argue that racialization and racialized subordination generate techniques of biopower, or the governance of life as life itself. Frank Wilderson offers one way to think about enslaved black bodies as the orginary category of "life itself." In "Gramsci's Black Marx: Whither the Slave in Civil Society?" Wilderson argues that the revolutionary subject of Gramscian/Marxist thought precludes the participation of the slave in revolution. Wilderson reminds us that, in the founding of racial capitalism, the worker and the slave are mutually incompatible categories. Insofar as the core of the revolutionary subject is the status of worker, the slave cannot revolt within the dialectics of capital. For Wilderson the point is not to reform the category of worker/revolutionary subject so it includes the slave. Rather, Wilderson emphasizes the fundamental incompleteness of a Marxist revolution that leaves untouched the place of slavery and the continued functions of antiblack racism in not just the economic order of capitalism but within the colonial-capitalist social order as well. For Wilderson, this social order includes oppositional anti-capitalist movements.

Here I want to dwell on a brief comment Wilderson makes in the course of building his argument. He writes, "The worker calls into question the legitimacy of productive practices, the slave calls into question the legitimacy of productivity itself."[30] I understand this observation to mean not only that the slave, as a form of property rather than an agent who sells the property of labor-power, is outside the relations of production. But Wilderson emphasizes here that the slave exists *only* as life, *only* as productivity. This insight is the kernel of Thomas Jefferson's radical innovation when he realized he could systemize the returns of investment in slave ownership by accounting for reproduction. That Jefferson also innovated in the use of slaveholdings as a form of insurance leverage points to the very embeddedness of life productivity in capitalism.[31] Perhaps Marx sensed this in distinguishing labor, an essence of human life, from labor power, an alienated commodity form of labor. But Marxian thought has failed to adequately deal with the violent denial of human status for those who could never alienate their labor power because they were already alienated forms of property in life itself, as enslaved life.

Following Wilderson's argument reveals that the ur-instance of biopower might be enslaved life, that the slave might be an originary case of life itself. As Achille Mbembe writes in his analysis of necropolitics, "Any historical account of the rise of modern terror needs to address slavery, which could be considered one of the first instances of biopolitical experimentation."[32] A contention with Foucault's work in recent years has been whether his account of discipline and the rise of the self-governing subject pushed concerns with direct forms of state violence out of view. "Self-governing" may accurately describe white middle-class subjects and their healthcare regimes, for example, but does not account for the over two million bodies, vastly disproportionately of color, locked in U.S. cages. Of course, governance regimes operate in multiple and contradictory modes. But we also can have a slightly different tack on this question, which is that the biopolitical formation of populations, of life itself at mass scale, was always first enslaved life. As Angela Davis demonstrates, the U.S. prison regime confirms this fact: the permutation of slavery into Black Codes and modern policing/prison regimes is just an inevitable and horrible expression of this.[33] Wilderson shows that we need accounts of biopower that do not add race and antiblack racism back in. They are there already, submerged under universalist accounts. In this present case of homelessness, we draw them back forward.

With this in mind, projects of state racism actually point to the vital connections between disciplinary racisms of individual subjection and biopolitical racisms of population control. While he does not pursue this connection, Foucault offers a way to think about it in his discussion of how "the norm" operates in regimes of biopower: "The norm is something that can be applied to both a body one wishes to discipline and a population one wishes to regularize. . . . The normalizing society is a society in which the norm of discipline and the norm of regulation intersect along an orthogonal articulation."[34] Here Foucault means "norm" in the sense of social hierarchies and their conventions of embodiment and behavior. He intends norms also as a statistical measure of pattern and tendency. Through their orthogonal relationship, biopolitical technologies of state racism may draw from an individualizing racism while tending toward what Patricia Ticineto Clough has termed a "population racism" that organizes and regulates life and death chances at mass scales.[35] The production of housing insecurity and deprivation offers an instructive example of the operations of the varied forms of race norm-ing that coalesce in projects of state racism to produce group-differentiated vulnerability to premature death, in Ruth Wilson Gilmore's words.[36] In fact, in a generally overlooked passage from the Collège de France lectures, Foucault uses the development of workers' housing in relation to town planning to illustrate how disciplinary and biopolitical poles work in concert:

> What were working-class housing estates, as they existed in the nineteenth century? One can easily see how the very grid pattern, the very layout, of the estate articulated, in a sort of perpendicular way, the disciplinary mechanisms that controlled the body, or bodies, by localizing families (one to a house) and individuals (one to a room). The layout, the fact that individuals were made visible, and the normalization of behavior meant that a sort of spontaneous policing or control was carried out by the spatial layout of the town itself. It is easy to identify a whole series of disciplinary mechanisms in the working-class estate. And then you have a whole series of mechanisms which are, by contrast, regulatory mechanisms, which apply to the population as such and which allow, which encourage patterns of saving related to housing, to the renting of accommodations and, in some cases, their purchase.[37]

To recast in the terms of the present discussion, we could say that Foucault is pointing to the ways that houses and homes (or the production of docile bodies in the enclosures of families and neighborhoods) intersect with housing insecurity and housing deprivation (or the production at population levels of access to health and life security). Given the endemic relationship of state racism to biopower—or the centrality of the production of death to projects of making live—it is no surprise that housing makes live and lets die. Housing necessarily builds up life and in so doing shores up racialized hierarchies and racialized subordination as well.

This is borne out in the history of housing in the United States, where homes have been made inaccessible through their reproduction as exchangeable and financialized commodities that belong to entities other than those that would live there. As a form of private property, housing is deeply implicated in the history of the coproduction of race and property. Cheryl Harris traces this coproduction back to the settler colonial founding of the United States through the "parallel systems of domination of Black and Native American peoples." The theft of Native lands and the enslavement of African populations created "racially contingent forms of property and property rights."[38] Race was not only an ideological project, but a project grounded and made in these forms of property and property rights. As Harris writes, "Even in the early years of the country, it was not the concept of race alone that operated to oppress Blacks and Indians; rather, it was the interaction between conceptions of race and property which played a critical role in establishing and maintaining racial and economic subordination."[39]

Harris demonstrates how biological concepts of race, including the supremacy of whiteness, evolved into legal categories articulated in relation to property forms and rights. During the early colonial era, as contractual periods for white indentured labor were shortened, the settler project relied more heavily on enslaved African labor, spurring a legal codification of these relations of production: "Racial identity was further merged with stratified social and legal status: 'Black' racial identity marked who was subject to enslavement, whereas 'white' racial identity marked who was 'free' or, at minimum, not a slave."[40] To be black was to be enslaveable, to be a form of property. At the same time, Harris argues, whiteness, rather than white people, also became a form of property: a "set of assumptions, privileges, and benefits that accompany the status of being white." As property, whiteness became recognized by the law as valuable, and hence given legal protections. The holding and exchanging of various forms of property is one such protected right. As imperial formations of white supremacy and black enslaveability become codified in law, this emergent legal framework instantiated European common law conceptions of property and property rights over and against various competing indigenous concepts and practices. As Harris explains, "Indian custom was obliterated by force and replaced with the regimes of common law which embodied the customs of the conquerors. . . . Indians experienced the property laws of the colonizers and the emergent American nation as acts of violence perpetuated by the exercise of power and ratified through the rule of law."[41] Andrea Smith has argued that this logic of enslaveability anchors capitalism and that this logic of Native genocide anchors colonialism; as such enslaveability and genocide function as what she terms "pillars of white supremacy."[42]

The result of these colonial implantations is a conceptualization of race through and as property forms and property rights. Property forms and rights in turn provide political and economic reinforcement of the racial subordination they put in place. As Harris demonstrates, these founding subordinations have been repeatedly entrenched throughout the history of the United States, and the protections of whiteness as property "became institutionalized privileges; ideologically, they became part of the settled expectations of whites—a product of the unalterable original bargain."[43] Consequently whites have greater access to property and property protection, and those organized as "non-white" have limited and insecure access. During the height of social welfarism in mid-twentieth-century United States, for example, the federal government literally invested in securing white home ownership while disinvesting from urban cores with large African American populations, shoring up what George Lipsitz describes as the "possessive investment in whiteness."[44]

From the nineteenth century on, an immigration system that produces some laborers as undocumented and criminalized and others as legally subject to racially exploitative and stratified labor markets has extended the exclusion from property and property rights to people of color more broadly, differentially by class, gender, and migration trajectory, but structurally nonetheless. Grace Hong explains this as the "ruptures of American capital."[45] Far from being outside property relations, these unpropertied populations are the included exclusions that have founded private property systems, animating private property through the production of scarcity and need. It is exactly these racialized populations that are disproportionately exposed to housing insecurity and deprivation—African American, white immigrant, and Native populations. A 1996 study by the Urban Institute estimated that the unsheltered population was 41 percent black, 11 percent Hispanic, and 8 percent Native American—all disproportionate for their representation in the overall population. A study conducted by the U.S. Department of Housing and Urban Development (HUD) notes:

> *Homelessness disproportionately affects minorities, especially African Americans.* Minorities constitute one-third of the total U.S. population and about half of the poverty population, but about two-thirds of the sheltered homeless population. African-Americans are heavily overrepresented in the sheltered homeless population, representing about 44 percent of the sheltered homeless population but 23 percent of the poverty population and only 12 percent of the general population.[46]

In the city of Seattle, a 2002 count of people utilizing homeless services identified 37 percent as African American, as opposed to 5 percent of the general population.[47] Similarly, based on shelter stay statistics from Fiscal Year (FY) 2011, we can determine that in New York City, about 54 percent of service users were identified as black and about 30 percent as Hispanic.[48] This pattern holds and increases for people who spend the longest periods in shelters. One study of "chronic shelter utilizers" identified around 71 percent of such users in Philadelphia and New York City as black,[49] and a project targeting people living on the street in downtown Los Angeles identifies 85 percent of those housed as African American/black.[50]

Housing insecurity can be understood as one of the key forms of antiblack racism in the United States, one that in turn especially impacts any populations positioned against whiteness and its properties. Thus we can recast the claim made in the introduction—that a house is a technology that makes live and lets die—and understand housing as a systemic form of state racism, making cuts that determine how the investments in health and life secured by homes will be distributed. As one form of private property, housing is produced by and reproduces projects of racialized subordination. The life that lives in systems of housing insecurity and deprivation is born of that life that dies on its streets and sidewalks.

RACE AND THE WELFARE STATE

If the preceding discussion updates and complicates the place of race and racism in Foucault's formulation, we still must attend to what the term "state" implies in "state racism." The use of the term is somewhat surprising. Most read Foucault as opposed to any state-centered theory. However, Foucault did not argue that the state is irrelevant or unimportant. Rather, his work responds to a certain strain of Marxian theory that centers the state exclusively in analyses of power and that considers the state simply an engine for economic domination by capitalists. Foucault argued against this view, proposing that power should not be analyzed as something held, and held exclusively by either the state or an economic class.[51] His views echoed those of contemporaneous anarchists who argued against a "take the state" model of revolutionary power.[52] Foucault's analysis of biopower seeks to recognize the diffuse and multiscalar nature of power, its production and circulation throughout the social where it is directed but not controlled by the enclosures of so-called civil society. Within this model, state apparatuses should not be disregarded, but must also be understood as significant though nonexclusive sites of power. This, too, connects with Wilderson's insistence that civil society, as imagined by Marx and Gramsci, is not outside the constitution of colonialism and antiblack racism.

Not only are the analytic methods of biopower outlined above compatible with accounts of the modern nation state. In fact, contra our expectations of Foucault, I argue that Foucault's account of the population actually *presumes* the nation-state form. The biopolitical population described by Foucault is very much a population that is aligned with a nation-state, and the nation-state in this model is deeply concerned with investing in and nurturing that population. This does not mean that states have a monopoly on state racism. A diverse range of non-state and quasi-private institutions, including nonprofit homeless social service agencies, do the work of state racism, making the cuts of investment and abandonment. But considering the evolution of welfare policy and administration will demonstrate how, insofar as the state takes on projects of distribution related to economic growth, state offices and policies have been key mechanisms for instantiating technologies of state racism across the social. From this view, the nation-state is always what David Theo Goldberg describes as "the racial state," a concept that points towards "the ways homogeneity has been taken axiologically to trump the perceived threat of heterogeneous states of being."[53] In other words, the modern nation state brings with it a notion of "the people" which is always cast in terms of a shared genealogy of racial sameness.

The racial state shapes its populations through processes of both homogenization and differentiation. In the twentieth century, these processes congealed as the social welfare state. Considering the social welfare state's emergence is an opportunity for us to theorize and observe the effects of both a racial state and the projects of what Cedric Robinson designates as "racial capitalism," a term he uses to describe the ways racialized divisions permeate the social order that emerges alongside capitalist modes of production.[54] Whereas normative views of the welfare state situate it in a progression of rights accorded to citizens—such that social rights to health and life follow the securing of political and civil rights—Marxist-feminist accounts suggest that welfare state apparatuses secure and guarantee the reproduction of labor within capitalist conditions of low wages and unemployment.[55] If this view might reduce state apparatuses to "the executive branch" of capitalism, it nonetheless points toward something significant—namely, that capitalist modes of production depend upon the optimization of life itself. As Foucault puts it, the development of technologies of biopower was "an indispensable element in the development of capitalism."[56]

> If the development of the great instruments of the state, as *institutions* of power, ensured the maintenance of production relations, the rudiments of anatomo- and bio-politics, created in the eighteenth century as *techniques* of power present at every level of the social body and utilized by very diverse institutions (the family and the army, schools and the police, individual medicine and the administration of collective bodies), operated in the sphere of economic processes, their development, and the forces working to sustain them. . . . The adjustment of the accumulation of men to that of capital, the joining of the growth of human groups to the expansion of productive forces and the differential allocation of profit, were made possible in part by the exercise of bio-power in its many forms and modes of application.[57]

Feminist theorists have argued that "social reproduction" is the generalizable category for capital, an argument that might dovetail with

Wilderson's emphasis on productivity itself.[58] Feminist attention to the labor and cost of social reproduction supports Foucault's suggestion here that capitalist modes of production force a reconsideration of the management, maintenance, and reproduction of human life. Foucault points to the ways that institutions and technologies of biopower organize and foster the synchronous growth of populations and money—"the adjustment of the accumulation of men to that of capital."[59] In the eighteenth and nineteenth centuries, as economic activity increasingly becomes consolidated as a national economy, population health emerged as a central concern of governance, giving rise to programs that became organized as the social welfare state. The social welfare state secures itself by securing a national economy, and this economy is understood to be positively correlated with the growth of a national population of productive laborers. Disciplinary technologies, administered through schools, barracks, families, neighborhoods, public benefits offices, and the workplace itself, prepped subjects to perform as organized labor. Meanwhile, biopolitical technologies, in the form of social and health insurance, allowed for the organization of a national economy by guaranteeing the growth and overall well-being of the population. Malthus's treatise of natural laws of population control may be the best known expression of these logics.[60]

The evolution of Social Security and Medicare in the United States points to the coproduction of the "two faces of biopolitics," technologies that make live and let die, and the ways they secure and reproduce racialized hierarchies.[61] If the welfare state occasions the rise of biopowerful investments in national well-being, it must bring along with it technologies of state racism for determining cuts in those investments. Comparative studies of the historical development of welfare states bear this out. The European welfare state arose as part of the history of imperial and colonial expansion. The surplus extracted through imperialism created the national wealth to underwrite social welfare programs, and so imperialism became the occasion for an investment in the life of the national body. In the context of capital accumulation through imperial conquest, national welfare programs served an integrative function, drawing subjects of home rule into cohesion with the state through investment in their health and well-being. At the same time, "the challenge of imperial rule demanded an 'imperial race,' which placed a burden on the state to ensure the health and welfare of its own citizens."[62] Social welfare programs demarcated the externality of colonized populations from the nation-state through exclusion from a socially secured well-being as well as discourses of racial inferiority. Robert Lieberman writes, "Thus the politics of welfare state building, the construction of a means of social solidarity at home, was connected to the process of drawing race-based distinctions between national citizens and colonial subjects across national boundaries. Seen in this light, the welfare state is potentially an agent of the political construction of race-based national solidarity."[63] The state-building project of welfare policy and administration was simultaneously a race hierarchy-building project. While subjects of the metropole were organized as national citizens whose health became an object of state concern, colonized populations were fixed in a subordinate status as a source for extraction, not as a site of investment.

Centralizing the role of imperialism in accounts of welfare state development recognizes the welfare state as a racial state. This challenges a common argument in political science that the United States developed a comparatively weak or laggard welfare state due to the ways that racial heterogeneity undermined possibilities for social solidarity.[64] As Lieberman points out, what distinguished the United States in the early twentieth century was rather the foundational presence of subordinated racial and national groups *within* the boundaries of the U.S. nation state, rather than primarily in "external" colonies, as was the case with European empires. The Black Panther Party's internal colony thesis recognized this reality as a necessary starting point for political resistance.[65] Thus, the integrative or social solidification functions of welfare state policies threatened the maintenance of the racial hierarchies of white supremacy in the United States. For the U.S. social welfare state, the dilemma became how to invest in the health and well-being of only *part* of the population and still solidify the nation.

During the early New Deal, key positions in the federal government were held by southern elites committed to maintaining a labor and social system of racial apartheid in the post-Reconstruction South. As what became the Social Security Act was first being drafted, these southern Congressmen were able to successfully exclude agricultural and domestic workers from eligibility—de facto denying African Americans and women access to national entitlement programs. Accompanying this limited national social assistance program was the development of public assistance programs (including what is commonly referred to today as "welfare") administered by subnational state and local governments.[66] Effectively, a bifurcated welfare apparatus arose, with social entitlements controlled by the national government and public assistance programs controlled by subnational governments. The federal entitlements programs served an integrative function by securing the health and economic well-being of the white male population of laborers (and women and children attached to them) and binding this population to the state. At the same time, it excluded from those investments internal racially subordinated populations.[67] Public assistance became the welfare apparatus available to African Americans who were excluded from Social Security, as well as women who were disqualified for entitlements designed for male heads of household. These benefits were "means-tested, relatively stingy, and stigmatizing."[68] Furthermore, being under local control and largely free of federal oversight, public assistance programs were amenable to arbitrary and discriminatory policies and practices that allowed whites to remain superordinate to local black populations by denying access to benefits and subjecting beneficiaries to punitive consequences for enrollment. Thus, whereas national Social Security programs invested in the reproduction of a laboring citizenry, public assistance functioned to maintain racialized and gendered hierarchies—in terms of both economic and national status—and to surveil and regulate the poor. Ruth Wilson Gilmore summarizes these results of the New Deal thus:

> On the domestic front, while labour achieved moderate protections and entitlements, worker militancy was crushed and fundamental U.S. hierarchies remained intact. The hierarchies map both the structure of labour markets and the socio-spatial control of wealth. Thus, white people fared well compared with people of colour, most of whom were deliberately excluded from original legislation; men received automatically what women had to apply for individually; and, normatively, urban, industrial workers secured limited wage and bargaining rights denied household and agricultural field workers.[69]

Federalism became the governance apparatus that could simultaneously serve the state-building demands of welfare policy and the race hierarchy-building needs of U.S. white supremacy. During expansion of New Deal programs under Johnson's Great Society, access to public benefits increased for excluded populations. Along with this expanded access came a racist backlash. As poverty alleviation programs became associated with populations of color, entitlements were challenged through populist and conservative Republican channels.[70] Of course, it took a neoliberal Democratic administration, under Bill Clinton, to fully roll back welfare and transform it into today's measly and punitive workfare.

If we think of social welfare programs as producing life by enabling and investing in it, and also by cutting out through abandonment weak life, it is not surprising that welfare reform in the 1990s revived discussion of making receipt of benefits dependent upon submission to sterilization.[71] The life-securing and life-promoting technologies of the social welfare state have always been accompanied by active and de facto eugenic measures designed to eliminate the "weak" or "unhealthy" elements that exert a drain on the overall wealth, well-being, and vitality of the population. From this view, we can understand Foucault's claim that all modern states are racist states. We can also understand, despite his emphasis in the lecture on state racism at the Collège de France on the Third Reich, that this does not apply to only the most obvious cases of explicit genocide. The modern state is necessarily racist because it makes and takes up population life, and in so doing enacts methods of state racism so that such life can live.

And so the presence of the term "state" in state racism is not incidental. Instead, as the evolution of welfare bears out, in engaging simultaneous projects of homogenization and differentiation, the state makes race in terms of investments in health and the organization and distribution of life chances. "So racism is bound up with the workings of a State that is obliged to use race, the elimination of races and the purification of the race, to exercise its sovereign power. The juxtaposition of—or the way biopower functions through—the old sovereign power of life and death implies the workings, the introduction and activation, of racism."[72] In other words, the charge of the state to organize and purify a national body puts state racism at the core of state-building and state power. Racism is the necessary mode through which biopower is taken on by the state—"racism is inscribed as the basic mechanism of power, as it is exercised in modern States."[73] This is not to say that other projects of distribution could not also be classified as technologies of state racism.[74] But it is to say that because of its concentrated power to distribute, the state is inevitably and unavoidably racist.

SURPLUS LIFE: POLITICAL ECONOMIES OF ILLNESS AND DEATH

If we have rethought the place of the state in organizing and distributing life, health, illness, and death through housing insecurity and deprivation, we must also rehistoricize biopower and its milieus of economy and governance. While Foucault's work has continued to inform scholarship across the social sciences and humanities, especially since the publication in English of his lectures at the Collège de France, little commentary exists about the historical limitations of Foucault's work in describing the contemporary moment.[75] I would argue that in particular we must attend to changes to the state form and to capital in order to reassess the methodological tools Foucault's work provides. Put bluntly, Foucault's model of biopolitics describes a twentieth-century social welfare state that no longer exists in the United States. The historical developments in neoliberal economy and governance since the time Foucault wrote require a historical reformulation of biopower.

One way to think about the historical limits of biopower as analyzed by Foucault is to point to ways in which a Durkheimian model is at play in the relationship Foucault posits between the species body of the population and the animal body of the individual human subject. Early sociologist Emile Durkheim compared modern social formations to a body writ large, suggesting that the different components of modern society functioned like the organs and systems of the human body. For Durkheim, social institutions work cooperatively to produce stability, allowing a society to function and stay alive.[76] I would argue that Foucault makes a similar move. In positing the "two bodies" of biopower, the animal body of the individual subject and the social body of the population, Foucault transfers a view of the human body onto the population. For Foucault, the biopoliticized population is something like the disciplined body writ large.

This translation between the individual body and the social body presumes that the biopolitical population, like the biological organism or individual human subject, would possess a homeostatic drive, an impulse to maintain overall systemic stability, to stay alive.[77] Thus, as described by Foucault, a biopolitical technology is directed toward maintaining equilibrium: "This is a technology which aims to establish a sort of homeostasis, not by training individuals, but by achieving an overall equilibrium that protects the security of the whole from internal dangers."[78] Consequently for Foucault, projects of state racism must identify illness and weakness in order to cast out those elements. Such elements drain the population body of energy and life, pulling it toward death. Foucault's model treats the undesirable parts of a population as something akin to a cancer cell in a human body—a dangerous internal element that must be expunged before it sucks all life away. In this model, the production and maintenance of population norms push away from death and embed the population in life. And so Foucault writes that the aim of biopolitical technologies

> is not to modify any given phenomenon as such, or to modify a given individual insofar as he is an individual, but, essentially, to intervene at the level at which these general phenomena are determined, to intervene at the level of their generality. The mortality rate has to be modified or lowered; life expectancy has to be increased; the birth rate has to be stimulated. And most important of all, regulatory mechanisms must be established to establish an equilibrium, maintain an average, establish a sort of homeostasis, and compensate for variations within this general population and its aleatory field.[79]

The model of homeostasis subtending Foucault's account of biopolitics demands a state that desires to grow and live on through its national population. The state seeks to do so by making population patterns knowable and predictable in order to direct the population toward life. Again, Malthus and his science of population growth express this perfectly.

That Foucault's account echoes Durkheim's points to the general emergence of biological models for interpreting and organizing state functions in relation to economic processes. I do not wish to argue that the social is or is not like a human body, or even that the human body operates always in terms of homeostasis. But I want to point out that the homeostatic-organic model that underwrites Foucault's biopolitics also underwrites the Keynesian welfare state and the concept of the national economy to which it is attached. Keynesianism introduced a set of state controls to mitigate the effects of capital's fluctuations. It did so by generalizing Fordist principles across economic and social realms. If Fordism aimed to systematize mass production through a regularization of labor in the factory, Fordist Keynesianism sought to bring that grid of regularization to labor outside the factory, to labor as a population subject to the ebbs and flows of economic cycles. As David Harvey writes, "The problem, as an economist like Keynes saw it, was to arrive at a set of scientific managerial strategies and state powers that would stabilize capitalism, while avoiding the evident repressions and irrationalities, all the warmongering and narrow nationalism that national socialist solutions implied."[80] In the United States, this took place through the introduction of the New Deal, which effected a "tense but nevertheless firm balance of power . . . between organized labour, large corporate capital, and the nation state."[81] By supplementing low wages and investing in the health needs of a race- and gender-stratified workforce, the New Deal regularized the well-being of labor while allowing for continued capital expansion. In this way, Keynes, like Foucault, assumed that the body politic, the national population of laborers, must thrive and grow in order for the nation, through its economy, to do the same; the health of one begets the health of the other.

By the mid-1960s, the contradictions of capital outmaneuvered Keynesian attempts to mitigate them. The restricted capacity of Keynesianism to stabilize the tumult produced by capitalist competition became apparent. However, critics of Keynesianism understood this not as an endemic feature of capitalism, but rather as evidence of the failures of regularization as a project. As Harvey observes,

> More generally, the period from 1965 to 1973 was one in which the inability of Fordism and Keynesianism to contain the inherent contradictions of capitalism became more and more apparent. On the surface, these difficulties could best be captured by one word: rigidity. There were problems with the rigidity of long-term and large-scale fixed capital investments in mass-production systems that precluded much flexibility of design and presumed stable growth in invariant consumer markets.

There were problems of rigidities in labour markets, labour allocation, and in labour contracts.[82]

In other words, Keynesianism demanded a rigidity that was out of phase with the irregularity of capital. Needed instead were political interventions that matched this irregularity. Patricia Ticineto Clough describes this as a shift away from viewing the economy as a closed system toward an engagement "in terms of disequilibrium in open systems under far-from-equilibrium conditions."[83]

Thus, post-Keynesianism introduces what Harvey describes in terms of a "flexible accumulation" that attempts to correct the rigidities of Fordism. Flexible accumulation involves a flexibility of production—a move to just-in-time, as opposed to simply mass, production. It demands as well a flexibility of labor, meaning its informalization and the shrinking or elimination of protections and securities won through the struggles of organized labor. Finally, flexible accumulation requires a post-social state, and so we have the introduction of neoliberal dismantling of social welfare programs. As Jacques Donzelot succinctly describes it, "Neo-liberalism wants intervention only if it serves competition. It neglects the social and even condemns it by only accepting social policy as a struggle against exclusion on condition, again, that it is not aiming to reduce inequalities."[84] Neoliberal reforms shift responsibility for managing the dangers of living in capitalism away from the state and once again directly onto reprivatized individuals, who must figure out for themselves how to survive low wages and endemic underemployment. As Ruth Wilson Gilmore puts it, "The sum of these displacements was socialised, in a negative way, by the state's displacement from its Keynesian job to produce equilibrium from profound imbalances."[85]

Of course, surviving in these conditions is not so easy, and the dismantling of social welfare nets and the related deindustrialization of the domestic economy has brought great social disorder in the form of deepened poverty and a widening racialized wealth gap.[86] This destructive restructuring has resulted in greater numbers of dispossessed populations alienated from the restructured labor market, which relies on overseas and domestically undocumented labor. This alienated labor can be described as "surplus populations." Some use the term only to mean Marx's reserve army of labor—those who, blocked from labor but capable of being brought back in, function to keep wages low by keeping competition for low-wage jobs high.[87] But in the contemporary context we see that this removal from formal labor becomes more or less, in Gilmore's terms, a "permanent redundancy" beyond the requirements of a reserve army.[88] The great masses of people living today without shelter are part of these neoliberal surplus populations.

If the neoliberal state does not protect against permanent redundancy, it must nonetheless deal with the populations generated out of it. The Keynesian welfare state directed itself to the laborer, and understood the maintenance and growth of labor as its goal. As feminist Marxists argue, this points to the centrality of social reproduction in the management of capital via the state. The Keynesian state targeted laborers who needed a supplement to their wages in order to reproduce their own lives, and in varying ways and degrees assisted those designated unfit to labor, due to being too old, too female, or too improperly embodied. Neoliberal social programs, on the other hand, have become in many ways detached from a strict relationship to labor. In the neoliberal context, the freedom of market mechanisms, and not the health of a population, is understood to guarantee the well-being of a national economy from which individual well-being is presumed to flow. The ongoing Affordable Care Act debates clearly illustrate this, as state-sponsored healthcare is understood as dangerous to the nation and the populace and a threat to a free market of healthcare services and goods.[89] In a neoliberal milieu, instead of securing the health of a labor force through investments in labor, social programs seek to manage unruly surplus populations. Thus, as Gilmore argues, "abandonment" to permanent redundancy is not a singular moment of casting-out, but rather unfolds in layers and requires active oversight and administration:

> Abandonment takes a long time and produces new agencies and structures that replace, supplement, or even duplicate old institutions. Many factors contribute to this complexity. One is that large-scale public bureaucracies are hard to take down completely, due to a combination of their initiative and inertia; another is the fear that a sudden and complete suspension of certain kinds of social goods will provoke uprisings and other responses that, while ultimately controllable, come at a political cost. Here's where non-profits enter the current political economy.[90]

Gilmore's reference to the political economy of nonprofit expansion points to another important distinction between contemporary neoliberal social programs and their earlier New Deal/Great Society counterparts. Today, rather than serve the economy by keeping labor happy, healthy, and alive, social programs serve the economy directly as *part of the economy,* as a social welfare industry. This social welfare industry includes governmental offices, private and quasi-private social service agencies, academic institutions, and commercial sectors, especially real estate developers in the form of Business Improvement Districts. Through this industry, the production of social scientific knowledge and the provision of social services circulate capital. Some have described the growing social service sector as the "nonprofit industrial complex," or NPIC. Others designate ours as a unique stage of "philanthrocapitalism."[91] As housing activist Tiny, a.k.a. Lisa Gray-Garcia, writes about her own organizing efforts, "We . . . no longer use the NPIC term 'homeless' because it is another way to turn our problems into profit for NGOs and NPICs across the globe."[92]

Here, Gray-Garcia names the category of "homeless" a technical apparatus of such philanthrocapitalism and recognizes as well the stake nonprofits have in stable categories such as "the homeless." In taking on population management of various categories, including "the homeless," as their institutional purpose, nonprofit industries leave in place the social, economic, and political conditions that produce massive inequality and diminished life chances in the first place. As Dylan Rodriguez argues, "the NPIC's (and by extension the establishment Left's) commitment to *maintaining* the essential social and political structures of civil society (meaning institutions, as well as ways of thinking) reproduces and enables the most vicious and insidious forms of state and state-sanctioned oppression and repression."[93]

The effect of the neoliberal shift from the social welfare state is a thorough reimagination of social programs as economic programs. Regarding the assimilation of social justice projects of redistribution into the nonprofit industrial complex, Rodriguez notes, "Incorporation facilitates the establishment of a relatively stable financial and operational infrastructure while avoiding the transience, messiness, and possible legal complications of working under decentralized, informal, or 'underground' auspices."[94] In his lectures on German and American neoliberalism, Foucault describes this as "a sort of complete superimposition of market mechanisms, indexed to competition, and governmental policy. Government must accompany the market economy from start to finish."[95] Donzelot characterizes this as the move from the social welfare to the social investment state. In a period of neoliberal restructuring, it is not enough for social programs to serve capital by mitigating the effects of capital exploitation. Rather, social programs are themselves subject to the logics and rigor of capital competition and must demonstrate capacity to survive in a competitive environment of limited resources. As Foucault puts it, neoliberalism demands and calls forth "a state under the supervision of the market rather than a market supervised by the state."[96]

In this shift from Keynesianism to the competitive management of populations through social welfare industries, risk is not just privatized, but reimagined. Efforts to bend flexibly to the fluctuating demands of capital growth force a reconceptualization of risk from a danger to a possibility. This includes the risk of social disorder. As Harvey describes it, the challenge becomes learning to "play the volatility right."[97] Under neoliberalism, risk and disorder are not understood as needing to be reduced or contained, as in the Fordist-Keynesian model. Rather they become opportunities for capital growth. This opportunistic view marks a general move to the *investment in* risk and disorder that characterizes neoliberal approaches to capital management. Investment in risk opens up a perception of social problems and their embodiment—permanent surplus populations—as economic opportunities. The opportunity represented is not a larger reserve army of labor. Rather, this potential is valorized through the development of new service and knowledge industries directed toward managing surplus populations. Neoliberal economic restructuring, including the selective destruction of city neighborhoods and infrastructures that produces mass housing deprivation, generates a disorder that from a Fordist-Keynesian model appeared as a threat to capital growth. Neoliberal technologies of governance transform that disorder into opportunities for investment and expansion by absorbing it into service and knowledge industries as surplus life. The homeless management industry investigated here is one such example of this, where post-social programs meet postindustrial economies.

We can thus update Foucault's original formulation of state racism to account for contemporary neoliberal economy and governance. In a context of the neoliberalization of social welfare programs as social welfare industries, illness and unproductivity may not need to be reduced or eliminated, as Foucault describes for the social welfare state. Neoliberal technologies reconfigure biopolitical governance such that waste and illness are not losses or drains that must be eliminated. Rather, illness and waste, and populations organized as such, become fertile sites for economic investment, as they multiply opportunities for developing and extending governance mechanisms, making the economic life of governance possible. They are the very conditions of possibility for neoliberal social welfare apparatuses. Furthermore, under post-Keynesian neoliberal restructuring, economic growth is not understood as dependent upon the well-being of a population. Instead, neoliberal investment demands a proliferation of risk, uncertainty, and instability. Surplus populations are not simply left to die, but in their slow deaths are managed by social service and social science industries. Gilmore writes, "What . . . distinguishes the expansion of social-service non-profits is that increasingly their role is to take responsibility for persons who are in the throes of abandonment rather than responsibility for persons progressing toward full incorporation into the body politic."[98] In reformulating biopolitical technologies of the neoliberal state, I want to emphasize that this responsibility accords economic and social value to abandonment itself.

This notion of the value of homelessness contradicts, of course, a popular and racist view that homeless populations are a social waste, draining the economy and offering nothing in return. That view is dangerously reproduced when social science fails to account for the ways that neoliberalism brings the persistence of social disorder into the economy. Some have argued, for example, that contemporary mass homelessness can be understood through Giorgio Agamben's concept of *bare life*.[99] Drawing from the political philosophy of Hannah Arendt, Agamben argues that "bare life" describes those populations excluded from the political order and stripped of political agency, incapable of assuming representation. This line of thinking has drawn necessary attention to the interrelations of symbolic and political disenfranchisement. For

example, Leonard Feldman documents how policy and police apparatuses increasingly make unsheltered life an illegal and impossible subject position, codifying into law a cultural figuration of unsheltered
populations as subhuman or animal.[100] The limits of this analysis result
from its neglect of the economic realm, its failure to account for the ways
in which neoliberal technologies are simultaneously governmental *and*
economic. As Aihwa Ong points out in her critique of Agamben's model
of bare life,

> Indeed, different degrees of political and moral claims by the politically
> marginalized can be negotiated in the shifting nexus of logics and power.
> There are conceptual limits to models that pose a simple opposition
> between normalized citizenship and bare life. Giorgio Agamben draws
> a stark contrast between citizens who enjoy juridical legal rights and
> excluded groups who dwell in "a zone of indistinction." But ethnographic
> study of particular situations reveals that negotiations on behalf of the
> politically excluded can produce indeterminate or ambiguous outcomes.
> Indeed, this is the complex work of NGOs everywhere, to identify and
> articulate moral problems and claims in particular milieus. At times, even
> business rationality may be invoked in seeking sheer survival for those
> bereft of citizenship or citizenship-like protections.[101]

Following Ong, we must notice the ways that political and social exclusion are forms of economic inclusion, occasions for moral claims set to
business rationalities. Another way to say this is that the processes of
extreme marginalization and dehumanization of unsheltered populations, which Feldman describes and others corroborate, take place *inside*
an economy and to the benefit of that economy. Rather than bare life,
these surplus populations constitute a form of surplus life—life that is
considered unnecessary, and that is nonetheless productive of surplus
value in neoliberal capitalism.

The past few decades have seen an expansion of federal funding
for homeless services as well as the growth of nonprofit organizations
focused on addressing unsheltered populations. The homeless management industry, as part of the nonprofit industrial complex, gains cultural
legitimacy through its moral claims on behalf of politically abandoned
populations; it gains financial backing through its promise to reduce the
negative impact of those neoliberal surplus lives on social and economic

order; the example of the Doe Fund, described in the introduction, points to this. Such social service sector growth has happened simultaneous to a continued growth of populations living without shelter. Like those founding exclusions that first made racialized private property systems possible, populations living without shelter are the internally abandoned populations that allow for neoliberal governance and economies. And so the post-social welfare state moves beyond Foucault's formulation of a zero sum game in which those marked as ill or unproductive, like "the homeless," would be treated only as negation or loss. Technologies of state racism in the neoliberal context enact processes of calculation and distribution as well as deprivation. Contemporary programs targeting unsheltered populations should not be mistaken for political and social rescue of abandoned populations. These programs emerge to manage the costs of social abandonment, and to transform the illness and death that result from housing deprivation into productive dimensions of postindustrial service and knowledge economies. Neoliberal forms of state racism allow for the continued reproduction of housing insecurity and deprivation as forms of racial subordination, even while transforming those "losses" into valuable economic enterprises.

For Foucault, death, through state racism, makes life because it eliminates that which would sap the population of its strength and vitality; it is a cutting out of loss and negation. But understanding death, the production of death, and the management of death as economic activities forces recognition that that which is ill or dying need not be eliminated to grant biopolitical life to a population. The activity of dying, of being ill, gives *economic* life as matter to be neoliberally and biopolitically managed. Social welfare policy and administration, as biopolitical technologies and economic enterprises, may invest in life and health as objects of governance without challenging the conditions that reproduce and distribute illness and exposure to premature death. In the neoliberal context, economic activity and biopolitical death grow side by side. Housing deprivation is one case of this, an instance of what Achille Mbembe has characterized as necropolitics, or "a subjugation of life to the power of death."[102]

Thus, biopolitical programs today, such as those discussed in the following chapters, should not be misread through the lens of the social welfare state. Rather, they must be taken on as what they are—competitive neoliberal industries of population management. As such, far from "ending homelessness," these programs secure the very economic conditions that expose populations to housing insecurity and deprivation. In so doing, they reproduce and extend the uneven distribution of life and death and the circulation of surplus populations as surplus life.

TWO

Homelessness as Method
Social Science and the Racial Order

IN 1991, AT THE CLOSE OF THE FIRST DECADE OF THE MODERN "homelessness crisis"—estimates of people in the United States living without shelter in the 1980s ranged from 300,000 to 3 million—the Fannie Mae Foundation published *Understanding Homelessness: New Policy and Research Perspectives*. The collection includes a contribution by James Wright and Beth Rubin titled, "Is Homelessness a Housing Problem?" The authors offer a careful but definitive "yes." They argue that obviously a diminishing supply of affordable housing is a direct cause of a rapidly expanding unsheltered population. And they carefully assert that, of course, just naming housing is not enough, as we must address access to the economic resources that make housing accessible. Wright and Rubin conclude that not only extreme poverty, but also "mental illness," substance use, and estrangement from family networks limit an individual's economic resources and thereby increase the risk of homelessness.[1]

That Wright and Rubin felt compelled to pose their opening question attests to the extent to which the material bases of housing deprivation were already obscured. Their article responds to a public discourse that divorced homelessness from housing. Through the 1980s, homelessness as a social problem was articulated through a post-Nixon racialized war on the poor that blamed those living in poverty for those conditions.[2] Joining this discourse, demonizing media portraits depicted people living without shelter as, at best, lazy individuals who chose streets over homes, if not as feral beings poised at the edge of reason and civilization.

And what has happened in the almost two and a half decades since Wright and Rubin first published their study? The "crisis" of the 1980s has stabilized to a permanent feature of urban life, in cities large and small. Most recently, the Department of Housing and Urban Development estimated that on a single night in January 2013, 610,042 people were homeless. Of this number, which includes people living in shelter systems, over one-third were estimated to be living in "unsheltered" locations, in cars or on the street.[3] Meanwhile, policy and punditry of the past twenty-some years have turned away from Rubin and Wright's question of housing, producing instead an almost singular focus on the homeless themselves. Poverty alleviation as a strategy for combating mass housing deprivation has been almost entirely neglected. The characteristics that Wright and Rubin argue produce vulnerability to housing deprivation, especially psychiatric disability and addiction, have become decontextualized and isolated as the focus of medicalized social service interventions that seek to fix pathologies of homelessness. This individual-reparative strategy has displaced a focus on the structural conditions of housing that produce vulnerability and elicit forms of illness and addiction as well. What to do with the homeless, rather than what to do about housing, has become the obsession of government policy, social service practice, and social scientific inquiry. Finally, the ways in which racialized subordination shapes housing vulnerability has become, if not addressed, taken as natural and inevitable, as homelessness has been accepted as a condition of racial otherness.

In many ways, the aim of the present project is simple: to recenter housing in discussions of homelessness. Of course, as Wright and Rubin argued years ago, to do so is not so simple a task. A central argument of this book is that the construction of "homelessness" as a problem has in fact obscured the material conditions that produce housing deprivation, proliferating expertise and management techniques while allowing housing insecurity to expand. Wright and Rubin were correct to call for attention to housing itself in analysis of homeless policy and programming. However, they misrecognize housing and individuals as ontologically distinct and independent. As the following chapters elaborate, in fact housing systems and their inhabitants are coformed through relations of capital and sociolegal regulation.[4] In other words, the life organized by systems of housing insecurity and deprivation does not precede those systems. Rather, housing systems produce the lives contained within, shaping, for example, vulnerability to living without shelter as an expression and experience of racialized subordination in labor markets and consumer economies. Had scholars wrestled with this during the crisis stage, perhaps it would have been harder to isolate individuals for intervention. Perhaps they could also have anticipated that a decade later something else would come to join the individual homeless subject as an object of intervention: the homeless population. Such a reframing is not a matter of idle philosophical speculation. As Gilles Deleuze wrote, the problem is not being too abstract, but not abstract enough. The chapters that follow strain toward a level of greater abstraction of housing and homelessness in order to reexpose the political consequences of the accepted configurations. One consequence of the accepted configurations is that the management of homelessness, rather than the eradication of housing vulnerability, has become the goal of a homeless services industry.

Moving beyond the accepted configurations requires methodological experimentation. As my experiences in social services taught me, we cannot take the categorical status of "homeless" for granted. We have to see not just how material conditions of housing insecurity are produced, but also the organization of the conceptual frame for understanding housing insecurity and deprivation. From this view, homelessness is a deployment of social policy, media narrative, and especially social service and social science practice. This deployment draws energy and resources toward the managing and knowing of its object—the homeless—and away from systemic interventions into the ways that capital, spatial organization, white supremacy, and racial subordination organize housing and life in vulnerable relations to one another. Thus, decades of homeless policy and discourse have not only detached homelessness from a material analysis of housing systems. The category of homelessness actually obscures housing, making an analysis of housing systems difficult to access. The present text is "against homelessness" as it strains alongside what homelessness has organized to bring other concerns to attention. To consider the ways that the construction of a homeless subject has obscured rather than revealed systems of housing insecurity and deprivation, we will turn to consider the role of social science in governance. This will help expose how, in the contemporary moment, a racial otherness underwrites the putatively neutral category of "the homeless" while evacuating a critical understanding of the operations of racial capitalism in producing and distributing unsheltered life.

SOCIAL SCIENCE AND RACIAL ORDER

From its first encounters with housing deprivation, U.S. sociology has grappled with questions of conceptualization and operationalization—how to define homelessness, and how to count it. In his 1933 study *The Hobo,* Nels Anderson recognized both the difficulty and significance of the task. Anderson defined the homeless as "a destitute man, woman or youth, either a resident in the community or a transient, who is without domicile at the time of enumeration. Such a person may have a home in another community, or relatives in the local community, but is for the time detached and will not or cannot return."[5] While acknowledging the significance of Anderson's research for the history of homelessness scholarship, Kenneth Kusmer points to the limits of Anderson's definition. In restricting "the homeless" to describing those who are immediately living "without domicile," Anderson potentially underrepresented the scale and reach of housing insecurity. Kusmer points to the various temporary and inadequate forms of domicile that many otherwise homeless people might be living in.[6]

The question of scope is at the heart of debates about how to define homelessness. The state has some interest in narrow definitions, in order to regulate access to apparently limited resources. But social science also has some motivation for investing in narrow definitions. In his survey of research methods employed in studies of housing deprivation, Peter Rossi notes a range of definitions for homelessness, from quite narrow (restricted, like Anderson's definition, to those literally living without shelter) to much broader and quite inclusive definitions (my own housing insecurity would be an example of this). Rossi writes:

> Clearly, more inclusive definitions imply a higher floor for the concept of decent housing, but they also enlarge the size (and change the composition) of the homeless population. More inclusive definitions also expand and considerably complicate the task for researchers; they set very fuzzy boundaries for homelessness, allowing guesstimates to range more widely.[7]

Like other scholars, Rossi is clearly concerned to adequately address a problem he recognizes as quite urgent. The discussion nonetheless accepts that the problem of definition must be resolved from the perspective of the capacity of research. In other words, the problem of definition becomes a technical problem of what research can practically capture. Rossi writes, "In all the homeless research, operational definitions tend to be less inclusive, focusing primarily on . . . the 'literally homeless,' as opposed to the 'precariously housed.' . . . The more restricted definition tends to be used in practice because the more inclusive ones are extremely difficult to implement, except at prohibitive costs."[8] Rossi concludes that no research program can resolve the limits of its conceptualization, so instead all research must be clear about the conceptualization employed.

The demands and exigencies of research thus foreclose the possibilities of broader and more inclusive definitions. These are real limits, and cannot be theorized away. Problems arise, however, when the material constraints of research fall out of view, and the categories produced in those constraints become naturalized. The historical forces that produce and organize housing deprivation, including, for example, the sociolegal coconstitution of race and property, are lost in the process of that narrowing as well. When that category then becomes the only available one for addressing the "problems of homelessness," a politicization of housing is pushed out by scholarly reification. The narrower definitions necessarily result in smaller and more conservative estimates of the number of people recognized as living with insecure housing. I remain skeptical about the power of numbers to reveal the truth, and skeptical as well about there being a direct correlation between knowing numbers and actually addressing the root causes of a problem. (As chapter 4 will show, the Department of Housing and Urban Development's efforts at accurate population counts have been mobilized primarily to regulate and limit the work of social service agencies.) Nonetheless, narrower definitions, in obscuring the extensive nature of housing insecurity, imply that housing deprivation is a bounded and containable phenomenon, rather than an endemic feature of racialized private property systems and the uneven impact of neoliberal social and economic restructuring. The narrower conceptualization also isolates "the homeless" as an enclosed category and as a special domain of expertise and intervention. Narrowed definitions employed in research have real intellectual and political consequences, as they make it difficult to shift focus from a technically organized and entrenched category to the complex set of factors that produce structural exclusion from safe, adequate, and permanent housing.

As Rossi points out, social science benefits from this limiting of definitions by getting a workable concept and manageable sample sizes. Social science is then positioned to further benefit from the opportunity to develop techniques to capture those marked out by this definition. In a sense, homelessness is a gift to social science, and the gift is that of a methodological conundrum. By focusing on the individual, social science organizes "the homeless" as a subject that lacks the attributes that count in social science, or what social science counts—a fixed, stable, legal identity; a more or less permanent and legal address; and a calculable and trackable income. So the homeless pose a challenge: How to count that which cannot be found? But the fact that the homeless slip away from quantitative social science is not evidence of a methodological failure, or a mere accident. Rather, sociology produces the homeless as an object that would escape it. The homeless are meant to escape— and, in turn, to be captured. Thus, the real question driving social science methods is how to render the homeless as a subject to be investigated and known. Quantitative studies of homelessness are rich with details about the statistical innovations developed to identify and count the homeless; these studies often dedicate more pages to a discussion of methods than to the results or their implications. The fixated attention to methods in quantitative studies of the homeless suggests that the studies are as much about the capacities of social science as about housing deprivation.

If quantitative methods strive to make the homeless countable, qualitative sociology in particular has responded by laying claim to that for which statistical analysis cannot account—the richly detailed "full sense" of the individual homeless person. Qualitative sociology often poses itself as an antidote to quantitative methods, promising depth and specificity to the supposed surface abstraction of statistical measures. But the relationship between quantitative and qualitative work is in fact reciprocal rather than antagonistic. The struggle for quantitative work to provide measurable definitions preps the field for the work of qualitative sociologists by focusing on bounded individuals. Qualitative research can then step up to fill in the details, providing those individuals with a human face. In this way, quantitative and qualitative work function together to co-organize the homeless in both statistical and narrative forms.

George Steinmetz argues that the rise of quantitative models in U.S. sociology in the postwar period was secondary to the triumph of positivism.[9] The tight match between statistical methods and the demands of positivism, especially as formalized by the federal government through the National Science Foundation, enabled statistical sociology's rise to dominance. While this relegated all forms of qualitative sociology to a secondary, less scientific position, ethnography has managed to grab some of the positivist pie. In its claims to "being there," ethnography meets and affirms one of the core principles of positivism—namely, that the world is observable and from there, knowable. As Patricia Ticineto Clough argues, by the mid-twentieth century, the twin positivisms of qualitative and quantitative methodologies worked together to form a "statistical personage" to be managed through scientific knowledge production: "With the further linking of a positivist empiricist methodology to a behaviorism that rejected any structural depth, a statistical personage is constructed as the subject of social science generally and sociology in particular."[10] Among various qualitative approaches, including critical interpretive modes, cultural studies, and historical studies, ethnography has assumed the greatest legitimacy in an institutional context of the supremacy of quantitative methods. In fact, ethnographies of the homeless have not only been central to the production of knowledge about the homeless, but central to the development of sociology as a discipline. Anderson's *The Hobo,* in addition to being the first census of the homeless, was also the first urban ethnography of what became the Chicago School; the study of hobo life gave sociology ethnographic practice. A few decades later, Douglas Harper's photographs of traveling unsheltered men would found visual sociology.[11] In this way, homelessness has served a discipline-building function within the social sciences.

Despite methodological differences, positivist approaches to housing deprivation ultimately attempt to answer the same root question: "Who are the homeless?" Ethnography does so through detailed portraits of specific individuals in context, whereas statistical study does so by analyzing broad population patterns. These methodological constructions of homelessness are situated in a larger context of social science and its relationship to the state and its urban centers. The development of domestic social sciences, especially sociology, has been coterminous with the founding of systems of racialized subordination and exploitation. Raewyn Connell argues that in the early decades of the twentieth century, a U.S.-dominated sociology rewrote its origin story, positing itself as a response to industrialization. In so doing, sociology has masked its actual origins in imperial conquest.[12] Of course, European and North American imperialism underwrote industrialization. Cedric Robinson and Eric Hobsbawm demonstrate this in the case of British textile production. The expansion of cotton farming, necessary to textile mechanization, would not have been possible without the enforced labor of the transatlantic slave trade and the appropriation of land in colonization.[13] So, to the extent that sociology as a formalized field of study emerges from colonial metropoles, imperialism materially makes sociology possible. But Connell demonstrates that sociology is *epistemologically* made possible by the imperial production of racial otherness. In surveying sociological writings of the mid- to late nineteenth century, Connell finds that the dominant theme of early sociology is not the social effects of industrialization and urbanization, as all introductory sociology textbooks claim. Rather, early sociological studies focus on the difference of the metropole from its agrarian past and from its contemporaneous colonies. In the early twentieth century, as the hegemony of European social science wanes and U.S. sociology assumes a globally definitive role, U.S. sociologists constructing a canon excised this imperial history. At the same time, early U.S. sociology directed the question of difference inward, to the internally colonized populations of the U.S. empire— Natives, immigrants, and ostensibly free and newly mobile African Americans. Thus, sociology departed from what becomes anthropology's domain—the overseas (post-)colonies—claiming the disorder of the domestic as its special realm of expertise and authority.

Roderick Ferguson reflects on the social, political, and economic transformations of the United States in these early decades of the twentieth century, placing the Great Migration of African American labor from the South to cities of the North in the center of a history of industrialization and urbanization. In the course of these transformations, Ferguson argues, the interests of capital and the state were not always aligned. Geopolitical upheaval and the reorganization of labor produced surplus populations with new and nonheteronormative embodiments of race, gender, and sexuality. These surplus populations served the needs of emergent industrialized production through a multiplication and diversification of labor. But these populations also challenged the homogenizing drive of the U.S. racial state, which sought to organize labor-citizen status through heteropatriarchal family structures that enforced normative embodiments of race, gender, and sexuality. Ferguson writes:

> Surplus populations point to a fundamental feature of capital: It does not rely on normative prescriptions to assemble labor, even while it may use those prescriptions to establish the value of that labor. Capital is based on a logic of reproduction that fundamentally overrides and often violates the state's universalization and normalization of heteropatriarchy.[14]

For the U.S. settler state, still in a slow process of consolidation post-Reconstruction, capital's overriding of heteropatriarchal norms and structures provoked "anxiety about the sanctity of 'community,' 'family,' and 'nation.' "[15]

Thus, even as the United States set the conditions for industrialization and the Great Migration, it perceived the resulting nonheteronormative surplus populations—forms of labor necessary for capital expansion—as threats to social order. The state desired to know this disorder in order to reduce, manage, and contain it. The call for knowledge was answered by sociology, which, as Ferguson documents, stepped in to observe, classify, measure, and narrate the shape of surplus populations for the benefit of the state.

> As sociology positioned itself as part of the state's reform agenda, its production of racial knowledge about African Americans as nonheteronormative subjects also mediated its relationship with the state. A whole set of methodologies was deployed to produce that exteriority as part of the racial knowledge about African Americans. The Chicago School sociologists . . . expressly used ethnography to measure the effects of economic change on black racial formations in the urban North and the South. Statistics emerged as the apparatus for tallying African American cultural dysfunction for the good of liberal capitalist stability. Statistics became an invaluable tool not only for measuring demographic changes around African American migration, urbanization, and employment, but for producing knowledge about the importance of such changes.[16]

Ferguson shows how sociology organized the disorder of industrial capitalism as new social scientific objects of knowledge amenable to governmental intervention. This intervention took the form of urban planning and new social programs of racial containment. Sociology thereby resolved the tension between capital expansion and state control. Producing racialized surveillance as a scientific discourse, sociology secured the continued reproduction of surplus populations, which now could be known and managed so as not to disrupt too much the working of the state. In its circulation of racial knowledge for the mutual benefit of the state and capital, sociology affirmed rather than challenged the discursive production of "non-white" gender and sexuality as always incipient aberrant threats.[17]

Thus, in Ferguson's terms, as both "critic and supplicant" of the state, sociology helps secure social order, allowing both governance and capital to thrive by entrenching the state in the midst of the upheaval produced by capital's reproduction of surplus labor.[18] But sociology secures more than just the state and capital; it secures itself as well. As Connell suggests, sociology accomplishes this through renewed processes of professionalization and institutionalization that mark out "urban disorder" as its exclusive domain of expertise.[19] In so doing, sociology makes itself indispensable to the state, aligning itself with the state and the state, in turn, with sociology. The expansion of National Science Foundation funding documented by Steinmetz points to this.

In return for offering up a science of difference for the racial state and racial capital, sociology gets an image of itself posited over and against its affectable others, to use Denise Ferreira da Silva's term. As da Silva writes, the "arsenal of raciality . . . produces both (a) the affectable (subaltern) subects that can be excluded from juridical universality without unleashing an ethical crisis and (b) the self-determined things who should enjoy the entitlements afforded and protected by the principle of universality said to govern modern social configurations."[20] In figuring the surplus populations of capital in terms of a set of failures— familial, gender, sexual, and laboring failures bundled together as racial inferiority—sociology produces itself as a self-determined form of labor, properly gendered, sexed, and raced. In the contemporary context of urban neoliberal capital, "the homeless" have been a key disordering problem for governance, and hence an opportunity for social science to secure and reproduce its universal self-determined status. The discussion below will consider ethnographer Mitchell Duneier's claim that social science derives its ethics from its methods for studying the homeless. I argue that these methods are figured as a kind of work, a "good" form of white, male labor. And so ethics becomes the special skill and purview of white masculinity, producing what I term the "whiteness/rightness" of social science methodology.

SIDEWALK WARS

In 2002, a decade after Wright and Rubin queried the connections between housing and homelessness, a debate ensued on the pages of the *American Journal of Sociology (AJS)* regarding the proper work of ethnographic research on urban poverty. The occasion for the debate was the publication of an extended review by Loïc Wacquant of three recent ethnographies, authored respectively by Catherine Newman, Elijah Anderson, and Mitchell Duneier. In addition to Wacquant's commentary, the *AJS* issue included responses from the three authors. Although there is much to say about each of those author's texts, here I will focus on Mitchell Duneier's *Sidewalk* and on the issues raised in Wacquant's review and Duneier's response. *Sidewalk* tells the story of the largely "unhoused" vendors of books and magazines who work along a stretch of Sixth Avenue in the Greenwich Village neighborhood of New York City.[21] Not only is *Sidewalk* taught in undergraduate and graduate classrooms around the United States (if not the world); it has furthermore proven to be a crossover hit. Reviews of *Sidewalk* have been published in the *New York Times, Chicago Tribune, Atlantic Monthly,* and *Village Voice Literary Supplement.* Duneier himself produced a follow-up documentary for use in teaching the text. *Sidewalk* developed out of many months of participant-observation research, conducted in several stages over many years, during which time Duneier worked with the vendors, selling magazines and books. As is well documented in the text, book and magazine street vending is difficult work with long hours, and Duneier's dedication to the task has been widely praised and celebrated.

Wacquant offered less laudatory words in his review of what he labels a "neo-romantic tale." In his discussion of *Sidewalk,* subtitled "The Saints of Greenwich Village: Duneier on Homeless Sidewalk Vendors,"

Wacquant accuses Duneier of depicting the sidewalk vendors as hard-working "saints" who dedicate their lives to following and enforcing strict moral codes. Wacquant finds this to be a simplistic portrait. But even more importantly, Wacquant argues that *Sidewalk*'s hagiographic mode dangerously feeds into and supports a neoliberal discourse of personal responsibility through a validation of the moral calculations that fuel welfare retrenchment and the contemporary war on the poor.

A small controversy ensued regarding the evidence marshaled by Wacquant in what is quite an aggressive and caustic critique of *Sidewalk*. To build his argument, Wacquant supplies a variety of citations from *Sidewalk,* which, as Duneier points out in his reply, are often truncated in such a way as to significantly alter the immediate meaning.[22] It is true that in his review Wacquant alters most of the quotations from *Sidewalk*. It is not clear, however, if this fact invalidates his central argument that *Sidewalk* offers an endorsement of neoliberal retrenchment of social welfare programs and the informalization of labor. Unfortunately, Wacquant's unique method of citation has perhaps discredited critique of *Sidewalk*—and if it did not, Duneier's forceful reply may well have stunned would-be critics into silence. Nonetheless, below I want to reopen consideration of *Sidewalk*'s implications in neoliberal discourses and technologies of governance in light of the role of social science in managing racial disorder as outlined by Connell and Ferguson. Both for its status in the field and for the ways it recapitulates core claims of social science methodology, *Sidewalk* offers a key opportunity to think about the problems of producing a sociology of the homeless.

Referencing all three works of his review, Wacquant summarizes the complicity of urban ethnography with what he terms an "ambiant [sic] neoliberalism":

> By leaving social movements, politics, and the state out of the picture and by acquiescing to extreme levels of class inequality, urban ethnography spontaneously accords with and even endorses the ambient neoliberalism. And its recommendations, anchored in the presumption of individual responsibility, the centrality of "values," and the sacralization of work, help legitimate the *new division of labor of domestication of the poor,* distributed among a dictatorial business class, a disciplining welfare-workfare state, and a hyperactive police and penal state, leaving a cosmetic philanthropic and private-foundation sector to mop up the rest.[23]

Sidewalk does pay what I would consider cursory attention to the operations of the police and state in the lives of the vendors. In my view, the most compelling section of *Sidewalk* is Duneier's documentation of the strategies employed by the management of Penn Station in midtown Manhattan to make the public spaces of the train terminal more amenable to surveillance, and to therefore undermine the possibilities for eking out a subsistence existence therein.[24] However, such social control mechanisms, and the larger political economic contexts in which they are embedded, are left largely in the background of *Sidewalk,* as individual tales of turmoil and triumph assume center stage.

The stories constructed in *Sidewalk* do carry along with them what Wacquant describes as a legitimation of moral ascription and sanctions tied to work ethics and personal responsibility. However, the limit of Wacquant's critique is that, like Duneier, he fails to consider the ways in which this ambient neoliberalism draws from and reproduces the racialized organization of heteronormative work and family structures. In other words, neither author accounts for the gendered and raced dimensions of both housing insecurity and the strategies mobilized to contain the impact of housing-deprived surplus populations on urban social and economic order. Lisa Duggan argues that such an analysis is central to the task of understanding the operations of neoliberal governance:

> In order to facilitate the flow of money up the economic hierarchy, neoliberal politicians have constructed complex and shifting alliances, issue by issue and location by location—always in contexts shaped by the meanings and effects of race, gender, sexuality, and other markers of difference. These alliances are not simply opportunistic, and the issues not merely epiphenomenal or secondary to the underlying reality of the more solid and real economic goals, but rather, the economic goals have been (must be) formulated *in terms of* the range of political and cultural meanings that shape the social body in a particular time and place.[25]

In their debate about whether or not *Sidewalk* endorses neoliberal economic restructuring, Wacquant and Duneier overlook the relationship of those economic programs to a cultural discourse of race, gender, and labor. Thinking of housing insecurity and its management as produced by and productive of gender and racialization draws attention to the ways that a latent discourse of family operates in Duneier's text. The ambient neoliberalism that Wacquant senses but inadequately documents emanates from that family discourse. *Sidewalk* is haunted by an earlier "culture of poverty" discourse that produced the black family as aberrant due to the supposed failed gender of black males—a failure to articulate a proper work ethic and do so within a heterosexual nuclear family arrangement.[26] *Sidewalk*'s neoliberal feeling is its rearticulation of black masculinity through heteronorms of family and labor, and its endorsement of neoliberalism occurs through its recapitulation of the culture of poverty discourse, which, though unnamed, organizes the narrative of redemption Duneier presents. Thus, what Wacquant does not offer but what *Sidewalk* demands is the kind of analysis Ferguson names "queer of color critique," a mode of analysis attentive to the interimplication of racial, sexual, and gender regulation through housing insecurity and deprivation.

BAD MEN DOING GOOD: THE HARD WORK OF POVERTY, FAMILY, AND MASCULINITY

The narrative of *Sidewalk* presents a strong validation of work and work ethics in its depiction of book and magazine vending. The text not only demonstrates that this is difficult and arduous work, which takes talent and skill, but also imbues this labor with moral quality. In the narrative of *Sidewalk*, selling books and magazines is not just a way to raise subsistence funds. These activities come to represent "moral" choices that constitute "decent lives." As Duneier wrote in his *AJS* reply, "A core issue of my work was to understand the ways in which 'moral' behavior and 'decency' are and are not constructed within settings seemingly unfavorable to such behavior."[27] What constitutes morality and decency is left unexplicated by Duneier; his use of quotation marks suggests that we all know, or should know, what those terms mean. It becomes clear that in the context of *Sidewalk* those words indicate participation in informal but legalized survival economies. For example, in response to the negative associations that passersby might have of the Sixth Avenue vendors, Duneier argues that this public should recognize that engaging in labor is an attempt to live a moral and decent life:

> When people sleeping *on these blocks* decide to stay there, it becomes questionable to many passersby whether they are really struggling to live "decent" lives. The answer, I think, is that such acts pose no challenge to what we saw in the first three chapters of this book: each of these men is engaged in such a struggle. This is most evident in the way they choose to support themselves: through honest entrepreneurial activity.[28]

Duneier presents the assignation of indecency as if it needs no critical inquiry or justification in research, and he counters his own claim with the value he assigns to sidewalk vending. In concentrating on the labor of the vendors, the political economic conditions that produce legalized informal labor as the best options for surviving in poverty fade to the background. In not only concentrating on this labor, but in fact celebrating it, *Sidewalk* revalorizes capitalist work ethics that have been leveraged against social safety nets in the context of the workfare state.[29] Validating this labor as moral and decent accepts as inevitable the social abandonment of these populations.

In response to Wacquant's accusation that *Sidewalk* bolsters neoliberal economic reform, Duneier describes his informants as "casualties of the neoliberal state, whose tenuous existence is continually threatened by the political leaders and business groups who vehemently seek their removal."[30] But the neoliberal state is not characterized only by withdrawal and abandonment. Rather, neoliberalism also involves the deployment of technologies of subjectivity that remake the individual within the context of increasing economic polarization and the erosion of social safety nets.[31] Processes of privatization have not only outsourced governing activities to nonstate and quasi-state entities, but have shifted responsibility for public concerns onto reprivatized individuals. Duneier concludes *Sidewalk* by arguing, "It is vital to the well-being of cities with extreme poverty that there be opportunities for those on the edge to engage in self-directed entrepreneurial activity."[32] I would say that in fact it is vital to the well-being of neoliberal capitalism that individuals be abandoned to self-directed entrepreneurial activity. In other words, entrepreneurs are exactly what neoliberalism demands—people who can figure out how to make something out of nothing, who can determine on their own how to survive eroding social welfare nets, sinking wages, and decreased opportunities for formal employment and job security.

Vendors may "self-direct" their labor, but those selves are neoliberalized selves, and that labor is certainly not in conditions of their own choosing. The subjects of *Sidewalk* should hardly be blamed for figuring out how to live through the increasing impoverishment of neoliberal inequalities, but the text's endorsement of this obscures the operations of state violence.

As a result of this framing of morality and decency, the historical conditions of capitalism and liberalism that have organized hard work and personal responsibility as laudable qualities pass without critical commentary in the text. Even without engaging contemporary scholarship on neoliberalism, we should recall from Max Weber's classic work *The Protestant Ethic and the Spirit of Capitalism* that we must be suspicious about the associations of moral worth with entrepreneurial activity such as that documented by Duneier.[33] The validation of the vendors' hard work as moral behavior derives from a historically specific arrangement of productive forces and legitimating discourses. In failing to address the historical context of the moral codes, Duneier neglects how those codes uphold the very systems of inequality that concern him—capital's stratified exploitation of labor. Furthermore, those codes are not universally applied, but are figured through race and gender systems. The sacralization of work is not only historically specific, but also produced through and productive of heteropatriarchal racial formations.[34]

The discussion of entrepreneurship and moral worth is made explicit in *Sidewalk,* even while the implications of the historical articulations of labor and decency are left unaddressed. Under the surface of this explicit conversation, a second, unacknowledged discourse unfolds. This is a discourse of how gendered norms of behavior, including the connection of proper masculinity to hard work, should relate to heteropatriarchal family structures. In addition to their willingness to engage in hard work, *Sidewalk* locates proof that the subjects are leading "decent" and "better" lives in reparative family relations. In seeking appropriate heteropatriarchal relationships—in the roles of father, brother, son, grandparent, and husband/boyfriend—*Sidewalk*'s subjects repair as well a black masculinity that decades of social science and social policy have depicted as damaged by and reproductive of a "culture of poverty." In narrating sidewalk vending in terms of attempts to "live decently," the text revalidates not only neoliberal expectations of personal responsibility, but also expectations of an indecent black masculinity that subjects must struggle to overcome. Roderick Ferguson points to an earlier history of this discourse in the context of the Great Migration and industrial capitalism. The contemporary recapitulation indicates the capacity of neoliberal governance to preserve and mutate earlier governance regimes and discourses while setting new arrangements among space, labor, race, and gender.

Hakim Hasan, the original inspiration for *Sidewalk* and the author of an afterword, presents himself to Duneier as a "public character," as described by Jane Jacobs in *Death and Life of Great American Cities*.[35] For Jacobs and Hasan, a public character is an individual who, as part of the local fabric of a street or neighborhood, helps connect otherwise alienated residents. Jacobs's text provides many of the conceptual frames for *Sidewalk,* and Duneier takes up Hasan's identification as a public character, connecting it to Elijah Anderson's concept of the "old head" who advises younger males in African American neighborhoods. Duneier emphasizes especially the relationship between Hasan and a nineteen-year-old identified as Jerome. Given that a narration of Jerome's own broken family is woven in with stories of how Hasan provides books to Jerome and encourages him to get a GED, it is hard not to see Hasan positioned as the father figure Jerome has lacked. Jerome is quoted as saying about his father,

> He used to be a carpenter the last time I talked to him, a year or two ago. He used to take care of us when we was younger, but everything changes. My parents haven't been together from when I was born. And my mother and I don't have a deep relationship. I mean, we talk, and I know she's my mother. I'm fortunate to just be alive, because she left me when I was a day old. And my father, I just don't know about it. We need to have a father-and-son discussion. I'm trying to have me and my daughter be close, so we can have discussions, because I don't want it to be like me and my father.[36]

Hasan's mentorship is cast as a reparative move that attempts to fix the broken black family. Hasan is quoted as narrating his mentorship in such terms, saying, "As I have developed a relationship with men like Jerome, they start to talk to me about their father and mother and the chasm between them. And I identify with that, because, when I was growing up, my father and mother didn't make it, and it was my mother who raised all of us. So I can identify very, very deeply with him."[37] Hasan's mentorship of Jerome is presented as breaking the cycle of the broken family for both of them.

We also see morality and decency tied to proper masculine-familial bonds in an exchange that Duneier has with a vendor, Marvin, regarding his work with another vendor, Ron. Early in the text, Ron is presented as a sometimes unreliable work partner due to his drug use. Duneier reports on his questioning Marvin about working with Ron:

> I asked Marvin why he seemed to sacrifice his own well-being and put up with Ron.
>
> "He's like the little brother I always wanted," Marvin explained. "I care kind of daily for him, 'cause I trust him. It's like a blinded love I have for another human being. His goodness is there, but it is blocked by his drug use. He still can be a good man, and I'm trying to teach him how to be good. There is a lot he doesn't want to go along with."[38]

Thus, this brotherly relationship, like the father/son mentorship, is connected in the text to the efforts to work in decent and moral ways.

For Duneier, the failure to live in proper family arrangements is a powerful force in his subjects' lives. *Sidewalk* argues that we can find evidence that the men do in fact care about some things when we look at their feelings about these failings: "Even if the 'Fuck it!' mentality is pervasive in its impact on a person's life, all of the men on Sixth Avenue do 'give a fuck' about certain things. This is illustrated by their sense of shame and embarrassment, emotions most firmly rooted in how they believe they look in the eyes of family members."[39] Ron's developing relationship with his aunt becomes the occasion for the subjects to reflect on the positive impact family relationships can have. Marvin is quoted as comparing Ron's relationship with his aunt to that of another vendor, Mudrick, with his granddaughter:

> "It's just like you," said Marvin. "When your granddaughter wasn't here, you were running around with the guys and blowing all your money. Soon as your granddaughter was born, you know you love your little granddaughter, you have a little responsibility for her, and you give her everything. He's supposed to give his aunt everything that he can."[40]

Ron is depicted as doing just that. In one scene, Duneier is asked to cover a shift at the vending tables for Ron, who wants to return to his aunt's house because he believes she may have left the stove on. Duneier writes this in terms of the redemption it evidences: "Ron's decision to get on the subway and go all the way up to Harlem was an example of his not saying, 'Fuck it.' A person who had given up on family and responsibility would have taken his chances that his aunt would discover the hot stove on her own. He wouldn't have cared."[41]

The connection between hard work, proper masculine family relations, and decent living is confirmed when Duneier returns to his research site after some time away:

> Six months later, when I was back in New York working on the street, Ron looked very different to me. Whereas once he'd had the disheveled appearance of a man who never shaved or showered, now he was clean-cut. He explained that he was still living with his Aunt Naomi, and had continued taking good care of her. Now that his cousin was gone, she had given him the spare bedroom.[42]

The narrative confuses the material results of living in appropriate and consistent housing as opposed to on the street—a clean-cut versus a disheveled appearance—with moral uplift. The improvement in Ron's appearance is not evidence that Ron is a better man; it is evidence that he is living in better conditions. Duneier and photojournalist Ovie Carter (whose images are published alongside the text of *Sidewalk*) accompany Ron on a trip home, where they witness him taking care of his aunt. The visit ends with a scene that takes place just after they leave:

> As we waited for the elevator, we heard Ron yell to [his aunt]: "Do you want your boiled milk now?"
> Ovie went back inside, and before they noticed him he made the accompanying photo of Ron serving the boiled milk. It illustrates, perhaps better than any interview might, the positive changes that Ron was making with the support of Marvin on the street.[43]

The fact that they were on their way out, and that Ron and his aunt did not realize Carter had returned, is meant to emphasize that the photo that accompanies the text is not staged. It calls to mind Patricia Ticineto Clough's argument about the function of narrative in realist ethnography: "In realism, then, narrativity is given a particular function: It permits characters to be presented as if they are completely absorbed in their own activities and therefore are seemingly completely unaware of the beholder and the painter outside the painting or the reader and writer outside the text."[44] This display of "good nephew" behavior, then, corroborates the narrative description with visual evidence, freeing the story from its technologies of construction and infusing it with objective realism. None of the photos in *Sidewalk* are captioned, and this is the only photo that is addressed directly by the text, according it a pivotal position in the narrative's development.

Finally, *Sidewalk* suggests that its subjects attempt to apply the lessons they are learning about family to their sexual relationships with women. When one subject discusses his girlfriend with Duneier, Duneier asks, "Do you curse in front of her?," which presumably is a measure of a decent and moral relationship. Duneier gets an affirming reply: "No! No cussing! No drinking beer! No smoking cigarettes! I cannot do that with her. She's a beautiful person. That's the respect she want from me. Not in front of her."[45] And so despite dedicating a chapter to how the vendors sexually harass women on the street, Duneier argues the following:

> While my analysis here centers on behaviors that some passersby find objectionable, it cannot be overemphasized that at other times on the sidewalk (and at other times in their lives) each of these men would be seen acting in "positive" and straightforward ways toward others, including the women in their lives—girlfriends, mothers, and granddaughters as well as general passersby.[46]

Thus, moral uplift is coded as an attempt to enter the sphere of heteronormativity, especially through hard work. *Sidewalk* realigns proper masculinity with labor and family, reproducing both an aberrant black masculinity and the possibility of its recuperation into the realm of moral labor.

Much of the material for this discourse on reparative family/masculinity work is provided by the subjects through stories and quotations. My concern is not whether or not these stories are true. In offering a critique of this discourse in *Sidewalk,* I do not mean to deny the reality of these relationships or the painful emotional experiences often suggested by the stories. But I want to raise the question of what it means to organize the narrative of the text through these stories, and what it means to tell these stories as opposed to others. These stories did not just magically appear in the text—they were solicited, selected, and organized by Duneier. They are the raw material out of which the text is produced. To say the experiences are real does not mean their existence in the text should be taken for granted. In emphasizing narratives of masculine redemption and reparative family and family-like bonds, *Sidewalk* dangerously recapitulates an individualized narrative that underwrites the culture of poverty thesis. Duneier's attention to critiques of literature on "the family," which is limited to one paragraph focused on a general issue of single-parent households, neglects the historical conditions of antiblack violence which his interview subjects navigate in their daily lives.[47] This emphasis is a methodological choice to reject engaging in a discussion of the historical state-produced violence against black families, from the Atlantic slave trade through to contemporary prisons, foster care, and welfare reform. That violence has produced a heteronormal nuclear model that punishes and pathologizes other familial arrangements, including queer, single-parent, and nonromantic households. In evacuating historical context, *Sidewalk* reasserts and revalorizes the violences of heteropatriarchy.

THE WHITENESS / RIGHTNESS OF SOCIAL SCIENCE METHODOLOGY

In his *AJS* reply to Wacquant, Duneier describes *Sidewalk* as part of a broader academic project to understand how individuals negotiate moral norms and how these negotiations reveal what he calls "the common elements of humanity."[48] In fact, Duneier argues that such a project is the important contribution that ethnographic research can make to social science: "The capacity of urban ethnography to humanize its subjects is one of its greatest strengths, providing an important antidote to the opposite tendencies among theorists of both the right and left who depict such people only in abstract terms, devoid of their quintessentially human qualities."[49] For Duneier, this defense counters Wacquant's claim that he depicts the vendors as saints. Rather, Duneier argues that *Sidewalk* offers complex portraits composed of both moral shortcomings as well as moral competencies, and that in revealing the latter, Duneier hopes to show that the vendors do possess those quintessentially human qualities.

At no point in *Sidewalk* or his *AJS* response does Duneier explicitly name what might constitute these quintessentially human qualities. The narrative thrust of the text suggests that to be human is at the very least to exhibit a capacity to understand and navigate codes of moral conduct. As Duneier wrote in *AJS*, "*Sidewalk* does not depict the vendors as saints, but rather brings to light their basic humanity, and yes, the desperate attempt of many, against nearly insuperable odds, to live 'moral' lives."[50] Perhaps because those human qualities are never specified, and the outlines of a moral life never filled in, Duneier fails to grapple with the historical specificity of the concept of humanity, and the ways in which a discourse of humanity is inexorably bound to categories of the inhuman. Feminist and critical race scholars have long pointed to the historical circumscription of the category "the human" and its emergence in relation to the modern state, capitalism, and imperialism in literature that Duneier does not address.[51] Duneier's use of the expression "quintessentially human" evacuates history, ignoring decades of feminist, critical race, and anticolonial critiques of just such universalism. Recently, Andrea Smith has emphasized not only the historical origins of "humanity," but also the continued violence of the category in the present. Because the legibility of humanity depends upon its distinction from inhumanity, discourses of humanity must continually reproduce and reinvest categories of the inhuman. Smith writes, "Unfortunately, the project of aspiring to 'humanity' is always already a racial project; it is a project that aspires to a universality and self-determination that can exist only over and against the particularity and affectability of 'the other.'"[52] Smith's comments are directed to one tendency in Native Studies to assert the common humanity of Native peoples, a move meant to counter racist and genocidal constructions of indigeneity, but her caution is equally applicable to the project of ethnography outlined by Duneier.

Establishing the humanity of sidewalk vendors requires a contrast, an other, the inhuman. *Sidewalk* finds its affectable others among its very subjects, those working and living on Sixth Avenue. In other words, in order to humanize the subjects of its narrative, *Sidewalk* must first dehumanize them. It does so in two ways. The first is in contrasting the vendors with others on the street, whom Duneier terms "panhandlers and layabouts" and describes as "unhoused black men on the street who refuse to take up the option of working as scavengers and vendors."[53] Putting this in terms of a refusal to work, with the strange Victorian language of "layabouts," and setting this in contrast to decency and morality, Duneier produces this "subclass" of Sixth Avenue as affectable others.

Secondly, to further make his case, Duneier devotes four chapters of *Sidewalk* to documenting a variety of what he characterizes as "indecent" behavior, including public urination and the sexual harassment of women. It is not beyond the pale of comprehension that these behaviors are performed by the subjects. They are performed by many people, in many contexts, and Duneier makes some effort to show the structural constraints, which already seem fairly obvious—the men have nowhere else to go to the bathroom, for example. But what must be called into question is the place of this behavior in the text. For Duneier, documenting the failure of some of his subjects to live "decent" lives proves that they are complex, and that his portraits are balanced and objective. While Duneier grants ethnographic justification to these portraits, I would argue that the images contribute to the race knowledge project of social science surveillance. Perhaps this would not be the case if Duneier spilled equal ink on detailing the indecent behavior of every other figure who appears in the text. While in a footnote Duneier acknowledges that he also "urinates and defecates," how he does that is not scrutinized; nor is the urination and defecation of other interview subjects, such as bookstore owners and lawyers.[54] Their relations with women and families, their sleeping habits, their drug and alcohol consumption all take place outside the confines of the sidewalk, and hence lie beyond scrutiny. The burden of bearing the ethnographic field—in this case, the sidewalk—is placed squarely on those least able to avoid the scrutiny and surveillance that regulate the poor and that, as Ferguson suggests, sociology has always played an important role in effecting. Thinking about how humanization produces affectable others helps make sense of the emphasis given to the photograph of Ron pouring milk for his aunt. Only with very low expectations could such an act be surprising, and so the text must enact those low expectations in other to then deliver on its promise of challenging them. For Duneier, some of those assumptions are justified no doubt by his expectations of who composes his readership as well as who composes the passersby. But this presumed audience enacts another layer of dehumanization, casting the vendors outside of the public, and enacts as well a naturalization and normalization of white middle-class values and expectations.

Furthermore, in focusing on the behavior of individual vendors, Duneier can pay only limited attention to structural forces. This is painfully clear in the accounts of bathroom use. While suggesting that we need more public restrooms, Duneier also notes their limits as a social control mechanism.

> On a recent trip to Paris, I walked the streets with a French sociologist, Henri Peretz, looking for one of the maintenance trucks that perform upkeep for the city's self-cleaning public toilets. When we tracked one down, and I told the driver (through Henri) of my hope that one day the people of New York would have such resources, he complained that in Paris some unhoused people had taken up nightly residence in the bathrooms, using them as shelters. This suggests that even public bathrooms will not always be available for people to do their bodily functions. Every policy has its unintended consequences.[55]

Duneier's fixation with decency and enforcing norms of behavior prevents him from commenting on how truly horrifying it is to think about locked toilets as the best option made available for some people to spend the night. By restricting his concerns to the performance of moral or indecent behavior, he dehumanizes people living without shelter once more by bypassing an opportunity to express moral outrage at the right target— social policies that create abject and horrifying conditions of poverty.

The submersion of inquiry into the violence of housing insecurity raises questions about the basic frame and premise of *Sidewalk*. Inspiration for the text comes from Jane Jacobs, and I think some of the problems of *Sidewalk* are inherited from there as well. With *Sidewalk*, Duneier takes up a central theme supplied by Jacobs—questions of safety in dense urban settings. In a passage that *Sidewalk* cites with no critical commentary, Jacobs presents the following argument:

> Nor is it illuminating to tag minority groups, or the poor, or the outcast with responsibility for city danger. There are immense variations in the degree of civilization and safety found among such groups and among

the city areas where they live. Some of the safest sidewalks in New York City, for example, at any time of day or night, are those along which poor people or minority groups live. And some of the most dangerous are in streets occupied by the same kinds of people. All this can be said of other cities.[56]

Although Jacobs attempts to be critical of racism against "minority groups," the frame of civilization employed derives from racial subordination and colonization. Like its related discourse of humanity, a discourse of civilization reinscribes colonial racist logics. Jacobs does not measure levels of civilization in "non-minority groups," those whose civilized nature can be taken for granted. Duneier makes a similar move by not detailing the indecent or immoral behavior of the other figures in the text, and thereby making their morality, decency, humanity— their civilized natures—beyond question. By accepting Jacobs's framework of safety and "eyes on the street," Duneier privileges the *feelings* of unsafety of passersby and "citizens" over and against the actual unsafety of the vendors, whose lives are threatened and shortened by poverty. It is exactly fears about safety and violence that tough-on-crime politicians have stoked and exploited for the past many decades of punitive carceral-welfare policies in the United States.[57]

Toward the end of *Sidewalk,* Duneier writes, "A new social-control strategy is needed. At its core can be unrelenting demands for responsible behavior, but there could also be new kinds of enlightened understanding from the citizenry, leading to greater tolerance and respect for people working the sidewalk."[58] In this call for enlightened social control, we see all of *Sidewalk*'s themes come together. Clearly the citizenry does not include the vendors, who must meet "unrelenting demands for responsible behavior" while hoping for tolerance and respect. In uncritically mobilizing the term "citizen," *Sidewalk* elides the violence of the concept and affirms what is always the purpose of the category, which is to exclude under the guise of universalism. The violence of housing deprivation is naturalized, and a law-and-order/war-on-the-poor discourse of safety is affirmed rather than challenged. In accepting the frame of "safety," Duneier marks out the public/citizens as in need of protection. By reassuring readers that the presence of legalized informal laborers on those streets will not disrupt that safety, Duneier renders the violence of housing insecurity normal and mundane. Here, then, we understand the ambient neoliberalism Wacquant senses as the racial and gender project it is.

Finally, we can understand the gift of homelessness to sociology in terms of how *Sidewalk* figures its own project over and against the lives it narrates. The call for enlightenment is central to the project of humanizing and civilizing that *Sidewalk* enacts. Pheng Cheah has argued that such enlightenment is itself a form of violence, which Cheah designates a "violent light."[59] And who should point out the path to enlightenment? The sociologist, of course, who can be trusted to provide an ethical guide for social control as he returns from the field unscathed, with facts and ethics intact. As Clough argues, "Staging the researcher's entering and leaving the field, . . . ethnography demonstrates that a boundary has been twice crossed, making possible the empirical correspondences, comparisons, and contrasts (across that boundary) that . . . ethnography presents as factual representations of cultural perspectives, historical events, and social situations."[60] The objectivity of the ethnographic enterprise, as characterized by Clough, grants credibility to its ethical dimension as well.

Duneier makes forceful claims that the ethics of his project are embedded in his research choices. Recall that he argues in *AJS* that what ethnography has to offer is the humanization of degraded subjects. We have already seen that the text also enacts the degradation it seeks to challenge. The discourse of ethics within *Sidewalk* effectively casts the subjects of the book outside the ethical, making the ethical the legitimate purview of sociology. In the appendix to *Sidewalk*, Duneier explains his approach to informed consent. Duneier writes:

> I did not believe that anyone could make an informed judgment about whether they would like their name and image to be in the book without knowing how they have been depicted. With this in mind, I brought the complete manuscript to a hotel room and tried to read it to every person whose life was mentioned. I gave each man a written release which described the arrangement whereby royalties of the book are shared with the persons who are in it. But I did not tell them that I would do so until the book was nearing completion.
>
> It was not always easy to get people to sit and listen to the larger argument of the book and to pay attention to all the places where they

were discussed. Most people were much more interested in how they looked in the photographs than in how they sounded or were depicted. I practically had to beg people to concentrate on what I was saying. It also did not help that they now knew they would share in the profits, a factor that sometimes made them feel less motivation to listen carefully, on the assumption that I could be trusted. The following conversation, while somewhat extreme, illustrates (among other things) that the effort to be respectful by showing the text to the person in it sometimes turns out not to seem very respectful at all. In this case, I end up insisting that the individual listen to me, and imposing my agenda on someone who seemed annoyed by my efforts.[61]

The transcript that follows details Duneier's efforts to get one of his informants to listen as he reads out loud sections of the text. Throughout the conversation, the informant interrupts, insisting that the ritual is not necessary while calling out for a friend to bring him a drink. Although in the passage above Duneier suggests that his efforts to be ethical may not "seem very respectful," the text does not question its research protocol. In fact, after the transcript, Duneier writes that because the informant was drinking a beer, he had to go back and repeat the process all over again.

What other possibilities for research are foreclosed in this process? Gayatri Spivak's famous call echoes here: "Can the subaltern speak? What must the elite do to watch out for the continuing construction of the subaltern?"[62] Rather than stick to the protocol, Duneier might have usefully abandoned for a moment his frames of morality and respect. Doing so perhaps would have allowed what was happening to register as informed and willful resistance to the sociological project. In not questioning the ethics of his own protocol, and in not taking the resistance seriously, Duneier makes the determination of proper, ethical research as belonging to the sociologist, not the vendor. The narrative ultimately confirms the role of the researcher, his proper work ethic and proper masculinity, his ability to recognize the appropriate place for bodies and activities even as he transgresses. The story thus reflects back an image of sociology and confirms the role of social science in governance. The role of sociology in governance is legitimated and marked as ethical. And the affectable others are marked as in need of sociological intervention— first to govern them, and then to grant them their humanity.

The sociology of homelessness, in accepting the restrictions of its categorical imperatives, neglects an understanding that the deployment of categories is never neutral and always carries with it political commitments and consequences. Following Tukufu Zuberi and Eduardo Bonilla-Silva, we can characterize such a sociology of homelessness as deploying white logic and white methods:

> By speaking of *logic* we refer to both the foundation of the techniques used in analyzing empirical reality, and the reasoning used by researchers in their efforts to understand society. *White logic,* then, refers to a context in which White supremacy has defined the techniques and processes of reasoning about social facts. . . . *White methods* are the practical tools used to manufacture empirical data and analysis to support the racial stratification in society. *White methods* are the various practices that have produced "racial knowledge" . . . since the emergence of White supremacy in the fifteenth and sixteenth centuries and of the disciplines a few centuries later.[63]

Through white logic and white methods, the racial order is reordered, as homelessness as a condition of blackness is naturalized, and the pathologization of black people resecured through narrativized overcoming. Governance too is granted once again its whiteness, in defense of white entitlement to the city—to feelings of safety, to bourgeois conceptions of community and cleanliness, to a naturalized order that in its circulation does violence to those designated as disorder. And, finally, the ethical place of social science is resecured once again, in the role of documenting and governing within the existing social order, or, in Denise Ferreira da Silva's words, for the benefits of those "self-determined things who should enjoy the entitlements afforded and protected by the principle of universality said to govern modern social configurations."[64]

THREE

From Pathology to Population

Managing Homelessness in the United States

AS CHAPTER 1 DETAILED, THE HISTORY OF SOCIAL WELFARE IN THE United States is a history of bifurcation between federal and subnational state programs. This splitting of the state has been an explicitly racial project. Federal programs have served the integrative projects of a homogenizing racial state, attaching a white, male citizenry to the nation and its economic investments and growth. At the same time, the exclusion from federal entitlements through cuts of race and gender and the subsequent dumping of those populations into subnational assistance programs have secured heteropatriarchal arrangements of labor and family along with the subordination of internally colonized populations.

Within this bifurcation of social welfare programs, housing and other services for populations living without shelter have been grouped with public assistance rather than federal entitlement programs. Hence, the responsibility for administering these programs has fallen on subnational state, county, and municipal governments, as well as on private and quasi-private organizations, from early settler-colonial churches to modern social service agencies. The federal government has played a limited but quite powerful role in this homeless management nexus. The current period of federal involvement begins in 1987. It is preceded by only one other such period, during the early New Deal, from 1932–1934. These two instances of federal involvement tell an important story about the changing nature of federal governance and the relationship of those changes to the pressures of economic restructuring. As we will see, while the early New Deal represents a stabilization of social and economic order through investments in labor, the return of federal involvement in the mid-1980s seeks a stabilization of consumption in the context of new service and knowledge economies.

Federal intervention into housing insecurity and deprivation must contend with long-standing discourses about the causes of homelessness and the most effective strategies for managing it. Those discourses shape federal responses and are being reshaped by them as well. Federal programs launched in 1987 introduced a new dimension of governance to a long-standing disciplinary dimension. If that disciplinary dimension seeks to mold individual homeless *subjects* by changing their thinking and behavior, this new dimension concerns the organization and regulation of a homeless *population* and its impact on government resources and local economies. Thus, the return of the federal government forces a biopoliticization of homelessness, a techno-conceptual reorganization of homelessness in terms of problem populations. Post-1987 biopolitical technologies of homeless management do not mark the end of discipline. To the contrary, disciplinary technologies of homeless management offer a track across which biopolitical technologies roll out. But in that process, disciplinary technologies—and the homeless subjects constituted through them—are radically transformed. In that transformation, they bring forward with them racialized systems of property and selfhood that demand management of populations that are understood to be fundamentally disordered and in need of governance.

Race, Space, and Federal Intervention from Bust to Boom

From the early days of white colonial settlement of North America through most of the history of the United States, people living without shelter have been considered a local problem to be dealt with by local institutions. In the nineteenth and early twentieth centuries, a period of reform known as the Progressive Era, the jailhouses of growing cities often allocated space for non-incarcerated individuals who needed shelter to spend the night.[1] During the same period, charitable organizations, usually church-based, built lodging houses to address shelter needs. In exchange for shelter, food, and prayer services, lodgers were required to perform what was known as a "work test," consisting of several hours of manual labor, such as breaking stone or cutting lumber.[2] The work served a small productive economic function—the sale of the stone or wood generated funds for maintaining lodging houses. But as the term "test" implies, its greater function was adjudicative, ferreting out those whose moral fiber failed to measure up to the standards confirmed by labor. The work test identified those willing to work, but temporarily unable to secure employment. At the same time, in language similar to contemporary evocations of the "deserving" versus "undeserving" poor, "tramps" who traveled illegally on railcars and lived in semipermanent camps outside the legal and moral purview of municipalities were disdained for what was understood to be a shunning of modern industrialized existence through a refusal to work.[3] While tramps opted out of the lodging house system, the task remained for lodging house administrators to identify and eliminate those among shelter-seekers with morally inferior tramp sensibilities. By the beginning of the twentieth century, municipally run lodging houses emerged alongside those that were privately run. These city shelters often did not require a work test and were thereby viewed more favorably by lodgers who resented the paternalism of the test.

The work test was petty and paternalistic, but it signaled an important conceptual and material connection between labor status and housing status. During this period, housing insecurity largely resulted from the economic insecurity of marginalization from work and was understood in these terms.[4] The number of people living without shelter and seeking shelter at lodging houses fluctuated along with economic downturns and upswings, as well as with seasonal cycles of agricultural and industrial production. The economic crisis that began in 1929 and became the Great Depression dramatically increased the number of unemployed and marginally employed. Therefore the numbers of impoverished people unable to afford private housing accommodations increased as well.[5] The Great Depression marked not only an increase and diffusion of housing insecurity and deprivation, but also the first time the federal government of the United States directly addressed unsheltered populations. This was not simply a case of responding to a growing need. As we will see again in the 1980s, national crises are not natural occurrences; the recognition of something as a national problem requiring federal intervention is a contingent and contested process. That housing deprivation became a "national problem" in the 1930s had to do with both the emerging federal governmental infrastructure of the New Deal and the fact that housing insecurity was becoming generalized across the white populations of the United States.[6] In fact, as chapter 1 suggests, those two facts are interimplicated, in that the emergence of a social welfare state in the United States was always a project of racial security and integration into the nation. During the 1930s, a national capacity for intervention, in the form of New Deal administrative initiatives, allowed housing insecurity to register as a national crisis, rather than one simply diverted back to local jurisdictions. Most significantly, as Kenneth Kusmer points out, this era of federal involvement marked a response to conditions that were considered acceptable for African Americans and Mexican migrants, but intolerable when white males were subjected to them.[7] Insofar as housing insecurity was seen as an epiphenomenon of general (that is, white male) labor insecurity, it fell within the purview of federal concern.

The federal response in the 1930s to the expansion of white labor insecurity and the growing unsheltered population was in fact fairly swift and bold. It turned out to be short-lived as well. At that time, local laws for unsheltered individuals were directed through settler colonial programs of indigenous land seizure.[8] Access to lodging houses depended on establishing settler rights, a local residency claim that secured white land access and ownership. To be admitted to a lodging house required proof of belonging in that jurisdiction. During the depression, the great masses of unsheltered people living on the road posed a challenge to these protocols. Many no longer had claims to settler rights due to being in transit for extended periods of time. Many others lacked the means to return to where those rights were held. The displaced white masses of this period pressured the existing settler rights system such that the federal government created the new category of "federal transient"— something like an internal refugee (exiled from local settler status) who was now granted a direct relationship to the federal government in lieu of a relationship to a local government.[9] Thus, the instability of white land claims was temporarily mediated through a new landless citizen subject position with a racialized access to federal protection.

Beginning in 1932, through the newly formed Federal Emergency Relief Administration (FERA), the federal government established or subsidized urban Federal Transient Centers as well as camps in rural regions. These supplemented the private and municipal lodging houses that were already in existence but overwhelmed by the dramatic increase in need. The urban centers connected residents to the contingent employment opportunities of the city. Older transients, those aged forty and over, were often directed to rural camps and therefore moved outside of urban labor circuits. As Peter Rossi notes, "From this distance the federal camps appear to have been rural warehouses for those considered unemployable."[10]

Within a few years, New Deal administrators turned their efforts to large-scale infrastructural public works projects, and FERA was quickly and somewhat unexpectedly dismantled in the summer and fall of 1934, less than two years after its founding, and despite the fact that FERA centers and camps had housed an estimated one million people.[11] Some centers continued to operate without federal funding and others permanently shut down, dispersing their residents to lodging houses or other communities.[12] The first era of federal intervention had come to a close.

By 1943, the war economy kicked in, and the phenomenon of unsheltered traveling masses began to die down. Tramp culture and camps also began disappearing as seasonal tramp labor was increasingly displaced by developments in industrial agricultural technology.[13] What remained was a population confined more or less to the "skid rows" of urban centers.[14] Much of this population (whom one scholar describes as "prosperity's discontents") would not fit contemporary conceptions of "homelessness," since for the most part they lived not on the streets, but in lodging houses and private hotels, or single room occupacies (SROs).[15] In addition to this housing, skid row districts provided a concentration of low-cost consumer services, social services, and opportunities for underground and contingent day labor.[16] Official perception of skid row residents retained the moral judgments of earlier eras. For example, a commentator writing in 1948 claimed, "The skid rower does not bathe, eat regularly, dress respectfully, marry or raise children, attend school, vote, own property, or regularly live in the same place. He does little work of any kind. He does not even steal. The skid rower does nothing, he just is. He is everything that all the rest of us try not to be."[17] The statement, typical of the era, projects the failures of industrialization onto individuals who are figured as embodying the antitheses of the American work ethic and gender/family norms. The notion of someone who "just is" anticipates formations of surplus life in the contemporary era.

Without accepting the moral judgment of the commentator cited above, we can ask what is new or distinct about skid row residents versus earlier unsheltered populations. The concentration of unsheltered populations in skid row districts represents a solidification of housing insecurity as a distinct phenomenon that can no longer be understood as simply a subset of unemployment. It is the beginning of a new permanent redundancy. From this time on, unsheltered populations became increasingly marginalized from all but the most underground forms of labor, as well as from the organizations and institutions of modern urban life other than those whose missions targeted unsheltered populations. A complex set of conditions coalesced to produce these new forms of housing insecurity and deprivation such that bringing someone into legal or regular employment became an insufficient redress. As a result, housing insecurity and deprivation became quasi-independent dimensions of the population, and unsheltered populations came to crystallize around a set of common characteristics. These developments occurred through a set of changes related to economic restructuring that began as early as the 1950s and produced what by 1975 historians were calling the "new homeless."[18] The category meant to capture a cluster of demographic characteristics: the new homeless were depicted as younger, more destitute, and extremely marginalized from employment, and their ranks were understood to include more women and greatly disproportionate numbers of people of color.[19] While reflecting significant historical shifts, the category of "new homeless" evokes the level of the individual subject, making housing deprivation something of an identity. We might instead think in terms of an emergent neoliberal housing insecurity. Considering the processes that produce housing insecurity within neoliberal economic conditions will clarify why housing deprivation took on the demographic characteristics it did, especially its consolidation as a feature and expression of racialized subordination. There is no neutral category of "homeless" that travels across time and space; how housing insecurity manifests and is interpreted are technical effects of political economic systems, popular discourse, and social policy frameworks.

The federal government began directing its attention to skid row districts in the 1950s, though not out of concern for the well-being of the people who lived there. Rather, government officials looked to skid rows through a financial lens, in terms of property values and opportunities for economic investment and growth.[20] Social scientific studies at the time dealt not with the plight of those living in subsistence conditions within skid row districts, but with how government and industry could "revitalize" the neighborhoods for what would turn out to be neoliberal postindustrial service economies catering to tourists and wealthy urban consumers. By the 1960s and 1970s, cities across the United States were tearing down their skid rows, emptying and demolishing residential hotels, and driving out the businesses frequented by skid row residents.[21]

The elimination of this form of housing had both immediate and long-term effects—immediate in the displacement of residents, and long-term in the erosion of a form of private housing on which future populations in need of low-cost shelter could no longer depend. James Wright and Beth Rubin document the loss of this housing stock:

> In San Francisco, 17.7 percent of the existing SRO units were destroyed or converted in a four-year period in the late 1970s, with further losses since. Similarly, in New York City there was an overall 60 percent loss of SRO hotel rooms between 1975 and 1981. The number of New York hotels charging less than $50 per week declined from 298 to 131 in that period; of hotels dropping out of that price range, the majority are no longer even hotels and have been converted to other uses, mainly to condominiums. Denver lost 28 of its 45 SRO hotels between 1971 and 1981, Seattle lost 15,000 units of SRO housing from 1960 to 1981, and San Diego lost 1,247 units between 1976 and 1984.[22]

Urban renewal efforts targeted not only skid rows, but impoverished inner-city neighborhoods generally, which were violently bisected by highway construction that facilitated white flight to booming postwar suburbs.[23] This flight was subsidized by the federal government through Federal Housing Authority programs that underwrote home ownership for predominantly white areas while denying loans to communities of color. The sum total of these developments was to increase and intensify housing insecurity for urban populations of color, who found low-income rental housing options disappearing and mortgages for home purchase out of reach. Thus, from the 1960s on, the size of the unsheltered population began to grow. Members of this population would find themselves struggling to survive in a reconfigured urban landscape created out of the ruins of skid row and increasingly hostile to their presence.

The destruction of Skid Rows and other inner-city neighborhoods was only one part of a large web of political, social, and economic changes, which together constituted a neoliberal restructuring of urban communities and economies. This was a creative destruction that cleared the way for the social and economic forces of gentrification to move in, in a process Neil Smith describes as a "new urbanism."[24] As Smith documents, this new era of gentrification, as part of a larger neoliberal remaking of the city and its economy, transformed formerly neglected or abandoned urban centers into sites of intense real estate speculation:

> This new urbanism embodies a widespread and drastic repolarization of the city along political, economic, cultural and geographical lines since the 1970s, and is integral with larger global shifts. Systematic gentrification since the 1960s and 1970s is simultaneously a response and contributor to a series of global transformations: global economic expansion in the 1980s; the restructuring of national and urban economies in advanced capitalist countries toward services, recreation and consumption; and the emergence of a global hierarchy of world, national and regional cities. These shifts have propelled gentrification from a comparatively marginal preoccupation in a certain niche of the real estate industry to the cutting edge of urban change.[25]

Further aspects of neoliberal economic restructuring multiplied the life-threatening effects of "renewal" and gentrification. Deindustrialization, the emergence of service economies, and the rollback of welfare programs increased economic disparity and alienation from labor markets for former skid row residents.[26] Beyond skid row, as with urban renewal programs, the strongest impact of these changes was felt by urban populations of color. Kenneth Kusmer points specifically to the intensification of African American exposure to housing insecurity through declining employment opportunities, barriers to education and new job industries, and the racialized effects of the 1970s economic recession.[27] From the 1970s on, the overexposure of these racially subordinated populations intensified and became entrenched. But rather than addressing the decisive break implied by the category "new homeless," neoliberal governance enacted a drawing out and consolidation of housing insecurity and deprivation as forms of racialized subordination.

What the "new homeless" wind up looking like was shaped not only by these political economic forces, but by social responses as well. This is what it means to argue that the techno-conceptual organization of housing insecurity is shaped by social services that are not merely responsive to, but also productive of the categories they manage. The average age of people living without shelter lowered due to the expansion of Social Security, which provided a greater level of economic security for those who aged out of labor. Women's housing insecurity became managed through public assistance and domestic violence programs that attached women to family structures.[28] This gendered and gendering apparatus did not eliminate women's experiences of housing insecurity, which grew alongside the gendering of poverty. It did, however, direct that insecurity through alternative channels of management. Thus, the population of people living on the street became, and still remains, disproportionately male. The police and prison systems scoop up the majority of this population, leaving behind a small fraction of the permanently redundant to be dealt with by the homeless services industry.[29]

Neoliberal economic and social transformations did not only increase the numbers of people living without shelter. As Kusmer writes, "by the end of the twentieth century a much enlarged homeless population was apparently on the way to becoming a permanent feature of postindustrial America."[30] Unlike periods in which economic upturns significantly reduced housing insecurity and deprivation, the recovery of the U.S. economy from the recession of the 1970s did not decrease housing deprivation; the numbers of people living without shelter continued to grow from the 1970s on.[31] I am not suggesting that economic recessions and labor structures no longer contribute to housing insecurity and deprivation. Rather, I wish to point to the ways in which neoliberal housing insecurity and deprivation can no longer be explained, or contained, by employment. In a neoliberal milieu, housing insecurity becomes an embedded feature of population dynamics, a permanent redundancy intrinsic to the national population rather than an epiphenomenon of something like unemployment. Neoliberal reforms also reveal that we cannot think in positivist terms of a dependent categorical variable—housed or not housed—that could then be simply related to a set of independent variables—gender, race, and age, for example.

Rather, housing insecurity is constituted out of those social dimensions, and "housing-deprived" is another way of naming the surplus populations produced by the inequalities of those dimensions. Housing insecurity has a "nature," and its nature is a concentration of vulnerabilities—vulnerabilities of racial exclusion from education, employment, social entitlement programs, property, and space.

HUD and the "New Crisis" of Homelessness

In 1982, a senior official in the Department of Housing and Urban Development (HUD) told the *Boston Globe* that "no one is living on the streets."[32] Unfortunately, such willful denial did not make this so. The residents of skid row districts did not simply disappear when those neighborhoods and the housing they supplied were destroyed. Far from it: the complex forces of neoliberalism increased the size of unsheltered populations, who were no longer concentrated and contained in skid rows but were dispersed more broadly through urban public places. In the emerging neoliberal city, they were considered threats to exactly those tourist and consumer economies for which the death of skid row was meant to make room. Thus, the contradictions of capitalism appear: neoliberalism produced its own problem population, its own uncontainable excess. It was in this context that housing insecurity reappeared as a national concern, this time as "the homeless crisis." The federal government, already involved in projects of urban renewal, stepped in to secure neoliberal urban economies by managing the disorder those economies created. This new moment of federal intervention evidences what Eva Cherniavsky has called "the duplicity of the modern nation-state," which, she argues, is "the double imperative to advance the public good and to secure private property in its myriad and proliferating forms."[33] Of course, what city planners and HUD officials imagined "public good" to signify would shift enough in this era that the protection of private property came to absorb the social. To secure city streets for consumption was imagined to be key the interest of the public.

A series of federal agencies charged with housing issues followed the dissolution of FERA but did not deal with unsheltered populations. Rather, these agencies, which were reorganized as HUD in 1965–1966, first dealt with increasing home ownership and providing rental assistance for low-income families, and later became involved in the urban renewal programs documented above.[34] Not until 1987, with the passage by Congress of the Stewart B. McKinney Homeless Assistance Act, did targeting homelessness become part of HUD's broad mission of urban development. The introduction to the act, later renamed McKinney-Vento, delineates both a crisis and a federal responsibility to respond:

> The Congress finds that—
>
> (1) the Nation faces an immediate and unprecedented crisis due to the lack of shelter for a growing number of individuals and families, including elderly persons, handicapped persons, families with children, Native Americans, and veterans;
>
> (2) the problem of homelessness has become more severe and, in the absence of more effective efforts, is expected to become dramatically worse, endangering the lives and safety of the homeless;
>
> (3) the causes of homelessness are many and complex, and homeless individuals have diverse needs;
>
> (4) there is no single, simple solution to the problem of homelessness because of the different subpopulations of the homeless, the different causes of and reasons for homelessness, and the different needs of homeless individuals;
>
> (5) due to the record increase in homelessness, States, units of local government, and private voluntary organizations have been unable to meet the basic human needs of all the homeless and, in the absence of greater Federal assistance, will be unable to protect the lives and safety of all the homeless in need of assistance; and
>
> (6) the Federal Government has a clear responsibility and an existing capacity to fulfill a more effective and responsible role to meet the basic human needs and to engender respect for the human dignity of the homeless.[35]

The McKinney-Vento Act was the first federal policy addressing populations living without shelter since the dissolution of FERA. The act responded to the new crisis of homelessness both by putting in place new mechanisms and by reorganizing systems that were already in place. McKinney-Vento founded the Interagency Council on Homelessness (ICH) "to coordinate the federal response to homelessness and to constellate a national partnership at every level of government and every element of the private sector to reduce and end homelessness in the nation."[36] The ICH works across all federal agencies whose missions intersect with housing insecurity and deprivation; in addition to HUD, these include the Departments of Health and Human Services, Labor, and Veterans Affairs. Under George W. Bush, the mission of the ICH was revitalized, and it was made a fully independent agency. Today the ICH plays a significant role in setting policy direction and shaping public discourse.

The McKinney-Vento Act also established funding for new programs that operate through subnational government offices and nonprofit organizations. HUD has been granted primary responsibility for managing these homeless funding tracks and programming initiatives, grouped together as Special Needs Assistance Programs (SNAPs). SNAPs include funding for emergency shelter, supportive housing programs for populations diagnosed with psychiatric disabilities, housing for unsheltered populations living with HIV/AIDS, and rental assistance for formerly unsheltered or "at-risk" families and individuals.[37] HUD's homelessness initiatives are situated within its Community Planning and Development office, or CPD.[38] An extension of its urban renewal efforts from the 1960s and 1970s, HUD's CPD efforts have been roundly criticized for increasing rather than challenging racial inequality in housing and business development. Like the urban renewal practices that destroyed neighborhoods, today HUD continues to produce housing insecurity. Under McKinney-Vento, it joins those efforts with responsibility to tidy up the messes left behind in the form of populations living without shelter.

The Obama administration reauthorized McKinney-Vento in 2009 with the passage of the Homeless Emergency Assistance and Rapid Transition to Housing Act (HEARTH).[39] HEARTH was included in the Helping Families Save Their Homes Act, which was meant to respond to the ongoing foreclosure crisis. HEARTH modified existing McKinney-Vento programs and was met with some opposition from advocates. The National Coalition for the Homeless, for example, argued that the new federal definition of "homeless" would preclude certain people living in precarious situations. They also argued that the act reduced community control over its responses and marginalized the role of homeless individuals and advocates in local funding decisions. Finally, they criticized data collection requirements that did not address privacy concerns.[40]

The differences between the role of the federal government in the 1930s and the current era illustrate the shift from the social welfare state that was just emerging during FERA to the contemporary post-social or neoliberal state. Today the U.S. federal government does not run its own shelters or programs, as was the case with Federal Transient Centers and camps during the 1930s. Rather, through the McKinney-Vento Act, the federal government provides funds to private agencies and subnational state and municipal governments to administer housing and related services. In 1987, the first year of McKinney programs, Congress provided $350.2 million in funding for those programs. In FY2013, HUD's budget for its Homeless Assistance programming was $1.933 billion.[41] Despite the outsourcing of service administration to lower levels of government and private agencies, I would argue that the McKinney-Vento Act instantiates an *increase* of federal authority, compared with both the time of FERA as well as the over fifty years of federal noninvolvement between FERA and McKinney-Vento. The nature of this federal authority is not simply a top-down hierarchy, but rather a heterarchic arrangement of "metagovernance," or the governance of governance.[42] Through the McKinney-Vento Act and its programs, the federal government enacts a multiplication and reorganization of the scales of governance, overseeing and linking up local municipalities, regions, states, and federal offices.[43] Within these heterarchic arrangements, the McKinney-Vento Act establishes programmatic parameters, including what kinds of populations can be housed, what kinds of housing can be built, and how services and outcomes must be assessed and reported. This funding never covers any more than a small part of an agency's operating costs—no nonprofit or municipal agency is fully funded by HUD. Agencies are however often required to secure HUD funding in order to qualify for funding from other sources, including subnational state and municipal offices and private foundations. In keeping with the neoliberal spirit of the times, federal policy on housing insecurity functions as a domestic form of structural adjustment, in which states, municipalities, and localities are "free" to innovate within restrictions attached to funding.

This picture of federal metagovernance contradicts both common assumptions about the state in neoliberalism and ideas the state might have of itself. Wendy Brown, cautioning against too dismissive a view of the state, suggests that one characteristic of U.S. neoliberalism is an "anti-Big Government" rhetoric that masks an intensification of federal authority.[44] Prison and military spending have, of course, expanded during a period of supposed shrinking of government. The case of HUD bears Brown's caution out as well. HUD has been a very powerful force in reshaping the techno-conceptual organization of housing insecurity and deprivation. Its funding parameters and reporting requirements are fundamentally changing the provision of housing and associated services for unsheltered populations. Its authority, though, is not the kind that clamps down. Rather, through the mechanisms of metagovernance, HUD plays a piloting role, setting parameters and facilitating transactions among state, municipal, and private entities. Metagovernance in this case is a grid of control overlaid on top of already existing networks, knowledges, and practices of a disciplinary homeless services apparatus. This dispersed and decentralized apparatus, in place long before the advent of neoliberal privatization and devolution, is shaped by HUD, but also creates the conditions of path dependency that partly determine what HUD is able to enact.[45] Through the McKinney-Vento Act, housing insecurity and deprivation have been organized as what is now accepted as a "crisis of homelessness." This crisis, established through responses to it, is shifting popular, academic, and governmental conceptions of homelessness. The next section will look at the long-standing conceptions of homelessness that are reworked in the contemporary era.

MAKING THE HOMELESS CRAZY

The dominant discourse on homelessness in the United States has its roots in medicine in general and psychiatry in particular. This is evidenced in American popular culture, which is saturated with images of "crazy homeless people." Newspapers and television news programs offer lurid crime and disorder narratives that depict the mental instability of street people as threatening the safety of "us" normal middle-class denizens of cities. As Robert Desjarlais argues, in such accounts, homeless figures provide a stand-in for social and political anxieties about modern existence in capitalist conditions of urban disorder and uncertainty:

> A common problematic vision is apparent in many accounts: the homeless live in an underworld; they are a ghostly, animal-like brood who threaten the peaceful, artful air of cafes, libraries, and public squares. Television shows and Hollywood movies . . . create pictures of ghostly, ragged vagabonds haunting the post-industrial wastelands of American cities, while newspaper accounts thrive on images of death, transgressions, and grotesque bodies. . . . The homeless themselves serve to counter images of health, wealth, purity, and high culture. The imagery passes swiftly, unquestionably, as if it was in the nature of sentences, of putting words onto paper, to set pain against beauty and wretchedness against form.[46]

In these popular and mass media productions, the homeless individual is rendered unmoored from the social and familial and also unmoored from their minds and the common morality and rationality thought to reside there, soldering a conceptual link between psychiatric disorder and urban disorder. The "mad homeless" are figured as less than persons. They are subhuman, animal-like in nature or appearance, parasitical. The mad homeless are also simultaneously figured as an excess of personhood—their bodies and possessions occupying too much inconvenient space, their bringing of the private practices of sleep and defecation into public spaces of subways, doorways, streets.

These excesses and shortcomings of personhood have served to reinforce feelings of disgust and to sanction social abandonment. But even more importantly for the present study, the figuration of the homeless as less than human also animates social rescue. Consider, for example, professor of psychiatry Stephen B. Seager's *Street Crazy,* which offers an account of the nine years Seagar spent providing mental health services to homeless patients in Los Angeles. The book opens with a story about "Mr. Smith," against whom Seagar sought a court order to continue treatment:

Mr. Smith was the first patient I'd taken to court to detain for further treatment. He'd come to our facility five days earlier having been found at the bottom of a drainage ditch soaking wet, babbling and bleeding. According to passers-by, a pack of feral dogs had mauled him. Not spotted, he would have died during the night.

Despite our ministrations, Mr. Smith still looked terrible. Save one molar and incisor on the left, his mouth was toothless. Our clean hospital clothing hung on a skeletal frame like drop cloths over attic furniture. A leg infection was barely beginning to heal. The facial lacerations, recently scabbed over, would cause permanent scarring. Mr. Smith was fifty-six years old, had been homeless for fifteen years and suffered from chronic schizophrenia.

The district attorney, representing the hospital, stood. "Do you think living under a car is appropriate shelter?" he asked.

"Shit, yes," Mr. Smith said.

"And eating garbage gives you enough nutrition?" he asked.

"I've been sick some but ain't dead yet. No maggots in me." He grinned crookedly.[47]

After affirming that Mr. Smith believed the underbelly of a car to be appropriate shelter because it kept him dry and that he also understood that garbage with maggots was to be avoided as food, the presiding judge released Mr. Smith from the courtroom, and from the hospital's supervision.

The passage certainly points to a variety of structural failures that have exposed countless "Mr. Smiths" to horrific violence and harm, including a social order that abandons people to barely survive in life-threatening conditions of poverty and a bureaucratic legal system that substitutes superficial inquiry for substantive engagement with cases. The emotional thrust of the passage, however, derives from the doctor-author's own failure, as he is reduced to bearing helpless witness to Mr. Smith's return to the feral dogs and maggots of crazy street life. Scarred, skeletal, more object of furniture than proper person, the hapless and grinning Mr. Smith unwittingly complies with his condemnation. Seagar ends the narrative recounting his own sudden outburst: "'He'll die out there,' I blurted to the psychiatrist sitting beside me. . . . 'Probably so,' she said."[48]

While cast as melodrama, *Street Crazy* points to the continuities between popular and professional depictions of homeless selfhood. It points as well to how that discourse of selfhood is mobilized in support of a medicalized homeless management. This management, as we will see, has taken the form of invasive and coercive social welfare technologies that promise to rescue the homeless from themselves. As should become clear, I do not mean to deny the reality of psychiatric disabilities among people living without shelter. But I want to point to the history of how ideas about those disabilities develop in order to unsettle presumptions about the best (or only) ways to meet mental health needs.

The image of the mad homeless draws power from a long-established American discourse about poverty that assigns to individuals blame for their own impoverished conditions, substituting personal failing for social, economic, and political explanatory factors. This social fantasy of personal responsibility has opened a ground for processes of medicalization, the techno-conceptual practices whereby a social problem becomes imagined and addressed as an individual or medical problem.[49] Medicalization should not be read in a narrow or always literally "medical" sense; rather, it is meant to evoke how the body and mind of the individual subject become targeted as the source of social problems. Medicalization deeply subtends conceptions of poverty in the United States, producing the failed inverse of liberal myths of individualism, such that case-specific explanations of individual blame trump social, economic, and political accounts of the reproduction of poverty and unequal distribution of wealth. Today, medicalization does its work broadly and flexibly, positing a wide range of disorders operative in numerous modes, including the surveillaint-punitive mode of welfare policing (targeting disorders of sloth and dishonesty), the social-Darwinist mode of education reform (targeting disorders of genetic limitations out of step with the evolutionary demands of modern capitalist life), and even a palliative-pastoral mode of social services (mitigating the effects of a mental sickness that is no fault of its bearer). The medicalization of homelessness has been well documented by social science.[50] But the medicalization of homelessness is not only a specific instance of the medicalization of poverty. Rather, the medicalization of homelessness is an intensified case that emerges from two forces: first, the relationship of modern mass housing deprivation to deinstitutionalization and, second, the impact of living without shelter on mental health.

As regards the first, the emergence of contemporary unsheltered populations has been understood as being linked to the closing of state mental health asylums in the early 1980s. The first asylums to house and treat those designated "insane," "imbecilic," or "feeble-minded" were constructed in the mid-nineteenth century.[51] As the numbers of people committed to asylums grew, and as government-sponsored asylums came to house poorer populations, the notion of the asylum as a safe haven for its patients gradually eroded. The asylum no longer served to protect the patient from disturbing or stressful conditions, but rather to remove the disturbed and disturbing patient from the family, community, or larger social environment.[52] The evolution of the asylum in the United States is part of the history of social welfarism as "race population control," as Kenneth Neubeck and Noel Cazeave term it.[53] Expanding projects of U.S. imperialism coupled with domestic anti-immigrant discourse and legislation produced a "race suicide" panic, a fear that white and middle-class America was being eliminated through population dilution.[54] In this context, asylum supervisors turned to eugenic measures such as sterilization to prevent their apparently incurable and increasingly indigent patients from reproducing.[55]

The second half of the twentieth century witnessed a continued decline in asylum funding and conditions, as well as new innovations in medical treatments, including frontal lobotomies and electroconvulsive shock therapy. Then, in the early 1960s, an unexpected alliance formed between antipsychiatric lobby groups and government reformers, with both groups calling for the deinstitutionalization of patient populations.[56] While the antipsychiatry movement criticized state asylums for their inhumane, unsanitary conditions and inhumane practices, government officials saw these institutions as economically inefficient means of managing the mentally ill. The passage of the federal Community Mental Health Act in 1963 closed great numbers of state- and municipal-run mental health asylums while funding was redirected to community health centers. As Robert Desjarlais argues, the results were less than advocates had hoped for:

> As is well known, the plans did not go as well as their architects envisioned they would. To begin with, the number of people released into the community was more than existing services could manage. In turn, many proposed community treatment programs went unrealized and

patients often left hospitals without any provisions for care, employment, or housing. In addition, many states proved reluctant to allocate funds for community-based services, community mental health centers delayed or resisted providing services to the chronically mentally ill, and many communities preferred not to have the mentally ill live in their neighborhoods.[57]

The net effect was a drastic reduction in mental hospital housing, which shrank from 559,000 beds in 1955 to 451,000 beds in 1965 and to merely 177,000 beds by 1980.[58] The impact of this shrinking resource was intensified in the 1980s, when liberal interest groups fighting involuntary commitment found allies in the Reagan administration. Together, these two entities helped dismantle involuntary commitment laws, the former on humanitarian grounds, the latter in support of neoliberal arguments about "economic inefficiency." Regarding the limits of this unlikely alliance, Alexander R. Thomas argues,

> Perhaps what is most interesting about the change in policies of involuntary commitment is the coalition that helped bring it about: a combination of "law and order" conservatives, economic conservatives, and liberal groups that sought reform in the provision of mental health services. But the policy shift had hardly anything at all to do with the mentally ill or the practitioners who treated them. It was designed to lower taxes and shift responsibility away from the federal government.[59]

As with the Community Mental Health Act of 1963, those seeking financial savings were the long-term winners, with people living with psychiatric disabilities paying the difference.

Though it is unclear to what extent the Community Health Act and deinstitutionalization can be held responsible for the growth of populations living without shelter, they did contribute to modern housing deprivation in at least two ways: first, by literally relocating former asylum inmates to city streets, and second, by removing a designated destination (however deplorable) for people with psychiatric disabilities. In the privatized U.S. housing market, the ability of any individual to access and maintain housing is dependent first upon his or her access to financial resources largely tied to labor. Insofar as employment capacity is determined in part by the successful performance of normative affect and behavior and embodiment of normative health, conditions of severe and persistent mental illness become obstacles to entering the labor market and, in turn, securing housing. As long as housing is not guaranteed to all people regardless of financial resources, psychiatric disabilities cannot but contribute to individual experiences of housing insecurity. Further, this deinstitutionalization has been taking place simultaneously with the erosion of social welfare safety nets, the destruction of SROs and other low-income housing, and the fiscal abandonment of urban cores to speculative investment and corporate tax evasion. The end of the asylum is the end of one particular technical system for managing and controlling racially subordinated and economically marginalized populations. Many would argue that jails and prisons are the new mental health asylums, and the vast numbers of imprisoned people living with psychiatric disability confirms this.[60]

Beyond its exact role in the expansion of housing insecurity and the growth of unsheltered populations, deinstitutionalization helped forge a link in the cultural imaginary about populations living without shelter. This link has been further corroborated by the well-documented and not surprising impact of living without shelter on mental and physical well-being. Enduring life without shelter involves an incredible confluence of mental stressors: risks and experiences of physical and emotional violence; the harms of being deprived of food and medical care; overwhelming daily experiences of instability, insecurity, and fear; and subjection to the degradation of police systems, welfare bureaucracies, and emergency shelters. Housing deprivation enacts a constant and intense exposure to trauma that for some people will undoubtedly materialize as states or behaviors diagnosed as mental illness.[61] Finally, even for those without psychiatric disability, living without shelter produces signs interpreted by others as "being crazy," such as carting possessions around or appearing dirty, which are in fact material consequences of housing deprivation.

Thus, while social scientists have discussed and debated the relationships between psychiatric disability and homelessness in terms of correlation and causation, the relationship has been made real in effect, in popular, government, academic, and social service imaginations and practices. This realization has been produced by the medicalization of poverty, by the historical role of deinstitutionalization in exacerbating housing insecurity, and by the effects of housing deprivation on mental health and physical appearance.

FROM MEDICAL PROBLEMS TO GOVERNANCE PROBLEMS

As a result of this historical confluence of factors, the medicalization of homelessness has produced "the homeless" as a category to which a pathological dimension is endemic. Among all of capitalism's cast-offs, the homeless in particular have been imagined as incapable of self-management and in need of direct and constant supervision and intervention. As lodging houses morphed into modern social service agencies, and as a professional class of social workers came to coordinate and execute their missions, the idea of "working on yourself" shifted from a moral model to a medical one. If early colonial and Progressive reformers sought to save the souls of those seeking shelter, in the modern era, the body and mind became objects of concern instead.

Disciplinary technologies of case management emerged that aimed to know and reform the individual homeless subject. In case management systems, a social worker, or caseworker, assumes responsibility for guiding clients, or cases, through a process of self-evaluation to determine the individual causes at the root of their problem.[62] Working together—although almost always within the confines of non-negotiable program requirements—worker and client develop a "case plan" to right the course of the client's life. For those living in modern housing programs, such plans might involve participation in educational or vocational programs and instruction in money management. Furthermore, case management programs frequently mandate treatment for psychiatric disabilities and drug/alcohol use, as such conditions and behaviors have especially been understood as barriers to what is called "housing readiness." Sobriety and compliance with psychiatric drug regimes are common preconditions for admittance to housing programs and minimum requirements for remaining housed. Finally, case plans typically include enforced waking and sleep times, limits or bans on outside visitors, and bans on sexual activity. In her important analysis of the emergence of the New York City shelter system, Theresa Funiciello refers to this case management model of welfare provision as a "tyranny of kindness," signaling the coercive nature of paternalistic programs that demand submission to reform protocols in the name of the client's own good.[63] Funiciello's term perfectly expresses the contradictions of disciplinary power as described by Foucault—that humanist projects of developing mental and physical capacities proceed through projects of submission and control, such that we come to believe that only through submission can the subject be improved and liberated.

This medicalized model and its disciplinary technologies for managing the case have not disappeared. However, the return of federal involvement in homeless management has brought another dimension to this discourse. This happened as part of what Jamie Peck and Adam Tickell refer to as the "roll-out" phase of neoliberalism.[64] Peck and Tickell argue that the ideological development of neoliberalism in the Chicago School was first followed by a "roll-back" phase. Ushered in through the administrations of Ronald Reagan in the United States and Margaret Thatcher in the United Kingdom, the roll-back phase involved the dismantling of social welfare programs, the increasing privatization of social administration as well as public space, and the devolution of authority to lower levels of government.[65] This dismantling was then followed by a roll-out phase, in which new, neoliberalized mechanisms of governance were developed and put into place. Rather than an expected and professed shrinking of the state, in this phase of neoliberalism, state institutions reassert authority over decentralized welfare apparatuses and reorganize the structure and delivery of social welfare services. Peck and Tickell argue that

> there seems to have been a shift from the pattern of deregulation and dismantlement so dominant during the 1980s, which might be characterized as "roll-back neoliberalism," to an emergent phase of active state-building and regulatory reform—an ascendant moment of "roll-out neoliberalism." In the course of this shift, the agenda has gradually moved from one preoccupied with the active destruction and discreditation of Keynesian-welfarist and social-collectivist institutions (broadly defined) to one focused on the purposeful construction and consolidation of neoliberalized state forms, modes of governance, and regulatory relations.[66]

Much of what gets rolled out aims to control the disorder of surplus populations created by neoliberal economic restructuring. This includes social welfare programs with intensified social control functions, such as workfare.[67] It also includes a much enlarged and increasingly aggressive prison and punishment system that serves a predominantly warehousing function; this occurs alongside an ever-expanding military and defense apparatus deployed overseas.[68] "Security" from internal and external threats becomes the dominant trope in response to neoliberal multiplication and intensification of social disorder. Homeless programs operate in the security state to stabilize cities in terms of perceptions of safety and cleanliness and in service of postindustrial consumer/tourist economies.

The federal programs discussed in chapters 4 and 5 are part of this roll-out phase. At first glance, the McKinney-Vento Act seems a kind of laggard social welfare initiative, arriving as it did during a period of fiscal and social conservatism in the mid-1980s. Its arrival is less surprising when we recognize that McKinney-Vento responded to the economic threat posed by unsheltered populations, the rendering insecure of the city by surplus populations. Increased funding and other forms of government involvement in homeless management must be understood in these terms. The first phase of McKinney-Vento programs attempted to insert some federal oversight over the already existing networks and practices of homeless services agencies. For example, the medical model of homelessness required that individuals move through tiered services, from emergency shelters, to transitional living programs, and finally into private housing or permanent supportive housing. McKinney-Vento formalized relationships between these tiers with its Continuum of Care model, which directed movement of clients through tiers of housing, from emergency shelters to permanent, private residences. By the mid-1990s, neoliberal ethics had caught back up with HUD in the shape of demands to reform its mission and its approaches to homelessness. In this latter phase of McKinney-Vento programs, from the late 1990s to the current period, federal involvement has become more active, more intrusive, and more radical, as the following two chapters will show.

The history of social welfare programs in the United States is a back-and-forth tension between a concern with social problems, or the structural impact of various forms of social and economic inequality, and medical problems, or the notion of failed individuals. The Keynesian welfare state addressed itself to social problems in a way that sought to care for the would-be laborer and "his" dependents. These social problems included structurally produced economic inequality in periods of un- or under-employment, poor health, and old age. As reforms to the administration of welfare programs increased access for populations of color in general and African Americans especially, a latent discourse of medical problems eclipsed a discourse of social problems. This is to say that while the Keynesian welfare state understood certain social adjustments would be made necessary for the smooth, regular functioning of capital, in the backlash period that led to the roll-back phase of neoliberalism, lazy or incompetent racialized individuals, rather than capital, were increasingly understood as the true source of social problems. Neubeck and Cazenave describe this succinctly as "welfare racism."[69]

In the current roll-out phase of neoliberalism, a third diagram of governance problems is layered on top of competing discourses of social and medical problems. If discourses of social problems and medical problems both offer fixes, though differently directed, a governance problem is concerned more with the ongoing management of a problem, rather than a resolution. Governance problems are organized through concerns foregrounded by neoliberal capital—fiscal responsibility, cost benefits analysis, standardization of responses, streamlining of central bureaucracies, and surveillance over decentralized bureaucracies. Governance problems concern allocating resources in the most efficient ways possible given a set of social problems that are viewed as intractable. McKinney-Vento has added to medicalized models a conception of homelessness as a governance problem—a problem of inefficient use of resources and nonscientific methods of management. Recasting homelessness as a governance problem means that administrative responses must mutate. While they do not lose all guise of social welfarism, responses to governance problems are perhaps best characterized as "technical solutions." As Aihwa Ong describes, technical solutions arise in a context in "which governing activities are recast as nonpolitical and nonideological problems."[70] Technical solutions are shot through with the abstracting and quantifying language of neoliberalism, which formulates all concerns as economic in nature and reconceptualizes all problems, including homelessness, as amenable to economic calculation and intervention.

In this context, the expected time-order of cause and effect is reversed. Neoliberalism can describe, as Ong has argued and others have corroborated, the application of technical solutions to diverse geopolitical contexts, from various nation-states under various political regimes, to both supra- and subnational scales. In such a generalized neoliberal milieu, we should not mistake governance problems as that which neoliberalism attempts to solve. Rather, governance problems are the retroactive *effect* of neoliberal technical solutions and their transformations of the social, political, and economic. Neoliberal techniques of governance instantiate governance problems in the social, such that they come to seem the obvious and necessary targets of governance. Homelessness must be cast as a problem of "bad government" so that neoliberal "better government" can fix it. The birth of a governance problem is neither inevitable nor given. Rather, it is the product of multiscalar processes and their interactions with already-existing norms and forms of governance.

The techno-conceptual reorganization of homelessness as a governance problem is pressuring a biopoliticization of homelessness, in which a homeless *population* and its patterns and costs become a privileged object of knowledge and concern. This biopoliticization follows from the ways in which neoliberal governance problems and conjoined technical solutions privilege technologies that can intercept and modulate the population. Such interventions make life quantifiable and hence commensurate with the financial. We can see the biopoliticization of homelessness, for example, in the proliferation of population counts and demographic studies, as well as in intensified concern with reorganizing funding through more "scientific" management, as documented in the following two chapters. The biopoliticization of homelessness pressures a reconfiguration of the medicalized dimension and its related disciplinary technologies of management. This does not mean that the contemporary era marks an end of discipline. Rather, the current discourse of homelessness as a problem of governance is changing how individuals are imagined and treated. The result is not a complete abandonment of disciplinary techniques. In some cases (as we will see in chapter 4), those techniques are forestalled or undermined by biopolitical imperatives. In other cases (as illustrated in chapter 5), they are reconfigured in service of biopolitical ends.

The diagrammatic shift to the population as a primary concern of knowledge and governance also does not mean that the pathological dimension of homelessness falls away, even if some of the disciplinary technologies associated with its pathologization are deemphasized. The staying power of these pathologizations can be understood when we attend to the race/property systems subtending the individual prior to his or her medicalization. Grace Hong offers a way to think about connections between liberal notions of the subject and contemporary neoliberal, biopolitical formulations of populations that require management. Hong expands on C. B. MacPherson's category of "possessive individualism," which proffers "a conception of self based on one's ability to own property privately and dispose of it as one chooses."[71] Possessive individualism adds another dimension to our understanding of a medicalization of homelessness that targets individuals as pathological and thus in need of intervention. Hong's analysis points to the ways in which racialized property systems are foundational to U.S. concepts of selfhood and the self's capacity to act for itself. Writing about the emergence of this conception in the nineteenth century, Hong argues "that subjectivity in this era is defined by the ability to own, and what the subject primarily owns is the self. That he 'owns' himself, or in other words, is self-possessed and self-determining, is demonstrated through the exercise of will. The subject is the propertied subject, the citizen-subject of the nation-state."[72] In other words, if Cheryl Harris's notion of whiteness as property demonstrates how race and property regimes coemerge in the United States, Hong reminds us that a symbolic-cultural system accompanies this emergence, forming the very notions of selfhood and its possibilities: "The concept of possessive individualism thus sutures together the condition of freedom and the condition of being propertied. Enslavement, on the other hand, is the condition of being subjected to the will of others, a condition that led to slaves being the figure for what Patricia Williams terms 'pure antiwill.'"[73] To lack the fundamental property of one's self is to be in your very nature in need of governance and management. Thus, housing deprivation, or dispossession, is naturalized and inevitable: those living without homes never had anything to lose; they are already constitutively without possessions as unpropertied unselves. Hong describes such remainders of capital speculation as "existentially surplus."[74]

The formulation of possessive individualism persists today, but becomes reconfigured as biopoliticization joins disciplinary regimes of self-management. Addressing our contemporary moment, Hong writes, "This new form of (bio)power is marked by the rampant proliferation of carceral and deadly regimes *enabled by* the *limited* incorporation and affirmation of certain forms of racialized, gendered, and sexualized difference."[75] Homeless management programs are a technical form of this incorporation. If medicalization casts the racialization of un/selfhood into the realm of psychiatrically conceived social service expertise and management, today's homeless management industry organized around governance problems scales this up to the level of population. The homeless population does not need individual subjectivity to be pathologized and reformed, because the racialization of housing insecurity means it has always been a population without selves. Thus we get a pathological population. In other words, the population itself is imagined to be endemically disordered and costly. Echoing Hong's argument, in an analysis of neoliberalism as "structural liberalism," Angela Harris has argued that the management of unruly surplus populations upholds liberal notions of the subject, such as those detailed by Hong, and its (failures of) agency. Harris writes,

> By structural liberalism, I mean two interrelated political-philosophical commitments: (1) the separation of family, market, state, and civil society into separate and independent "spheres" which should in principle be governed differently; and (2) a commitment to the ideal of the self-governing subject, through which individuals and groups deemed incapable of self-government may be subjected to kinds of regulation that would otherwise be deemed incompatible with liberty.[76]

Just as the privatization and concomitant racialization of property forms and relations depend upon included exclusions, the free subject of neoliberalism requires those for whom freedom is an impossibility. This is not only a symbolic unfreedom. Permanently redundant populations are the economic as well as political conditions of possibility for neoliberal consumer capitalism and its constitutive individuals endowed with free choice.

Those concerned with housing deprivation must contend with the complicated ways in which the population arises as an object of knowledge and intervention, and the ways it preserves and transforms medicalized models of pathological subjects, of those unpossessed individuals. If we take on only the limited task of deconstructing medicalized discourse to reveal the social bases that lay beneath, we risk being left behind by a diagram of governance that has begun to lose interest in reforming the individual. A critique of medicalization remains relevant, but it cannot account for the techno-conceptual organization of unruly surplus populations in terms of a problem of governance. Furthermore, as chapter 1 introduced and the chapters that follow further evidence, the social sciences have been drawn into the realm of governance problems, assigned with setting out the technical knowledge parameters that render homelessness available to intervention. This has occurred thus far with little critical social scientific reflection, not only in terms of the role of the academy in governance, but as regards the broad reconfiguring of the social, political, and economic by a neoliberal translation of medical and social problems into problems of and for governance.

FOUR

Governing through Numbers

HUD and the Databasing of Homelessness

IN 2001 CONGRESS MANDATED THAT HUD COLLECT NATIONAL
data on populations living without shelter as well as data on the effec-
tiveness of federally funded programs targeting this population. The
2001 congressional directive required that local jurisdictions receiving McKinney-Vento funds produce "unduplicated counts" of clients
they served, meaning that all agencies in that jurisdiction coordinate
data collection so that every client was counted, and counted only once.
As a Senate report stated:

> HUD must collect data on the extent of homelessness in America as well
> as the effectiveness of the McKinney homeless assistance programs in
> addressing this condition. These programs have been in existence for
> some 15 years and there has never been an overall review or comprehen-
> sive analysis on the extent of homelessness or how to address it. The
> Committee believes that it is essential to develop an unduplicated count
> of homeless people, and an analysis of their patterns of use of assistance
> (HUD McKinney homeless assistance as well as other assistance both tar-
> geted and not targeted to homeless people), including how they enter and
> exit the homeless assistance system and the effectiveness of assistance.[1]

Efforts to meet this directive have subsequently become embedded in
the requirements attached to McKinney-Vento funds. Since 2004, HUD
has required all agencies receiving McKinney-Vento funds to implement
the use of a homeless management information system—also called an
HMIS. "HMIS" designates any information management software,
of which many versions exist, that a service agency uses for recording
"client-level information on the characteristics and service needs of
homeless persons. . . . An HMIS is typically a web-based software application that homeless assistance providers use to coordinate service
provision, manage their operations, and better serve their clients."[2]
Promoting HMIS among agencies it funds has assisted HUD with the

two tasks named in the Senate report cited above: producing a national count of homelessness and assessing patterns of use in programs targeting homelessness. HUD has also developed a number of technical support programs to facilitate these efforts.

Though HUD's initiative is fairly recent, the use of computer-based applications for managing client records is not new in the homeless services industry. As with other sectors of social and medical care, the move from paper to databank has been in motion for some time now, a shift designated the "electronic turn" in social work.[3] Within a history of social work practices, the use of HMIS has been understood as replacing a case notes system of an earlier era of service provision, in which a social worker produced narrative accounts of clients in terms of their needs, services accessed, and changes in their condition and circumstance. An HMIS is not, however, simply a computer-based repository of notes (which might imply, for example, typing up case notes in a word-processing program). Rather, it is a database management system that provides fixed inquiry fields, including demographic details, categories of need, and kinds of service, in which standardized measures are input. The use of an HMIS does not signal simply a shift from the pen stroke to the keystroke, but from qualitative to quantitative records and assessments. Consequently, an HMIS changes not just how case notes are recorded, but what can be recorded, and in what forms. This electronic turn takes place in a generalized field of quantification that characterizes neoliberal imperatives of cost/benefits assessment. As evidenced in the congressional directive cited above, the "necessariness" of counting goes unquestioned; an unspecified but taken-for-granted value is accorded the gathering of numbers. In this context, HUD promotes HMIS as simply making the work of case management easier and more efficient. However, many in the homeless services industry take another view. As the financial officer from one agency told me, "My advice to any nonprofit would be to not seek federal funding. If you can do it without, it's so much easier. You have so much less reporting to do if you have foundations and individual donors—the stuff is so much less onerous. The government just makes it impossible, and there's so many restrictions." From the view of this and many other service providers, HUD's HMIS program looks more like a bureaucratic hindrance than a help.

The databasing of homelessness enacted through the HMIS program produces a biopoliticization of homelessness. Despite concerns of service providers and scholars that such databases represent an intrusive form of surveillance, HMIS concerns less a one-to-one correspondence between individuals and their data doubles. Rather than spy upon individuals, the primary use of HMIS is to produce knowledge of a population. This population production has great consequences for individuals, but those consequences are in many ways indirect, secondary effects. Furthermore, as much as HUD's HMIS program instates the population as an object of knowledge and governance, it produces the population as a mechanism *for* governance. The homeless population produced through HUD's HMIS program is used to regulate the service agencies that generate the data composing that population. This techno-conceptual organization of housing deprivation secures a form of decentralized federal control over the dispersed and multiscalar homeless services industry. In so doing, it also puts in place putatively race-neutral technical conceptions of housing need that obscure systems of race/property without interrupting them. This is the form of post-racialism in neoliberal homeless management, as populations circulate in relation to "objective" economized measures of service success.

The chapter that follows considers the capacities of the database in relation to the technical requirements of HUD's HMIS program. It also considers the ways in which HUD promotes the use of HMIS as an improvement over earlier case management technologies. I look to critiques of the electronic turn but set them in a broader context of techno-conceptual management. With this in mind, we can see that the primary use of HMIS data by HUD is to regulate agencies, rather than to track individual clients. In this way, HMIS becomes an opportunity for new forms of metagovernance over a dispersed social welfare apparatus. Finally, the chapter concludes with some thoughts on the consequences of the biopoliticization enacted by the HMIS program.

In this and the following chapter, I draw from interviews I conducted with people working in the homeless services industry—program directors, social workers, outreach workers, and staff psychiatrists—at agencies in New York City, Philadelphia, Los Angeles, San Francisco, and Seattle. All interviews were conducted on condition of anonymity.

When necessary, I specify the bare minimum to identify the speaker's position. I do use the actual name of agencies when discussing material that is drawn from public records, rather than from my interviews.

Databasing the Homeless

A database is a system for the classification, organization, and retrieval of heterogeneous elements.[4] It is not the first such system; various other methods have obviously existed for quite some time.[5] Eugene Thacker notes dictionaries, encyclopedias, anatomical atlases, maps, and statistical charts as the forebears of the contemporary computer database.[6] In the context of social services, another obvious historical precedent is the filing cabinet stuffed with manila folders, containing everything from case notes to identity documents, photographs, medical records, and copies of bureaucratic forms related to health benefits, income support, and legal proceedings. All of these systems employ a specific method of organization that "depends on the technical specificity of the system; whereas the dictionary and encyclopedia utilize an alphabetic system, the anatomical atlas utilizes a diagrammatic logic, and statistics utilizes a series of tables, charts and quantitative graphical elements."[7]

Each of these systems offers a means to organize various elements into some sets of relationships, particularly with an eye towards ease of retrieval. But the possibilities are neither endless nor neutral. Each system carries a logic of organization that constrains not only the organizational mode—or sets of possible relationships between elements—but constrains the form of the compositional elements as well. For example, in a dictionary, while an illustration of an "apple" may supplement a textual description of the word "apple," it cannot stand on its own. The illustration's lack of an alphabetical attribute denies its entry into this system, except as back up for the word-element "apple" (which possesses an appropriate attribute—it begins with the letter "A"). A statistical chart that displays how many respondents to a survey are white, black, Asian, or Hispanic cannot include the narrative descriptions of family lineage, ethnicity, and migration that people commonly use to describe their own "race." Such narratives must be operationalized, or assigned attributes that make them organize-able within this system. Otherwise, they cannot materialize in the chart. Finally, while a summons for creating a public nuisance can easily find its way into a social worker's manila folder, warmly tucked between case notes and a photocopied birth certificate, a plate of food refused in protest of the police at mealtime cannot. This is to say, the refused meal cannot enter into the official record, as the structure of organization (a folder within a system of folders) cannot accommodate such an element. So while the computer database is not the first system of classification, organization, and retrieval, it is unique in its capacity to integrate any number of other systems into itself: the database can organize and present elements as alphabetical lists, as statistical graphs, as a series of illustrations. This multiplicity occurs through a process of digitization, or the translation of the raw material into binary form.

The kinds of data that HUD generates through its HMIS program are not specific to this historical moment, but belong to a long history of number-gathering and its evolution into the modern statistics of which HUD's HMIS program is a part.[8] While gathering numbers predates the rise of the modern state form, statistics (the etymology refers to "state data") marks the shift from a gathering of numbers for numbers sake to the production of numbers put to work. As such, the development of statistics and a bureaucracy to support their generation is central to the rise of the nation state. The "numbers work" of the state might solidify as natalist policies, electoral districts, unemployment forecasts, or insurance rates.[9]

At first glance, HUD's HMIS program could seem to be simply an extension and perhaps an intensification of what Ian Hacking calls the "avalanche of numbers" that has washed across the Americas since the time of European colonial invasion.[10] But some important shifts are provoked by the use of the database. If governmental number-gathering has always been activated, here we have a kind of data—which is to say, digital data—that realizes that action component in its very form. In other words, a database is not simply a collection of numbers, but it is numbers constructed in relation to action—the algorithmic functions of the computer, or, more specifically, the database management system (DBMS). While other systems of organizing heterogeneous materials, such as dictionaries, atlases, and filing cabinets, may have struggled with how to allow for the efficient retrieval or reorganization of those materials, the computer database organizes matter in the form of matter-set-to-retrieval. In fact, the computer database departs from older systems in that referring to a process of retrieval is something of a misnomer. Within a database system, the process of retrieval is really more a process of generation. A dictionary can contain only those elements entered into it (even, say, an online dictionary that can be frequently updated). A database, on the other hand, makes more than what was already there. The DBMS allows for the *production* of data, not simply its organization and retrieval. What might be "processed data" at the end of one algorithm is available to become "raw data" for another set of computations, or retrievals. Thus, data entered into a database should not be thought of as fixed or stable. Data are mobile points of connection that facilitate the dynamic algorithmic functions of a computer, organizing data into new combinations, new relationships and, most importantly, new calculations to make new data.

These dynamic properties of digital data are brought into the realm of homeless social services through HUD's HMIS program. Agencies participating in the program may choose to develop their own version of an HMIS or, more likely, purchase an already existing, customizable HMIS program from any number of private vendors.[11] HUD itself does not provide an HMIS application. Nor does HUD require that agencies use any specific version of an HMIS. This is not unusual or unexpected in a neoliberal context. What HUD does require, and what marks its entry into the HMIS model, is the collection of "universal data elements" by every HUD-funded agency on each client it serves. The universal data elements required by HUD are Name, Social Security Number, Date of Birth, Race, Ethnicity, Gender, Veteran Status, Disabling Condition, Residence Prior to Program Entry, Zip Code of Last Permanent Address, Housing Status, Program Entry and Exit Dates, and Personal and Household Identification Numbers.[12] The universal data elements must be collected in forms that meet data standards set by HUD. The data standards ensure that the universal data elements will be commensurate across agencies. For example, data standards outlined for the universal data element "Disabling condition" are as follows:

> *Rationale:* Disability condition is needed to help identify clients that meet HUD's definition of chronically homeless and, depending on the source of program funds, may be required to establish client eligibility to be served by the program.

Data Source: Client interview, self-administered form, or assessment. Where disability is required to determine program eligibility, the data source is the evidence required by the funding source.

When Data are Collected: At any time after the client has been admitted into the program (unless a disabling condition is required for determining the client's eligibility for the program).

Subjects: All clients served.

Definitions and Instructions: For this data element, a disabling condition means: (1) a disability as defined in Section 223 of the Social Security Act; (2) a physical, mental, or emotional impairment which (a) is expected to be of long-continued and indefinite duration, (b) substantially impedes an individual's ability to live independently, and (c) is of such a nature that such ability could be improved by more suitable housing conditions; (3) a developmental disability as defined in Section 102 of the Developmental Disabilities Assistance and Bill of Rights Act; (4) the disease of acquired immunodeficiency syndrome or any conditions arising from the etiological agency for acquired immunodeficiency syndrome; or (5) a diagnosable substance abuse disorder.

HUD's data standards then specify possible responses to this question, which are No, Yes, Don't Know, or Refused, each of which is assigned a numerical code. Similar data standards are provided for each of the required elements.[13]

According to HUD, the collection of universal data elements in standard form will correct miscounts of homeless populations accessing services at multiple locations. Collected from dispersed locales by agencies using any number of software applications, these data will then provide the raw material for aggregate population counts and trends analysis required by Congress, as data produced at each locale will be commensurate in form and thus can be set to calculation together.

> The universal data standards will make possible unduplicated estimates of the number of homeless people accessing services from homeless providers, basic demographic characteristics of people who are homeless, and their patterns of service use. The universal data standards will also allow measurement of the number and share of chronically homeless people who use homeless services. The standards will enable generation of information on shelter stays and homelessness episodes over time.[14]

Data gathered through the HMIS program is reported and analyzed by HUD in its *Annual Assessment Report to Congress*. It has thus far published ten such studies, including Part I of the 2014 report.[15] It has also published a number of supplemental reports on homelessness among veterans. The 2012 report points to the success of HMIS implementation, which HUD not only requires for agencies it funds, but encourages for any agency that provides homeless services. Whereas the initial 2007 report used data collected from 80 communities, 427 communities contributed data for the 2012 report.[16]

HUD argues that the use of an HMIS benefits not just the federal government, but also the agencies providing services. According to HUD, an HMIS allows a variety of tasks to be completed more efficiently and accurately, "bringing the power of computer technology to the day-to-day operations of individual homeless assistance providers."[17] These are the familiar terms of the turn to quantitative models in health and social services.[18] The first set of tasks an HMIS improves upon is related to service provision and involves the use of standardized intake and assessment procedures. This is meant to replace the largely "anecdotal" methods of earlier eras of case management. Rather than each caseworker developing an individualized, subjective assessment, one method of accounting for something like "disability status" is developed. Using equivalent measures allows for the translation of one worker's notes to any other worker and eliminates the labor of producing those measures case by case.

Additionally, HUD argues that HMIS make for better collaborative work across agencies, "knitting together housing and service providers within a local community into more coordinated and effective delivery systems."[19] Although privacy protections prevent the sharing of unique identifiers such as names and Social Security numbers with HUD, these data can be shared between agencies. Hence, an HMIS allows for the tracking of clients utilizing multiple agencies within a Continuum of Care in a local community. HUD offers the example of an agency being able to determine if a client requesting service has already received that same service from another agency. This clearly serves to police the poor from "double-dipping." HUD, however, sells it as a way for agencies to better allocate resources where they are needed and useful.

In addition to benefiting service provision, the use of HMIS is understood as creating more accurate "pictures" of homelessness. These accurate pictures are presumed both to serve agencies and to allow HUD to produce an unduplicated count of the national homeless population. Thus, the unique goals of both service agencies and the federal government are met through the implementation of HMIS:

> HMIS can help local communities understand how many people are homeless in shelters and on the street; how many people are chronically or episodically homeless; the characteristics and service needs of those served; and which programs are most effective at reducing and ending homelessness. HMIS can help HUD and Congress understand: how many people are homeless in the United States; who is homeless; where people receive shelter and services and where did they live before they became homeless; the patterns of homeless residential program use; and the nation's capacity for housing homeless people.[20]

A presentation prepared by Abt Associates (a private, for-profit research corporation that contracts with federal agencies) for HUD's use in "recruiting" agencies to HMIS explains that "HMIS is a tool, not the goal."[21] This phrase is meant to show that HUD is not attempting to change what service providers do, but only trying to help them along—with funding attached to the *requirement* that the agency use an HMIS. Comparing service provision and counting methods with and without the use of an HMIS, the Abt presentation demonstrates how HMIS not only accomplishes what traditional methods cannot, but also better realizes the accomplishments of older methods. According to this presentation, traditional service provider reports are not able to produce unduplicated counts, as the same client may be counted as a unique individual at two or more different agencies. Traditional reports are also not able to assess patterns of "entering and exiting homelessness," with patterns here understood to be statistical portraits. On the other hand, not only can an HMIS accomplish these two goals, it can also capture "in-depth information on clients and needs," the one accomplishment accorded traditional, narrative-based service provider accounts. HMIS can do this through user configurability, such that areas of need or service specific to an agency can be tracked with an HMIS, in addition to the data required for producing the compliance reports containing an agency's universal data elements. From this perspective, HMIS offers the best of both worlds: it captures the universal (such as names and exit/ entry dates) and the particular (the specific data interests of agency and locale); allows for accurate counts of homeless populations; adds a longitudinal dimension of patterns over time; and preserves the richness of caseworkers' understandings of clients and their needs though an amassing of quantitative detail.

HMIS thus introduces the technical capacity for a biopolitical reorganization of housing deprivation. This does not mean that "the homeless" were never before imagined to exist as a population. Quite the contrary: one effect of the dehumanization of those living without shelter is the long history of their treatment as an anonymous mass. To imagine that the homeless would share a set of generic characteristics and exhibit "patterns of shelter entry and exit" is already to biopoliticize. HUD's HMIS program draws out this latent biopolitical dimension, making a "homeless population" knowable and amenable to governance. In some ways, earlier case management technologies tried to counter the massifying effect of housing deprivation by introducing the idea that each individual client of a program had a history that must be understood in order to be changed. The quantification of services through HUD's HMIS program does not undo this pathologizing individualization, but it does re-abstract it to the generalizable level of a statistical population. As a staff person at one agency told me about the agency's work prior to HMIS, "The type of data we kept about them was much more personal and much less statistical." What might it mean to shift from the personal to the statistical?

AGAINST THE ELECTRONIC TURN

HUD's promotion of HMIS recites a familiar fetishization of technology, or technophilia: HMIS makes things easier and faster, saving money and time. On the other side, critics in social work studies recapitulate technophobic themes that warn against handing control over to "the machine." To appreciate these concerns, we must remember that disciplinary social work understands that an intersubjective relationship between client and caseworker, as described in chapter 3, forms the foundation from which social service provision can most effectively operate. By the late 1960s or early 1970s, just as the Fordist-Keynesian pact was also becoming undone, this relationship became insecure, as psychiatric-based theories and practices came under fire.[22] The inability of psychodynamic practices to produce cures in patients, especially as evidenced by the growing and burdensome indigent populations of state-run mental health asylums, offered an opportunity for the rise of neuro-scientific models that located mental illness not in the history of the case, but in the misdirected activity of the brain.[23] The erosion of psychodynamic authority cleared room for the introduction into social work of the demands of evidence-based medicine, in particular the requirement to produce the "hard science" of numbers about diagnosis and treatment. HMIS is one more instance of evidence-based medicine catching up to the "soft medicine" of social services.

Thus, the liabilities that HUD understands the use of an HMIS as correcting—the ad-hoc, interpretative, anecdotal practices of the well-meaning but unscientific social worker—are what critics of the electronic turn understand to be precisely the unique resources that social workers offer. These resources are threatened by the use of machines. Bob Sapey, for example, draws from studies of the relationship between decision-making and communication media to argue that the complexity of the social worker's milieu demands the "richness" of interpersonal conversation:

> Messages which are sensitive or complex and which require a greater degree of explanation to be understood, will require a medium that will permit more direct interaction between the sender and receiver. The richest medium is generally face-to-face talking, in which non-verbal communication can be incorporated and there is opportunity for response and exploration of the issues.[24]

Thus, the depth offered by psychodynamic casework contrasts with the superficiality or surface-iality of electronic data. As the interpersonal relationship gives way to an impersonal information exchange, the electronic turn instates an evaporation of the multidimensional knowledge structures of social work. Technologies like HMIS are understood to intensify, if not enact, a rationalization and instrumentalization of knowledge. Along these lines, Nigel Parton argues:

> Identities are constructed according to the fields that constitute the database, so that in striving for clear and objective representations and decision making, the subjectivity and social context of the client can be deconstructed into a variety of lists and factors associated with, in particular, "need" and "risk." Categorical thinking, based on the binary either/or logic, dominates, which puts individuals into categories and, in the process, obscures any ambiguities. Rather than be concerned with presenting a picture of the subject, as previously, social work increasingly acts to take subjects apart and then reassembles them according to the requirements of the database. Practitioners are required to produce dispersed and fragmented identities made up of a series of characteristics and pieces of information which are easy to input/output and compare. In the process, the embodied subject is in danger of disappearing and we are left with a variety of surface information which provides little basis for in-depth explanation or understanding.[25]

Such a criticism would counter HUD's insistence that databasing social work can preserve the richness of the social worker's understanding of clients. In the passage above, the use of computer technologies not only damages the caseworker/client relationship, but also erodes the client him- or herself. From this point of view, the amassing of data that HUD argues adds up to a complete picture is simply a quantitative increase in superficial content.[26]

Such criticism falls short, however, by imagining that the introduction of computers effects a complete eclipse of qualitative approaches. In fact, program managers and caseworkers describe the use of HMIS as layering upon existing practices. Many case managers have continued to keep their own private anecdotal records on clients while also keeping records through an HMIS database. The explanation offered for this practice does corroborate the critique made in social work literature— that too much is left out of the HMIS program, and that it cannot record much of the information upon which case managers rely. Many workers told me about entering HMIS data retroactively, when it is time to submit the information to their supervisors who prepare reports for HUD. Some described turning handwritten records over to supervisors, who then translated that material into an HMIS. In these ways, the quantification of clients coexists with subjective/anecdotal accounts. Agencies participating in HMIS produce a kind of double-speak, in which they explain their clients and services both in traditional case management terms and in the quantitative-technical terms of HMIS applications.

If scholarship on the electronic turn has overstated the extent to which databasing pushes out other approaches, in arguing for the advantages of HMIS over older forms of case management, HUD overstates the fail-safe aspects of this technological form. It is fairly easy to anticipate the fallacies embedded in HUD's promotional materials for HMIS. While HUD contrasts the clean data produced by an HMIS with the subjective and incomplete accounts of case managers and "one-night counts," database programs, of course, also fall short or fail—systems crash, networks go down, files get mysteriously deleted.[27] Furthermore, in the process of retrofitting case notes into HMIS or of supervisors inputting subjective notes gathered by case managers, there is no guarantee that the data collected by HUD is as accurate as HUD presumes. In fact, in conversations, agency supervisors readily admitted to inputting false information as they begrudgingly complied with HMIS requirements. "There was general consensus in our Continuum of Care that this was a piece of crap. People would do whatever they needed to do to secure their funding but were in no way eager to give HUD this information. It just felt unpleasant. You know, here's another thing we're gonna tell you you have to do."

Entering inaccurate information sometimes resulted from incomplete records, so that necessary missing information was guessed at. Other times, the inputting of false information was a deliberate effort to appear to be in compliance with HUD requirements. For example, one agency that began using an HMIS during the early years of HUD's program worked with many women from sex work industries. Given the criminalization of sex work and the overexposure of poor women to criminal prosecution for sex work, many of the targeted clients of this program experienced periods of imprisonment.[28] HUD's technical definition of "homeless" requires that an individual have spent at least the past thirty days without shelter. Living in a jail or prison is considered being housed, so clients could not be taken into the program directly from jail or prison and would have to spend thirty days without shelter before qualifying for entry. Obviously, living without shelter would put these women at great risk for re-arrest, and exposing them to this harm was considered by this organization to run counter to their mission. As one staff person explained it, "We weren't allowed to take women who'd been in jail but we took women who were coming out of jail all the time and just lied about it. Our attitude was, 'These are ridiculous restrictions upon us, so we're just going to do whatever we can.'" This required that the agency enter false universal data elements regarding the client's previous address.

The danger of both the social work literature critique and some of the resistance from agencies is that it may romanticize earlier eras of the homeless services industry and naturalize earlier technological practices of case management. By basing critiques on the intrusion of the computer itself, critics fail to consider the long history of the technological configuration of social work practices. When past technologies are accounted for, their role is understood in very much the sense that HUD understands HMIS—as a tool taken up by the social worker in support of the central, intersubjective tasks. For example, Nigel Parton points to a set of technologies central to social work prior to the electronic turn, from the 1950s to the 1970s:

> While "the relationship" was the primary tool or "technology" of the work, there were also a variety of other technical devices that were drawn upon so that individuals would be rendered as knowable, calculable and administrative "subjects." These devices were in the form of a variety of written reports but also included other devices, such as the car and the telephone, which made it increasingly possible to negotiate time and place more efficiently and quickly.[29]

Here Parton offers an important analysis of the technical apparatuses that made earlier models of case management possible, and recognizes the interpersonal relationship itself as a technological form. However, unfolding within a technophobic reaction to computer-based technologies, this analysis renders the written report, the telephone, the car, and the relationship less technological and therefore less dangerous. Thus, Parton argues,

> What becomes evident is that, increasingly, such [technological] developments not only acted to support and refine the work, but become a major influence in reconfiguring the form of knowledge itself. Such developments become increasingly evident with the introduction of new systems of information technology (IT) and, more recently, ICTs [information and communication technologies].[30]

The ways in which computer technologies make the technological configuration of social work "increasingly evident" is mistaken for proof of social work being *increasingly technological*. A guilt by association is projected onto practices that rely on computer information technologies, producing in turn a foil of innocence for those practices that relied on "tools" thought to be less technological and more genuinely human/ humane. This view suggests an apolitical version of social work divorced from governance regimes, rather than a set of technologies that shift within evolving political economic contexts.

But, of course, the management of housing deprivation is already technologized. The use of any one technology in social work neither enhances nor degrades a core or true practice of the service provider. Rather, the act of service provision is always a set of technical operations. While the forms of knowledge production may change along with changing technologies, there is no form of knowledge absent a "technical substrate": knowledge is always bound to the technologies that allow for its registration and distribution.[31] The written report, the car, and the telephone did not simply aid the intersubjective relationship between caseworker and client; they made it possible, and did so through the disciplinary production of the client *as* a case: an individual subject technically open to intervention, which is to say, available to be studied, known, and treated. The knowledge of the caseworker, the loss of which cautionary tales currently bemoan, is not simply a heuristic position that offers depth against the gleaming surface of digital transfers. Rather, it is a technology that binds together the individual subject— the case—and draws that subject into relations of what we must recognize as disciplinary management. From this perspective, we can understand case management as a technical apparatus of disciplinary power. And the humanism that critics of HMIS worry is being undermined by the electronic turn can be understood less as a palliative program of assistance than as a constitutive political project.[32]

With this insight in mind, we must ask not what HMIS simply degrades or enhances, but what it produces. Surveillance studies has offered a way of recognizing the productive capacities of surveillance technologies in an already technologized environment. While this work often picks up on technophobic themes of anticapitalist critique, it also draws attention to what information technologies of surveillance create and make possible, not simply what they corrupt.[33] This is to think of how surveillance technologies organize possibilities and kinds of living, rather than simply record life as it is. Surveillance technologies are not just tracking individuals, but are actively generating objects of intervention—data. In this sense, surveillance technologies are not seen just as repressive, controlling people and their movement, but productive of something new. Accordingly, Kevin D. Haggerty and Richard V. Ericson designate an emerging "surveillant assemblage," or the coming together of once-independent systems of surveillance. One result of this new assemblage is the production of what they and others call the "data double":

> Today . . . we are witnessing the formation and coalescence of a new type of body, a form of becoming which transcends human corporeality and reduces flesh to pure information. Culled from the tentacles of the surveillant assemblage, this new body is our "data double," a double which involves "the multiplication of the individual, the constitution of an additional self." . . . Data doubles circulate in a host of different centres of calculation and serve as markers for access to resources, services and power in ways which are often unknown to its referent.[34]

Here, Haggerty and Ericson offer an alternative understanding of information technologies such as HMIS. Pointing to the diffusion and linking up of surveillance technologies across the social, they argue that the surveillant assemblage does more than "spy upon" past actions. Rather, these technologies orient toward the future, determining the distribution of access to resources and life chances in arenas of health, education, employment, consumption, and civic life.

This is true, but I want to push this analysis a bit further. To argue that the data double "serves as a marker" for access does not say strongly enough how information technologies open and close channels through which possibilities of life itself circulate. The marker is an active agent, drawing capital and bodies towards it. And I would say that not only does this happen in ways unknown to the data's referent, but in fact, in its circulation and especially in its form as statistical probabilities, data becomes divorced from its referent and takes on a life of its own. Statistical data that comprise consumer and risk profiles, for example, derive from the calculation of aggregates that exceed an individual referent. HUD's population counts are one such excess of data. To consider this excess is to point to the existence of a field of data of which any one individual is only an incomplete compositional piece, but in which all individuals are caught up. This is also to challenge the assertion that surveillance data form "an additional self" or a "new type of individual," as Haggerty and Ericson propose.[35] The concept of a data double hovers too closely to the individual subject, reducing data to a shadow, or a reflection, of a specific person, and therefore it cannot account for what is produced by the technology above and beyond the scale of an individual body/subject.

In other words, the data double as formulated by surveillance studies has been chained to the object of disciplinary management—the subject's body and its movement in space. But HUD's effort to produce a national homeless population must be considered in terms of a biopolitical project that disciplinary models of surveillance studies cannot fully describe. Within that project, the population becomes useful in powerful but not always obvious ways.

HMIS and Subnational Governance

Technologies of biopolitical governance allow for biological life processes to be set in relation to economic calculations. In treating life en masse and describing life in terms of overall processes and patterns, biopolitical technologies can begin to think of populations in terms of inputs, including financial entitlements, like social wages and health resources and insurances, and outputs, or what kind of economic activity the population produces in turn. HUD's HMIS program brings a set of biopolitical technical and economic concerns into the field of homeless management. It does this by standardizing and quantifying the assessment of clients and services. It also does this through a kind of economic restructuring enacted by its funding requirements. While these funding requirements have a trickle-down effect on clients, in shifting from the register of disciplinary surveillance to biopolitical management, HUD intervenes more directly in agencies than clients. Agencies are the economic actors that HUD seeks to regulate, and the population of homeless clients becomes the access point for HUD's intervention.

One of the most direct and obvious ways that HMIS impacts agencies that receive McKinney-Vento funds is that, despite HUD's claims to the contrary, HMIS compliance creates more work for agency staff. This includes the labor of being trained in an HMIS and using the database. The HMIS program also creates more work through additional reporting requirements. An agency staff member told me, "We talk about this all the time, like how the paperwork just changes slightly every year. Less than a quarter of our annual budget comes from this money. But it's this huge hassle, and our other money is kind of dependent upon it." HUD promotes HMIS as if the information it generates is transparent, or will simply "analyze itself," rearticulating a mythology of digital information as instantaneous and self-contained. But in fact the aggregation of data requires quite extensive and complicated record-keeping and reporting to generate the numbers and make them work. It also requires plenty of extra-database, human-based computations and analyses, including seemingly endless forms upon forms that agency staff must manually complete. As the financial officer at one organization told me,

> Honestly, it is hundreds of hours per year spent. . . . To get this money we do the McKinney application, and there's bidder's conferences that we go to to learn how to fill all these things out and every year there's new components to it. And then we do a technical submission and an Annual Progress Report [APR]. There's just reams of paperwork and it all kind of asks the same questions but then your outcomes on your APR affect your next year's funding cycle and you'll have to do it a year in advance, so everything's happening really far out.

The impact of this new work is even greater for many agencies due to digital divides. A common practice in housing programs is for clients to "graduate" from being residents to being staff. Thus, many people move into social work with inadequate training and preparation for the technical skills demanded by HMIS.

If you think about who often staffs these direct service projects, it is often people who are in recovery themselves, or maybe don't have any computer skills to speak of. This was very much the case with us, where it was much easier for them to take case notes and just handwrite them—a ton of unfamiliarity with computers, and distrust and awkwardness. And so it was a much more onerous task for them to have to enter stuff into an unfamiliar database.

There are many reasons to be critical of the practice of hiring former clients, and in noting the differential impact of HMIS on organizations that employ former clients, I in no way mean to endorse it. For one, former clients rarely move up in the nonprofit hierarchy, but rather are generally contained in lower level, low-wage positions. Furthermore, the work itself is quite stressful, and many providers note high levels of relapse into unhealthy drug use among clients who become staff. Nonetheless, this hiring practice helps explain why the work of inputting data into an HMIS might be done by people who do not have personal knowledge of the case. It also suggests an unfair and uneven burden on agencies that employ members of the population they serve, a burden that is erased by HUD's insistence that computers simply make things faster and easier.

The layering up of quantitative work on top of qualitative work, or the insertion of information technologies into an already existing milieu of case management technologies, produces additional labor demands at all levels of an organization, from the case managers and supervisors who must use the databases to financial officers who must adjust budgets and file reports. The net effect, as a staff person at one agency explained it, is to deemphasize services in what science studies would call another instantiation of an actuarial turn:[36]

It's another bureaucratic piece. We all have to learn how to use the software, we all have to add it into our budgets. You now have to allocate at least one percent of your budget for [an] HMIS. Even if it doesn't really cost you that much, you need to say that you're spending that money. So everyone had to redo their budgets. Each piece is yet another hurdle. We're moving you further from the services that you provide, taking person-hours away from any kind of direct service and putting them in more bureaucracy.

As the statement testifies, in the context of the actuarial turn, the tasks of financial calculation come to permeate more and more aspects of life, including occupations previously considered more strictly interpersonal or humanistic.

Making clients and services quantifiable also makes them calculable in relation to financial resources, and it is here that we see some of the biggest impact of the HMIS program. This is not the first introduction of financial concerns by the federal government into the homeless services industry. Far from it. As the financial officer cited above explained, "Even before HMIS, if you look at the [McKinney-Vento] application, that's what HUD wants to know. They want to know income at entry, income at exit. How many people did you connect them with [in terms of] connecting residents with mainstream benefits. It's one of the main criteria." "Mainstream benefits" in this statement refers to public assistance (that is, "welfare") and income support (such as disability payments). These are forms of financial support that are not coordinated through HUD and are not limited to those designated homeless. Hence, the goal is to move clients off of "homeless money" and onto general support systems. While not entirely new in its concerns, HMIS allows for a tighter regulation of the financial cost of service approaches and a reorganization of services along lines of supposed economic efficiency.

The concern with money follows logically from HUD's role as financier of housing and related health services. The Senate report cited at this chapter's opening expresses dismay at what was a fifteen-year lapse in federal oversight of homelessness initiatives, a lapse that would seem symptomatic of social service provision in the bifurcated post-welfare state. With services provided by such great numbers and kinds of agencies, the federal government's capacity to monitor and assess these programs has faced obvious challenges. HUD's HMIS program is an exemplary case of neoliberal or post-welfare state governance in that it permits the state both to disperse and contract. Putting in place database systems allows for any number of nodes, or agencies, to operate independently within a structure that is decentralized but nonetheless subject to parameters or controls. In many ways, this arrangement may be more powerful than a centralized database, or even perhaps a centralized state. The network is mutable and can survive even when nodes in the system fail; for example, one local jurisdiction's bad data would not stop the flow of data to HUD overall. Furthermore, as demonstrated above, the labor of generating data does not need to be centrally organized or coordinated by HUD. The use of universal data elements produces commensurate materials that can operate both at local levels (within the agency and its target constituencies, as well as in local Continuum of Care jurisdictions) and at national levels. At the local level, the data can be attached to a unique client and can therefore serve an agency's work of case-by-case monitoring. At the national level, the data sheds its unique identifiers and becomes part of an aggregate, thus satisfying claims for privacy and drawing together to form a national count—which is to say, the universal data elements organized by each local database can be used to generate other data that can be processed again into the shape of a national count that Congress demands. This aggregation of data can be thought of as something like the collectivization of labor that produces more than the sum of each laborer. In this case, "the population" is the surplus of the collectivization of the universal data elements.

This population is not only an object of regulation. The population in this case acts as a mechanism *for* governance, a technology deployed toward regulating the economic activity of agencies that receive HUD funding. This regulation occurs in a kind of de facto way in the new demands on labor already discussed. It also occurs through more direct ways by setting information about clients in relation to money being spent. As a manager put it, HUD wants to know "what are we getting for our money": "We want to know the size of the problem and we want to know dollars per capita. How much are we spending per person, per unduplicated homeless person in the United States, what are we spending?" HUD's assessment of what it is getting for its money is happening in a number of ways at subnational levels.

The use of HMIS data by the Washington, D.C., Continuum of Care offers a good example of the valuable surplus generated by universal data elements, as well as the practices of "governance of governance," or the use of a homeless population to regulate service agencies. Working with the Department of Health and Human Services, the D.C. Continuum of Care has developed an Annual Performance Plan that all D.C. service agencies receiving McKinney-Vento funds are required to submit. These plans are used to evaluate agency performance and to help determine how D.C. will allocate its McKinney-Vento funds. As a report on this initiative notes,

> The ability to use HMIS data for more than required reporting is a tremendous asset to the CoC [Continuum of Care]. The D.C. Performance Measurement System has enabled CoC staff to collect data on each program's performance and monitor progress toward individual program and broader community goals. As shown . . . the Annual Performance Plan is a well-defined, structured way in which to hold providers accountable and ensure everyone clearly understands what is expected.[37]

Three accountability factors are tracked by the Annual Performance Plan using HMIS-generated data: the occupancy rate of the program; the income clients obtain while in the program (including public benefits); and either the successful transition to or maintenance of permanent housing. The income streams tracked by D.C.'s HMIS program reflect the statement about mainstream benefits quoted above. "Mainstream" means both income from employment as well as public assistance benefits not specific to homeless management, disability, and unemployment insurance. In other words, this factor signals non-dependence on HUD-funded services.

The three factors tracked in D.C. are used to create comparative quantitative measures of agency performance, which are in turn used, though not solely, to determine D.C.'s funding priorities. While we do not want to misread this as some sort of automated technocracy that matches dollars to scores, we should note what a far cry this use of HMIS is from HUD's promotion of it as a way to do what agencies already did, only better and faster. These three measures, which translate client experiences into agency scores, operationalize better and faster as commands that agencies must respond to in order to remain competitive in a context of scarce and restricted funding.[38] Individual experiences of finding and maintaining appropriate shelter or accessing income necessary for survival are absorbed into a governance mechanism in which the regulation of the poor functions not only as social control, but also as a mechanism for the regulation of social services. Being a target of homeless social services here becomes a kind of labor used to produce a population *for* governance and *as* governance.

The State of Arizona has gone even further in systemizing its use of HMIS universal data elements to regulate and fund agencies, and provides another telling case of how data generated through an HMIS is put to use toward the production of not just a population, but of subnational governance. In Arizona, McKinney-Vento funds are channeled through a central state agency, which then distributes those funds to municipal and county governments and nonprofit organizations. For agencies receiving its McKinney-Vento funds, Arizona has developed what it calls a "self-sufficiency improvement score."[39] The score is generated through the use of a matrix that measures fifteen different domains considered part of self-sufficiency, including Income, Employment, Adult Education, Mental Health, and others. For each of the domains, clients receive a score representing the following levels of self-sufficiency: 1 = In Crisis; 2 = Vulnerable; 3 = Safe; 4 = Building Capacity; or 5 = Empowered.[40] The state provides guidelines for what constitutes each level for each of the domains. For example, in the area of Employment, possessing no job earns a score of one; a temporary, part-time, or seasonal job with no benefits and inadequate pay earns a score of two; a full-time job with adequate pay but few or no benefits earns a three; a full-time job with adequate pay and benefits earns a four; and the maintenance of such a job earns a five. Thus, a client's self-sufficiency would range from fifteen, for a client determined to be "in crisis" in all fifteen domains, to a highest possible score of seventy-five for a client determined to be "empowered" in all fifteen areas.

These data for the self-sufficiency matrix are required to be collected when clients enter and exit programs. Agencies can then calculate a self-sufficiency improvement score by looking at the increase from time of entry to time of exit; a client who moved from "in crisis" to "safe" in all domains would be said to have increased his or her self-sufficiency by fifteen points. In terms of the clients of service agencies, this score accomplishes two things. First, it creates a standard measure of self-sufficiency, thereby operationalizing what HUD would otherwise consider vague and subjective outcomes; now a number can be attached to clients' abilities to care for themselves. Secondly, it allows their progress over time with an agency to be measured, giving a longitudinal dimension to this data. The self-sufficiency score serves as a good example of exactly the concerns raised by critics of the electronic turn. The self-sufficiency improvement score represents an amalgamation of various areas of need and service but also their quantification. Here, the subjective sense of being able to care for oneself, as well as the caseworker's interpretation of this, is eclipsed by a numerical measure. As described by critics earlier, this is the client decomposed and recomposed as data points.

However, the State of Arizona's and HUD's commentary on this program makes clear that how these data will be used to serve clients is of almost incidental concern. Arizona plans to use the scores to create aggregate rates of self-sufficiency improvement for *agencies*. Thus, Arizona can compare and rank agencies, and funding can be directed at them based on their successful generation of data that improves—marking the introduction of "performance-based contracting" in the homeless services industry.[41] For agencies, making their numbers "get better," and not necessarily their clients, will draw in more money. Improving rates of self-sufficiency may not be the same thing as improving the lives of people living without shelter in Arizona. Here we can see the quick movement from an individual who might look something like a case, to his or her reconfiguration as a data profile of numerical scores, to these scores' absorption as part of a larger data body (clients of an agency) out of which are generated numbers to draw in funds. If anything, HUD here is successfully regulating agencies, not clients, and it is doing so through "flexible regulation." Arizona operates within a given set of parameters—namely, the gathering of universal data elements by each agency supported with HUD funding—which can be actualized in any way the State of Arizona deems appropriate. It is "free" to make other uses of HMIS, and it has done just that. By providing flexible limitations, HUD allows states, cities, and Continuums of Care to innovate. They thereby function as test laboratories, producing new uses of HMIS that HUD can circulate as models, to be repeated and further elaborated upon by other locales.

While these were early innovations in the use of HMIS at subnational governance levels, the Obama administration's reauthorization of McKinney-Vento via the HEARTH Act of 2009 has put in place requirements that in effect mandate such metagovernance practices. The 2009 act requires that HUD evaluate Continuums of Care based on outcomes organized around a stated goal of the act that people experiencing homelessness should be relocated to permanent housing within thirty days.

In response to these demands, the National Alliance to End Homelessness has developed a Performance Improvement Clinic to help agencies meet the evaluation requirements of the HEARTH Act. The clinic includes the use of a Performance Evaluator Tool that works along the performance indicators that the alliance has identified as key to the act: reducing new episodes of homelessness, reducing returns to homelessness, and reducing lengths of homeless episodes. Training materials produced by the alliance suggest measurements agencies might generate to meet those requirements. For example, regarding returns to homelessness, they recommend measuring clients who return to the system at three-, six-, nine-, and twelve-month intervals from exit.

An alliance presentation for the clinic uses as a model the Columbus, Ohio, Continuum of Care. The alliance designates Columbus a "data driven system" and notes that agencies are paid only for programs that lead to reductions in homelessness. We must keep in mind that "reductions in homelessness" is within the terms of housing-deprived populations' techno-conceptual organization in the homeless management system. The inability of the CoC to impact housing options outside the shelter system means its organizational responsibility is to displace individuals from the homeless management system. To where is unclear. The reductions in homelessness mandated by the HEARTH Act in fact mean the disappearance of numbers from HUD tracking systems—that is all. Anything outside the purview of HMIS literally does not count.

While the National Coalition for the Homeless criticized the HEARTH Act for the marginalization of homeless program residents and advocates in decision-making processes, here we see a radically technocratized version of governance.[42] The narrowed scope—data about entries and exits and numbers in programs—evacuates any context about the production of housing insecurity and deprivation. Rather, we have nonprofit agencies spending funds to attend professional trainings organized by other agencies. Here agencies learn not how to provide housing or how to structurally interrupt the production of racialized housing insecurity, but how to meet the performance criteria of HUD. This is not to be too cynical about the work of the alliance and its Performance

Institute. It is inevitable that nonprofit structures like this would proliferate in the context of both ongoing privatization and the demands of a federal government that still plays a structuring role within these heterarchic arrangements.

What is homeless assistance in this model? Assistance extended to homeless agencies whose own data is turned against them in a competitive funding context that makes resources scarce. Clients of programs become a way of determining where money, resources, and technical information will flow, and what the life of an agency might be. This is a case of the governance of governance that operates through disciplined bodies mined for population data. And the population generated, which is a population of agencies overlaying a population of housing-deprived, feeds back on those disciplined bodies, the raw material out of which this data generation takes place. So, for example, an individual in Arizona or in Washington, D.C., or in Columbus, Ohio, will find the service options that become available to him or her will be dependent on (1) how that individual is sorted within the general population; and (2) how population data for that track has determined what agencies exist for that track and what services they offer. This is not a population as a representation of "the people," but rather a plane of intervention formed from the raw material of homeless clients that draws bodies back into itself. The answer to critiques that HMIS signals an invasion of privacy has been the creation of "masked data" that cannot be traced back to a specific client at the federal level. But whether or not a specific individual can be related back to data generated out of that individual, the life of that data will absorb and transform the life of that individual. The population is a living entity injected with biopolitical force that acts back upon that which made it.

The Biopoliticization of Housing Deprivation

HUD's effort to produce a national homeless population, then, must be considered in terms of a biopolitical project that disciplinary models in critical social work and surveillance studies cannot fully describe. In the contemporary context, discipline does not fall away. Rather, disciplinary mechanisms serve as flashpoints between an individual and a population. In this case, HUD's data standards allow for translation between these two political registers. Technologies of disciplinary psychodynamic case management—including the intersubjective relationship of caseworker and client, as well as institutional arrangements of nonprofit agencies, service plans, and federal mandates—provide a track across which biopolitical techniques of information management can roll out. Understood as inadequate to the task of population management, disciplinary case management is absorbed in a weakened state into a biopoliticized terrain in which its technologies continue to reproduce, though in mutated form. And so social work is neither simply enhanced nor eroded by a technology it deploys, but rather is itself deployed inside this technically reconfigured context. In order to survive, social work must transform to move within the contours of this new milieu. The innovations of the Washington, D.C., Continuum of Care, Columbus, Ohio, and the State of Arizona are examples of these creative adaptations; the adoption of those models as mandates are a reminder of the force of the federal state in this decentralized context. Though the disciplining techniques of case management may continue to accomplish some of their older goals, they survive insofar as they hold the subject available to biopolitical interventions that will in some ways leave the subject behind, as service agencies become privileged objects of governmental intervention.

The consequence, then, of scholars and critics remaining at a disciplinary register is not that such analysis is wrong. The problem is that when an individual subject is assumed as the object of intervention, such analysis cannot fully account either for the productive operations of power at play or for the consequences of this for individuals dependent upon federally reconfigured social service provision. Whereas HUD would imagine the "unduplicated population counts" of its HMIS program as simply a statistical reflection of what actually exists, we can rather understand HUD's program as arranging homelessness *as* a population, and therefore as vulnerable to biopolitical calculation. Thus, clients of homeless service agencies are caught in a field of data not tied directly back to them, but to which they are very much bound. Contrary to HUD's claims, this population does not merely present an accurate picture of homelessness in the United States, but it rather remakes homelessness by reconfiguring what needs are allowed to register and what services can address those needs. In fact, the population precedes the lives that made it, as the individual becomes drawn into the possibilities of life determined by biopolitical technologies. As an incarnation of surplus life, the individual must come to reflect the population, not the other way around. And so, far from being merely a reflection of the people that make it up, the population of universal data elements works toward "making up people," to play with Ian Hacking's formulation.[43] With this phrase, Hacking points to how the categories of statistics determine not only what kinds of people can be conceptualized—what kinds of laborers, for example—but also that people can be categorized in terms of the labor they perform at all. I want to point to how the production of populations makes some kinds of living possible, while foreclosing others. HUD's HMIS program produces a population of universal data elements that circulates powerfully in the biopolitical context of contemporary governance. Providing privacy protections for individual homeless clients—as critics demanded and as HUD has done—does not shield those individuals from such feedback effects of this population data. Surveillance technologies in this context do not "clamp down," but rather let loose. They let loose a biopolitical register toward the proliferation of governance and its populations—which is to say, they free new objects of intervention that may not look like any one individual, but of which the individual client, in order to survive, must become a part. The client gives life to the population, and this life is organized not only as an object of governance, but as a mechanism for governance. In a context of renewed federal intervention, the universal data elements allow for the roll-out of new kinds of oversight that reorganize homeless services in terms of quantified outcomes set in relation to financial costs and savings. Those managed by the homeless services industry come to manage it, in the sense that they have become a population that governs service provision. And for "offering" themselves up as raw material for the productions of HMIS, clients receive life in return: access to the bare minimum of food, shelter, and healthcare. In this sense, the "surplus" of life must be read as extraneous and leftover. Within biopolitical homeless management, for individuals in desperate need of resources controlled by social service agencies and basic to survival, there may be no life outside the surplus life given by the population.

The conditions of housing insecurity remain intact even as the technologies of homeless management are recalibrated and modernized.

HMIS produces limits within which the homeless services industry operates while reproducing it as the nonprofit industrial complex. As the statements from homeless industry workers attest, this process is not complete. Social workers find ways to work around the tasks of databasing or outright lie in performing them while also doing the work they think is essential. Regardless, HMIS produces a new techno-conceptual of housing deprivation: a population of homelessness defined in terms of patterns and tendencies and set in relationship to economic data and quantified measures of service and results. This population offers another level of abstraction from a material analysis of housing insecurity and deprivation in terms of racial capitalism's organization of space and the racial state's projects of managing and investing in health, life, illness, and death. Here we have a technical problem managed through technical means. While of course HMIS collects data on the race of those it databases, this too is an abstracted race, leaving behind the coconstruction of race and property so we have rather a free-floating set of data points that, in the terms of a post-racial imaginaries, just happen to be black or just happen to be Latino. How that happens is cut outside of the bounds of this population as well as the service industry it is set against to manage.

In the measures it does not seek, HMIS reproduces this post-racial racialized housing insecurity as inevitable, given, and unworthy of investigation. But this does not mean that race and its measures are not engaged. As the next chapter will show, race as population has its own role to play in putting surplus life to work.

FIVE

The Invention of Chronic Homelessness

IN 2007, A COALITION OF LOS ANGELES GOVERNMENT OFFICES AND nonprofit organizations launched Project 50, a social service and housing program targeting what researchers, politicians, and journalists have recently begun calling the "chronically homeless." As defined by the United States Interagency Council on Homelessness, "A chronically homeless person is . . . an unaccompanied homeless individual with a disabling condition who has either been continuously homeless for a year or more *or* has had at least four episodes of homelessness in the past three years."[1] Unlike individuals or families for whom living without shelter is a temporary episode, the chronically homeless are understood to exhibit long-term patterns of cycling in and out of shelters, hospitals, and jails, interspersed with periods of living unhoused and on the streets.

Following a model tested first in New York City, Project 50's team of outreach workers set out to identify chronically homeless individuals concentrated in downtown Los Angeles in a neighborhood still called Skid Row. Mortality rates are so high in Skid Row—three times that of the surrounding county—that in the 1970s, one group of researchers referred to the neighborhood as a "death zone."[2] In recent years, Skid Row has been undergoing a dramatic revanchist turn as it is reterritorialized by luxury housing developments and consumer amenities.[3] As described by Neil Smith, "revanchism" names a model of gentrification that seeks revenge on poor populations who occupy spaces that capital now wishes to reclaim for investment.[4] An expanding and increasingly hostile police presence has accompanied this real-estate push-out. After a pilot launch in 2005, the so-called Safer City Initiative targeted unsheltered individuals in Skid Row for criminal punishment from 2006 to 2007; it represented one of the greatest concentrations of police force in the United States.[5]

Armed with outreach questionnaires, Project 50 workers initiated face-to-face conversations with Skid Row residents. In these conversations, they gathered targeted information about the lives of their interview subjects, including how much time they had spent in hospitals, shelters, and living on the street, their medical backgrounds and histories of substance use, as well as any current health conditions. For each Skid Row resident interviewed, the information obtained was measured against what is known as a "vulnerability index." The index used by Project 50 identifies eight conditions linked to increased mortality among street populations:

> more than three hospitalizations or emergency room visits in a year
> more than three emergency room visits in the previous three months
> aged 60 or older
> cirrhosis of the liver
> end-stage renal disease
> history of frostbite, immersion foot, or hypothermia
> HIV+/AIDS
> tri-morbidity: co-occurring psychiatric, substance abuse, and chronic medical condition.[6]

The index is based on medical research demonstrating that possessing any one of these indicators significantly decreases an individual's lifespan. The "50" in Project 50 refers to the goal of the outreach efforts: to use the index to identify the fifty people in Skid Row most likely to die in the coming year. These individuals were offered immediate placement into a housing program, with none of the typical case management requirements regarding social services or sobriety. One radio program described Project 50 residents as those "fortunate enough to be determined the most unfortunate."[7]

Project 50 is just one among hundreds of chronic homelessness programs launched in municipalities across the United States in recent years. Chronic homelessness programs depart from long-held assumptions about people living in poverty and long-established technologies for managing those populations, and thus their emergence and rapid spread defies easy explanation. As chapter 3 argued, popular conceptions of poverty in the United States have maintained that individuals living in poverty produce their impoverished conditions, not social or governmental institutions. Such discourse of personal responsibility has been accompanied by intensive networks of social welfare technologies that seek to regulate the poor by intervening in individual behavior. As chapter 3 also demonstrated, persons living without shelter have been understood as being especially incapable of self-management and in need of invasive social assistance. Many decades of formal and informal policy have made treatment for substance abuse and psychiatric disabilities a mandatory condition for entering and remaining in housing programs. Such earlier policy argued that drug/alcohol and psychiatric treatment, as well as social services focused on money management, job training, and a wide range of other so-called life skills, make formerly "shelter-resistant" individuals "housing-ready."

Thus, chronic homelessness initiatives are quite surprising, as they facilitate immediate access to housing with no social service or work requirements, bypassing the coercive social control technologies associated with the contemporary workfare state and the war on the poor.[8] This departure in policy is even more surprising considering that those categorized as chronically homeless are disproportionately men of color who actively consume drugs and alcohol and lack close family ties.[9] Far from finding themselves the privileged targets of housing programs, members of this population, typically demonized as the "undeserving poor," are more commonly barred from social service agencies and housed in prisons and jails.[10]

Long before the advent of chronic homelessness initiatives, advocates and activists organized against mandatory health and social services in housing programs. Socially progressive service organizations, convinced that mandatory services actually kept people out of shelters, experimented with making services optional.[11] This model, known as "Housing First," remained marginal within the homeless services industry until its adoption by the federal government for chronic homelessness initiatives. How did this unexpected moment arrive, and through the efforts of the neoconservative administration of George W. Bush?[12] Should this be taken as a compassionate turn in social policy and administration? Does it represent a reversal of social abandonment, as vilified populations deemed most likely to die became targeted for life-saving housing interventions rather than displaced to zones of exclusion?

In my use, "chronically homeless" should always be read as if in scare quotes. As will become clear, I want to foreground the provisional and constructed nature of the term, even as I investigate its deployment.

Due to its very real material consequences, we must take the term seriously while nonetheless understanding it to mean populations *targeted* as "chronically homeless." How those quotes fall away and this subpopulation achieves a taken-for-granted status are investigated in the chapter that follows. The rise of chronic homelessness as a concern results from the convergence of two historical forces. The first is a counterdiscourse in homeless social services that challenges medical models and technologies of homeless management. This is the early Housing First movement and a related discourse of public health. The second is the production of an economic analysis of homelessness that emphasizes the financial cost of leaving populations housing deprived. This economic analysis is produced first by social scientists and then picked up and circulated by government offices and mass media. Uncovering the intersection of these historical forces makes the arrival of chronic homelessness initiatives less surprising, and points toward the limits of these initiatives as well. Despite the promise of chronic homelessness programs—namely, the lifting of barriers to access and the immediate provision of housing—I propose a cautious interrogation of the relationships between the technical calculation of death chances and the securing of health and life resources. This is to take seriously the tension expressed by a social worker with an activist background who told me:

> I mean the good thing is that we're really making an impact. We're really housing people. At times I'm like, oh my god, I'm just so "the Man" right now, selling out big time. But then at other times, you know, I see the folks that we're able to get inside. And they're the people that nobody else has ever been able to really talk to, or have wanted to talk to. You know, the quote-unquote "resistant to services" people. And we spend time with them, and we don't give up on them.

This social worker communicates some dismay at working within the government—"I'm just so 'the Man' right now"—while also asserting the incontrovertible fact that the program is housing exactly the people who have been most blocked from social welfare benefits. Ultimately, the contradictions that statement points to, and the surprise of finding a progressive housing agenda picked up and promoted by the U.S. federal government, arise from the ways in which managing vulnerable populations enables neoliberal economic expansion.

"Housing First" and the Demedicalization of Homelessness

As discussed in the previous two chapters, the primary mode for managing homelessness within the dominant medical model has been through case management technologies. In contemporary social work practice, the medical logics embedded in case management technologies comprise an inherited culture that has made case management seem obvious and necessary. This has been formalized by the Department of Housing and Urban Development (HUD) in the Continuum of Care (CoC) model, which mandates progression through stages of housing, from emergency shelter, to transitional housing, and ultimately in either private marketplace or supportive permanent housing. Thus, the old Progressive-era work test has survived in a new form. Rather than cutting stone or lumber, modern shelter aspirants demonstrate worth through commitment to working on themselves and making it through the Continuum. As a former caseworker and current director of a housing program told me, "I think there's just this really old-fashioned treatment approach to things, where you have to earn your way to housing. I can't really say that I've ever seen any kind of formal funding requirement of sobriety or anything like that. You basically worked your way up the Continuum." As the statement suggests, notions of deserving versus undeserving poor are embedded in practices that withhold housing and other services from those who have not "earned" it. As it also suggests, associations of homelessness with alcohol abuse and drug addiction have especially called forth the presumed necessity of professional intervention in the form of social work technologies. That informant continued, "People thought that they needed to have folks that were clean and sober. It was sort of just a requirement that was handed down but never really written anywhere." A staff therapist of another organization explained that mandatory treatment draws legitimacy from the popular conception that "addicts" require shaming and direct intervention. But it is also produced by the professionalization of social work, and the organizational status of the case manager over the client.

> I think to some degree it's a thing we're conditioned to about substance use generally. But I think it's sort of a natural extension of being in the social services world as well. Because just the logic of social services is

that we're being paid to make life better for these people. Therefore, our judgment is paramount. And they ought to be following that. And so going into a setting where we don't just impose our judgment on things I think doesn't feel right to some people. And then you complicate it further with our conventional view of addiction stuff, where it's all about, you know, shaming someone until they come around and start making better decisions for themselves. . . . The whole thing just becomes a big mess I think.

Thus, moral, medical, and popular conceptions of selfhood and homelessness naturalize the compulsory deployment of case management technologies. As a result, the provision of housing services has almost always been conjoined to coercive attempts at fixing problem individuals.

In contrast to compulsory case management technologies of social and health services, Housing First represents a potentially radical break from medicalized models by separating shelter provision from social and health services. Housing First programs make available traditional social and health services, but as the designation suggests, housing is the first thing provided, and services are not required for admittance. Housing First represents a social commitment to the principle that all people deserve housing at all times, and an organizational commitment to putting resources into supporting all residents. The Downtown Emergency Services Center (DESC), which is based in Seattle and has become a model for agencies around the country, outlines the following core components of a Housing First approach:

> Move people into housing directly from streets and shelters without preconditions of treatment acceptance or compliance.
> The provider is obligated to bring robust support services to the housing. These services are predicated on assertive engagement, not coercion.
> Continued tenancy is not dependent on participation in services.
> Units targeted to most disabled and vulnerable homeless members of the community.
> Embraces harm reduction approach to addictions rather than mandating abstinence. At the same time, the provider must be prepared to support resident commitments to recovery.
> Residents must have leases and tenant protections under the law.
> Can be implemented as either a project-based or scattered site model.[13]

Before being named as such, Housing First practices were being put in place by a small number of nonprofit agencies targeting unsheltered populations. These organizations, each of which was attempting to reach what one informant called "the hardest to house" and another "the worst of the worst," came to a reverse logic about the relationship of services and housing. Compulsory psychiatric and drug treatment, rather than enabling people to stay housed, came to be seen as barriers that kept people on the streets. Compulsory requirements set up residents to fail (at sobriety, for example), and thus to be evicted and deprived of housing once more. A self-fulfilling prophecy was put in place: residents in fact appeared not to be ready for housing. Speaking of this process that leads to eviction, one caseworker told me, "It deepens people's impressions that these clients are impossible to house. Every time that happens, then they feel more strongly about that."

As suggested in the DESC principles cited above, proto–Housing First programs evolved out of contemporaneous harm reduction movements in AIDS activism. In the realm of HIV/AIDS prevention, harm reduction argues that abstinence models do not keep people safe and that education efforts should rather be aimed toward developing safer practices. Services must meet clients "where they're at" and provide tools for making healthier choices in how to have sex or use drugs.[14] Translated to the realm of housing, harm reduction suggested that rather than coercing residents to accept an organization's concept of housing readiness, organizations should simply provide housing; housing is a safer option than living unhoused, and once housed, clients can be supported in making informed choices about their needs and interests regarding services. Since many housing organizations were already working with populations targeted by harm reduction HIV/AIDS prevention, they were already prepped for Housing First. "It wasn't some huge internal dialogue we had to go through to get comfortable with Housing First as an idea. There was some pushback from some of the staff. But those values were pretty much in all of our seminal documents, part of orientation, part of ongoing supervision, part of service training. It wasn't a huge thing for us; it just felt like a very natural evolution."

The early adoption of Housing First did not occur all at once. Rather, it was a piecemeal effort that required reevaluating long-held assumptions rooted in the disciplinary case management model. Service providers describe a kind of organic process of trial and error that led their respective agencies to develop "low-demand" environments that would eventually be named and organized as Housing First. The director of one such agency describes the shift at that agency from "housing readiness"—the notion that only some people were prepared to accept and stay in housing, and that others must first go through mandatory treatment.

> We employed a readiness concept. "So-and-so" is not ready for this housing because he's not keeping his appointments with their case manager. Or "so-and-so" is not ready because he's a crack addict and he's not doing anything. And yet, because of who we are . . . we were sort of known in the community as the organization of last resort. If you were so crazy, or so into drug and alcohol use, and the Y[MCA] didn't want to serve you anymore, they would refer you to [us]. Social workers and emergency departments, police officers—if they encountered someone who was very disorganized, very dysfunctional, they would take them here. So we had all that experience. But we were right out of the box with a housing project and we sort of, to a certain degree, followed this readiness thing. But because we had all this experience, we also stretched that a little bit, and took some risks with people.

As the statement indicates, an organizational commitment to finding ways to house those populations who were most neglected by compulsory services drove these early experiments in Housing First.

Of course, the medical model and its technologies of compliance proved quite sticky. Even as agencies experimented with low-demand environments with optional treatment services, pathologizing assumptions about homeless populations were not automatically or easily abandoned.

> When we developed [our first permanent low-demand housing,] we sort of had this naïve assumption that this group was gonna trash the building. And so we built in this humongous line item into the budget for repairing things. Because our thought was, "We're not gonna kick them out, we're just gonna fix the things that they break." And it turned out, that didn't happen. And I think that was part of the change in our thinking to "these people are really not any more difficult to house than anybody else."

> Even though we were close to these people, I think we bought into the same stereotypes. That they're a bunch of animals who are gonna rip the place to shreds. It's embarrassing to think about it now.

Despite some of these reservations, organizations that experimented with low-demand or Housing First approaches quickly saw that freeing clients from mandatory services did not render them incapable of staying housed.

> And over the first few years of operation we discovered that the people that we were taking risks with were just as likely to succeed in housing as those people that we predicted were housing ready. About the time we were coming to that realization, the Safe Haven idea was introduced at the federal level. And the next housing project . . . we decided that we wanted to build this housing project, and we wanted to use it as an engagement tool. So we set our caps to recruit residents that we knew to be crazy and homeless and not connected to anybody's [services] program, including our own. [15]

As the experiments bore results, the idea that some populations possess an untamed desire to live on the street came undone. Along with it, the notions of "service resistant" and "housing ready" seemed increasingly implausible.

> There was all sorts of mythology out there about, this is the one group of homeless people that is just not gonna come inside. They would prefer to be outside and just drink themselves to death. It turned out that was not the case. We had to make seventy-nine offers of housing to get seventy-five people to accept housing.
>
> I think we're experiencing evidence that homeless people want housing, and can maintain it. When I started . . . what they told me was, homeless people won't talk to you, they don't want housing. They would be labeled as "service resistant," which is just meaningless. It's just a meaningless thing to call a person, it doesn't mean anything. It's not rooted in behavioral science, it's just a cop out.

As the director of one program pointed out to me, these early experiments succeeded because agencies were offering permanent housing, as opposed to temporary placement in an emergency shelter while clients got clean and sober. An organizational recognition was emerging that clients respond to the conditions of housing opportunities, as anyone would. Rejection of heavy service requirements or the lack of privacy and comfort in emergency shelters was being recognized as a reasonable reaction that agencies must take seriously. "Everybody knows that shelter is not a place anybody wants to be. So quote-unquote 'shelter resistant,' I never believed a word about it. If you give somebody housing, they're gonna go in. So why even tag somebody with that description? I'm resistant to shelter, anybody would be."

Slowly a new logic developed: clients who refused compulsory services would accept no-strings-attached housing. This led to new outreach approaches, as Housing First principles got structured into every stage of work.

> So we focused on going out to the folks on the street. They started to ask people, "Will you work with us toward permanent housing?" They didn't talk to them about, like, you need to get clean, you need to go into [emergency] shelter, you need to get mental health services. The first question was, "Will you work with us toward permanent housing? Your own apartment—your own place with a door that locks. And if you're willing to work with us, we will stick with you until it happens." And that's how they were able to reduce [street] homelessness.

As the bind between housing and compliance technologies loosened, pathological conceptions of homeless populations lost their logical force. Housing First technologies edged out disciplinary logics that individuals must be reformed to be housing ready. Rather than a war on the poor mentality that assigns individuals personal responsibility for conditions of poverty, a new view of institutional responsibility emerged. From this view, government and nonprofit organizations, not individuals living without shelter, bore responsibility for housing failures.

> If this person goes back on the streets, then you the housing provider need to realize that you failed the individual. It's not the individual that has failed himself, but we have failed to figure out how to work with him. And you need to be confident that you have exhausted the possibilities. I think too much still we just give up on people and say, "Well, they didn't jump through all the hoops we wanted them to, so they clearly don't want this housing." Well, that's nonsense, nobody wants to go to sleep back on the street.
>
> I think we should be held accountable for outcomes that are really difficult to achieve. . . . For a long time, we as a sector put the onus on

the individual to figure out how to work with us. And now I think the shift is . . . [that] it's our job to figure out how to work with that individual, and it's not ok just to say, "They don't wanna come inside." We have to figure out how to get that person inside and how to negotiate with them and serve them.

For organizations to accept and understand the ways that technologies of compliance perpetuate housing deprivation requires fundamentally reconceptualizing the role of nonprofit organizations within the nonprofit industrial complex. It requires understanding the provision of housing—rather than the reforming of the individual—as the appropriate goal. This means, as many described it, that "housing is an outcome" rather than a tool for enforcing compliance in self-help regimes.

A lot of people can't seem to accept the idea that being housed is an outcome for homeless people. They want to know, "So, what's happening to their mental health symptoms? And are they getting jobs, and are they abstinent from substance use?" and all that kind of stuff. Which for some people, certainly it's the route they end up taking and it helps and all that. But the point of housing is housing. It's an outcome for all of us. It isn't to facilitate something else for us. It's to have a home base. Why can't it be for them as well?

Housing First principles demand a rejection of the polarizing pathologization embedded in disciplinary social work regimes. Rather than marking out "the homeless" as a special category of individual, Housing First insists that housing-deprived populations deserve the same access to housing as any of us who are able to pay for that privilege.

Thus, throughout the 1990s, before being named as such, Housing First approaches developed organically through organizational experiments with housing under-served populations. When Pathways to Housing, an early advocate of this approach, published research indicating that mandatory services do not impact ability to find and maintain housing, Housing First was organized as a named concept, and began to formally travel around social service networks.[16] Thus, the leader of an effort to convert service-heavy supportive housing to Housing First describes recognizing the new common sense of Housing First. That manager, charged with dramatically reducing the street population of a tourist urban core, described hearing about Housing First

149

and recognizing almost immediately that it would be the most "efficient and effective way" of getting that population housed.

In challenging pathological conceptions of homelessness and attempting to address the needs of underserved populations, Housing First advocates enacted a demedicalization of homelessness. In other words, in this approach, the idea of homelessness as an incarnation of a failed selfhood is undermined, and along with it, the compulsory use of case management technologies is undermined as well. Accompanying this demedicalization has been a new discourse that reframes homelessness as a public health issue. This discourse also concerns medical issues, but does not treat housing deprivation as a pathology that must be cured. Rather, this new discourse draws attention to the health consequences of living without shelter, such as those outlined in chapter 1, including greater exposure to tuberculosis and HIV and much higher mortality rates than housed populations. Through this discourse, advocates emphasize that living without shelter dramatically harms health and shortens life—hence Project 50's goal of locating those most likely to die in the coming year. Insisting on the health needs of unsheltered populations has been an attempt to undo the stigmas attached to cultural conceptions of the homeless:

> The health piece is less stigmatized. We're able to use it as a more powerful advocacy tool. If you scratch an alcoholic you're gonna get liver disease. If you scratch, unfortunately, someone with severe and persistent mental illness, you're gonna find diabetes and heart disease from the secondary [effects] of taking the psych meds. So you can find a way to less stigmatized manifestations of all the things we see on the streets and use that.

This counter-discourse of public health also seeks to mobilize political sympathy against demonizing portraits of the undeserving poor. Advocates describe it as a means of redirecting attention and garnering support. Referencing an agency's work doing public presentations on the health consequences of housing deprivation, one staff member told me:

> Almost always . . . it's common for one of [the government officials] to start weeping. And then publicly, because it's framed as a life or death issue, not as a behavioral health issue, they have the clearance to take bold decisive action. They're like, "Oh my god, they're gonna die." And

they have this little mini freak-out on Thursday, and then on Friday, they step up.

Another worker, describing efforts in the local community, echoed this sentiment:

> The number one most vulnerable guy we found . . . was in the middle of going through chemotherapy on the street when we found him. How can you as a public official not act? I mean, that's just ridiculous, there's no reason that man should be on the street. And so it takes away, I think, a lot of the "people are drug users, or they're crazy, or they're undeserving of our services." And brings it down to a level which everyone can relate to, about being how awful it is to be sick, and especially sick on the street.

While there is no doubt that for advocates, the public health discourse is a powerful mobilizing tool, it is not clear how much credit the discourse deserves for changing the political landscape of homeless social services. As it turns out, economics is playing at least as important a role as empathy.

The Costs of Chronic Homelessness

Looking at how public health concerns get rolled out suggests that we must attend to an economic dimension of those health concerns. This economic dimension follows from what I would call the "invention of chronic homelessness." By "invention," of course, I do not mean to deny that some people endure much of their lives deprived of housing. Nor do I mean to downplay the incredible risks to health and life posed by housing insecurity and deprivation. Rather, I want to draw attention to how a certain conception of a subcategory of homelessness— the chronically homeless—becomes the condition of possibility for the mobilization of public health discourses and Housing First practices. And in turn, I want to attend to how that condition of possibility sets limits on what becomes of those discourses and practices.

The terms "chronic homelessness" and "chronically homeless" start appearing in media discourse as early as the 1980s. The usage at that time, and up until the mid-1990s, was fairly loose.[17] The terms were used to describe a state any person might be in. So, for example, a newspaper article might describe someone by saying, "Throughout his 20s and 30s, John was chronically homeless"—as in, John was frequently without a home. Beginning in the mid-1990s, however, the meaning of these terms began to congeal, and they came to refer to a specific *subset* of homeless people, rather than a state any person might be in. This solidification of the concept happened as a result of research conducted out of the University of Pennsylvania by Dennis Culhane and Randall Kuhn. In a series of studies published in 1998, Culhane and Kuhn argue that people who stay in emergency homeless shelters can be organized into three categories: the transitionally homeless, the episodically homeless, and the chronically homeless. In the first study, Culhane and Kuhn explain: "The *chronically homeless* population could be characterized as those persons most like the stereotypical profile of the skid-row homeless. These are people who are likely to be entrenched in the shelter system, and for whom shelters are more like long-term housing than an emergency arrangement."[18] Thus, the chronically homeless are one part of all those who use shelters. Culhane and Kuhn described them as "over-utilizers"—their shelter stays last the longest, and they are most likely to return. In the second study, Culhane and Kuhn argue that the chronically homeless tend to share a number of characteristics and that "in general, being older, of black race, having a substance abuse or mental health problem, or having a physical disability, significantly reduces the likelihood of exiting shelter."[19]

Culhane and Kuhn's research not only solidified the concept of chronic homelessness. It also introduced an economic dimension to the category. The extended stays and high rates of recidivism attributed to the chronically homeless are understood to be most significant in terms of their drain on the shelter systems; Culhane and Kuhn argue that chronically homeless individuals use a "disproportionate amount of resources" in the homeless service industry. In other words, with their long and frequent shelter stays, they are the most costly. Subsequent research by Culhane, Kuhn, and others went further, correlating shelter stay statistics with data from hospitals and jails to show that the chronically homeless in fact brought high costs to these other institutional sites as well.[20]

The concept that there exists a distinct subset of chronically homeless people has turned out to be quite compelling, and since the publication of Culhane and Kuhn's study, it has circulated widely through mass media. In the years just around the publication of their study, newspapers began to consistently use the term "chronically homeless" to refer to a specific set of people. In this circulation, the concept has brought the economic analysis along with it. Media accounts frequently refer back to the idea that chronically homeless populations are expensive. Malcolm Gladwell's widely read 2006 article for the *New Yorker*, "Million Dollar Murray," follows one of the chronically homeless as he moves about draining institutions of money. In the piece, Gladwell summarizes further research that tracks the impact of the chronically homeless on hospital systems:

> Boston Health Care for the Homeless Program, a leading service group for the homeless in Boston, recently tracked the medical expenses of a hundred and nineteen chronically homeless people. In the course of five years, thirty-three people died and seven more were sent to nursing homes, and the group still accounted for 18,834 emergency-room visits—at a minimum cost of a thousand dollars a visit. The University of California, San Diego Medical Center followed fifteen chronically homeless inebriates and found that over eighteen months those fifteen people were treated at the hospital's emergency room four hundred and seventeen times, and ran up bills that averaged a hundred thousand dollars each.[21]

Many social service agencies have produced their own studies, making note of some of the same costs. As a program manager told me, "We had someone run the Medicaid numbers on about one hundred clients, and they were costing $24,000 a year pre-housing. It was costing us $24,000 a year to do nothing."

In 2001, HUD named ending chronic homelessness one of its programming priorities. By 2003, the Bush administration included this goal in the fiscal year budget; it was followed by an endorsement of such efforts by the U.S. Council of Mayors.[22] Chronic homelessness programs have been a central feature of what are known as 10-Year Plans, or municipal initiatives to end street homelessness in a decade. Currently, at least 243 communities in the United States have established 10-Year Plans.[23] As partnerships among municipal governments, nonprofit organizations, and business leaders, the 10-Year Plans are typical arrangements of neoliberal governance. Like the destruction of skid rows that began in the 1960s, 10-Year Plans today aim to clear space in city centers to improve opportunities for capital investment and growth.

Social service models that require psychiatric and drug/alcohol treatment have been considered an obstacle to 10-Year Plans, insofar as they keep the chronically homeless out of housing programs and on the streets, in the way of business ventures, wealthy residents, and tourists. Thus, the federal Interagency Council on Homelessness and HUD have called for a "paradigm shift" in social services and housing. As stated by *Strategies for Reducing Chronic Street Homelessness,* a report prepared for HUD, "The people on whom this project focuses are, by definition, those for whom these programs and services have not produced long-term solutions to homelessness. Their resistance to standard approaches has been a challenge to communities committed to ending chronic street homelessness."[24] While the statement still emphasizes individual-level resistance, rather than the institutional barriers indicated by my informants, its suggestion that mandatory requirements be lifted gels with what housing program residents and advocates have long argued—namely, that there is a mismatch between organizational requirements and clients' needs. This, rather than an untamed desire to live on the streets, explains resistance to shelter.[25] The paradigm shift called for in *Strategies for Reducing Chronic Street Homelessness* would remove barriers to access by delinking "housing and service use/acceptance, so that to keep housing, a tenant need only adhere to conditions of the lease (pay rent, don't destroy property, no violence), and is not required to participate in treatment or activities."[26] HUD's programs also call for harm-reduction, rather than zero-tolerance, approaches, "where sobriety is 'preferred but not required,' which often translate into a 'no use on the premises' rule for projects that use HUD funds."[27]

The federal government understands that chronic homelessness programs may be a difficult transition for housing providers, who have traditionally relied on more directly coercive measures for controlling resident populations, as well as the funds attached to such approaches. One director of a program, who formerly managed a housing program as it underwent a transition to Housing First, recounted feelings of resistance when first confronted with "hard to house" clients. "I'd say—he's not ready for our housing. You gotta send him to the shelter, you gotta send him to transitional housing, and then he can apply from there. With us doing this project there was a real tension in our organization, with one part of our organization trying to house people, and the other part saying they're not housing ready." HUD has recognized the organizational challenges, and the organizational resistance they are likely to bring:

> For mental health and social service providers, low-demand environments mean they cannot require tenants to use services, and they have to deal with both mental health and substance abuse issues, and do so simultaneously. In addition, tenants may not use their services consistently, thus reducing reimbursements on which the providers may rely. For housing providers, a low-demand residence means that tenants may not act as predictably as the property managers might wish. For both, the challenges are as much philosophical as financial, in that the new model demands that they conduct business in ways that had formerly been considered not just impractical but wrong.[28]

Despite these obstacles, HUD has made programs that incorporate chronic homelessness initiatives a strong priority of its Homeless Assistance grants. This includes funding allocated through the Samaritan Housing Initiative to develop permanent housing exclusively for populations designated chronically homeless.[29]

Thus, as a result of its attachment to chronic homelessness initiatives and 10-Year Plans, Housing First has become not only prioritized but even a mandated approach. In a sense, the target of "the compulsory" has shifted from individual clients to organizations. And this compulsory has the force of the financial behind it. Many leaders of a loosely conceived Housing First movement argue that the traditional funding structure of the homeless services industry encouraged leaving populations unhoused.

> You know, to get the provider community . . . rethinking the way that they've been doing business for 20 years has been enormously challenging. Because what's the incentive for doing that? If the money you're getting isn't changing, if no one is paying you to do anything different than what you've been doing? If there's no consequence . . . then it's kind of understandable, why would you change what you're doing?

The reorganization of federal funding now provides this financial incentive for taking on Housing First approaches. Organizations that previously received government contracts based on outreach (or what is described as "contact") are now being required to document placements and placement duration. "In the past, the contracts were really only based on contacts. So you could be constantly contacting people on the street and not housing anybody, and it wouldn't make a difference." The shift has required a willingness to work with and for demonized populations. One municipal program director remarked that many organizations that saw their work as providing health and treatment services rather than housing were unable to make this shift, "So we put them out of business." The change in federal funding priorities has been reproduced at all levels of government, including city contracts. City funding often provides the bulk of money for an organization, along with private foundation grants. Federal funding, though underwriting only a small portion of the work, functions as something like a "seal of approval": agencies must secure federal funding to qualify for other kinds of funding. In that way, federal funding requirements often "trickle down" to lower levels of government.

> And so when we demonstrated that there were results from this program, the city ended up withdrawing all of its outreach contracts and reissuing an RFP [request for proposals]. So they reissued that money. What they've now started paying outreach workers to do is to house people. And since they've done that, they've housed 1,100 people. So there's just been a huge shift . . . in part because of this shift from an approach which is about making contact to one which is about a census reduction in street homeless people, and therefore [about] requiring housing providers, and especially providers who were supposed to be serving this population, to take the hardest to house, and figure out how to keep them in housing.

Thus, the reinterpretation of housing deprivation as an economic burden on city resources has forced an economic overhaul of housing services as well. It is not surprising, then, that in taking up chronic homelessness as an object of knowledge and intervention, the federal government has translated the economic dimensions of the category into business plans for its management. An Interagency Council on Homelessness presentation on 10-Year Plans offers the following reasons to focus on chronic homelessness:

This group consumes a disproportionate amount of costly resources.

Addressing the needs of this group will free up resources for other homeless groups, including youth/families.

Chronic homelessness has a visible impact on your community's safety and attractiveness.

It is a finite problem that can be solved.

Effective new technologies exist to engage and house this population.

This group is in great need of assistance and special services.[30]

The presentation is a textbook example of neoliberal post-social thinking in action. The first two points make explicitly economic arguments. The third point makes an implicit economic argument, evoking the cost to urban economies posed by perceived danger and dirt. The fourth and fifth points make pragmatic arguments—it can be done—and only the last point makes something like a social welfare argument about the needs of the population itself. The presentation elaborates on only the first point, regarding the disproportionate consumption of resources, positing that the chronically homeless represent only 10 percent of the overall homeless population, but consume 50 percent of resources.[31] This data is also not correct. The 50 percent figure is rounded up from the 46.9 percent established by Culhane and Kuhn's research, which applies only to number of shelter days "consumed" by chronically homeless residents in the shelter systems they studied.[32]

That chronic homelessness demands savvy economic responses is made even more explicit in a second presentation entitled *Good . . . to Better . . . to Great: Innovations in 10-Year Plans to End Chronic Homelessness in Your Community*.[33] The presentation draws from *Good to Great*, a study by Jim Collins, which identifies the attributes of corporations that sustain long-term competitive edges over other corporations and perform "above market." The Interagency Council presentation applies the principles of Collins's study to analyze chronic homelessness programs and identify how "great" programs employ the same principles found by Collins as key to corporate success—"disciplined people, disciplined thought, disciplined action." The presentation not only encourages partnerships between government offices, nonprofit agencies, and private sector business leaders, but also suggests that 10-Year-Plan leadership be placed in someone "of high standing in the community who is *not* primarily associated with homelessness." This is meant to lend credibility to the efforts, providing a sheen of respectability and distancing them from touchy-feely social programs.

According to the presentation, a key element of "disciplined thought" is the implementation of a business plan to combat chronic homelessness. Great plans include the following elements of disciplined thought:

> Business Principles—familiar concepts, such as investment vs. return, that bring a business orientation to the strategy
> Baselines—documented numbers that quantify the extent of homelessness in the local community
> Benchmarks—incremental reductions planned in the number of people experiencing chronic homelessness
> Best Practices—proven methods and approaches that directly support ending chronic homelessness
> Budget—the potential costs and savings associated with plan implementation.[34]

Thus, the invention of chronic homelessness becomes an opportunity for a thorough reimagining of social services as economic ventures. The problem of chronic homelessness becomes a problem of inefficient use of resources. The solution becomes better management of social welfare administration through the application of business principles.

Thus, the federal government's interest in Housing First is not so surprising after all. As one advocate told me, "From a conservative's perspective, it saves money. It saves taxpayers money. Research has even shown it's even cheaper in the long run to fund Housing First programs because it reduces recidivism rates. And it's really expensive to go from shelter to street to psych hospital to jail to community courts, through all these revolving doors." Recognizing the limits of political empathy, advocates have been able to leverage the economizing of health to advance their social agenda. "Asserting the cost savings offers an apparently irrefutable logic. So that's what I use sometimes when I'm talking to a government type. I'll talk about how it's really beneficial for people, but then if I'm really trying to sell somebody on it who hates homeless people, that's what I'll tell them about it. So that's why they're interested."

While advocates argue that the economic costs of housing deprivation become a way to translate across political divides, connecting advocates and politicians, it represents instead a new political constitution of housing needs. In this context, the economizing of life, health, illness, and death may provoke unexpected investments in vilified and long-abandoned populations. As a part of biopolitical governance, these programs serve to shore up and extend neoliberal economic industries that produce housing insecurity in the first place.

Economizing Race and Death

While many agencies and advocates are enthusiastic about this move to Housing First models, some have critiqued the language of chronic homelessness discourse. A report issued by the National Coalition for the Homeless states, "The term 'chronic homeless' treats homelessness with the same language, and in the same fashion, as a medical condition or disease, rather than an experience caused fundamentally by poverty and lack of affordable housing."[35] Of course chronic homelessness programs have a complicated relationship to medicalization. On the one hand, although the concept of "chronic homelessness" does carry a pathologizing taint, in practice the programs actually leave behind many of the disciplinary techniques of pathologization. If "chronically homeless" codes shelter needs as medical problems, as if some people are addicted to being homeless, we must nonetheless note that it is exactly the technologies of medicalization that chronic homelessness programs undo, insofar as they allow for immediate access to housing without service and treatment requirements. Policy reports on chronic homelessness initiatives continue to stress the responsibility of the individual, evoking some of that old moral argument. But rather than the individual's self-work being a necessary first step toward housing provision, the current model provides housing regardless of an individual's willingness to submit to medicalizing, disciplinary regimes.

On the other hand, in its adoption of Housing First through chronic homelessness programs, the federal government does not offer a critique of pathologization. While federal chronic homeless programs suppress the compulsory use of case management technologies, they do so through the argument that requiring services is not cost effective, insofar as that requirement acts as a barrier keeping people on the street where they cost cities money. Pathological conceptions of homeless populations did not disappear with the rising validity of Housing First approaches. In fact, some argue that the persistence of these pathological conceptions provides a stumbling block for the adoption of Housing First in anything more than name. "If these providers feel like there's some kind of a gravy train for working with high utilizers and they don't know how long it's gonna last, and they want in on it, they're gonna say they're doing Housing First but they're afraid to do it. What I've seen at [our Housing First project] is people come to visit and they have all sorts of fears about what it would really be like to house this group of people in our community or wherever." The persistence of pathological conceptions opens a space for the rearticulation of medicalized notions and the reassertion of disciplinary technologies of compliance. Chronic homelessness programs allow for two ideas to exist side by side: that there is something wrong with these people, but nonetheless we need to house them. In the context of medicalized social problems, sympathy and disdain peacefully coexist.

Not only do federal chronic homelessness programs leave the pathologization of housing deprivation in place. These programs also expand housing opportunities only for people designated chronically homeless. So, as much as chronic homelessness initiatives function to bring people into permanent housing, they also serve a population-sorting function that excludes other people from housing. As Foucault wrote, "Knowledge is not made for understanding; it is made for cutting."[36] Those that chronic homelessness cuts from housing are populations whose costs are not directly carried by city institutions, but whose health and housing are nonetheless quite precarious. Keeping in mind that the federal government defines the chronically homeless as "unaccompanied adults," we can see that if you have a family that can absorb the work of the welfare state, you are considered a bad investment and unworthy of housing; only those with absolutely no familial safety net are brought into housing.

The earlier history of the concept of chronic homelessness indicates something about this cutting function. "Chronically homeless" as a category was introduced prior to Culhane and Kuhn in New York City by

Rudolph Giuliani. During his first mayoral campaign in 1993, Giuliani released a position paper in which he promised as mayor to limit shelter stays to ninety days for all shelter users except what he called the "chronically homeless." So the category has always served a sorting function, cutting out those who deserve investment from those who do not. While the public reacted with confusion to Giuliani's term, and some with hostility to his plan, soon enough Giuliani's suggestion that there was a chronic subset of shelter-stayers would be accepted as commonsense, and Culhane and Kuhn would provide the economic justification for what has in effect been a national policy that instates what Giuliani called for: the privileging of one part of the unsheltered population and the exclusion of the rest. As a population-sorting mechanism, chronic homelessness preserves the idea that some deserve housing and some do not. But if an a previous era, you proved you were among the deserving poor through a willingness to submit to mandatory case management technologies, today, the determination of who deserves housing moves from a moral calculation to an economic one.

Further, even within those targeted for chronic homelessness programs, distinctions continue to be made. Agency managers describe a process of "creaming" for chronic homeless housing—as in picking the cream of the crop among clients they already know. This is especially the case for "scatter-site housing," when programs rent apartments in buildings that also house private tenants with no program affiliation. The push for scatter-site responds to the pressure of white and wealthier residents to keep concentrated housing forms like shelters out of their neighborhoods, a sentiment described as "NIMBYism" (for "not in my backyard"). In cases of scatter-site housing, questions of sobriety, and even stratification of kinds of substance use, arise.

> The big thing now in Philly, and also in New York, in some scatter-site programs . . . is that they won't take people that are active crack users. Heroin is fine, schizophrenia is fine, but crack—no. Because they say that it attracts more criminal activity, more groups of people that are taking over apartments, and more dangerous behavior, sex work, and all of this. And that, you know, one lonely heroin addict is easier to deal with when you have to deal with landlords and an apartment building with other people in it that aren't in a Housing First program.

The stratification of need points to the lack of a structural critique in the rush to Housing First. The National Coalition for the Homeless report cited above goes on to point out that in addition to reproducing homelessness as a pathology or addiction, chronic homelessness programs will do nothing to alter the structural conditions that produce housing insecurity and deprivation. And at the same time, the adoption of Housing First by federal, state, and municipal governments runs the risk of emptying Housing First of its disrupting potential, instrumentalizing it as financial incentive rather than as a social or political commitment that directs agencies to adopt (or claim to adopt) Housing First approaches. "Now, because it is ensconced in policy, and it's everybody's priority—federal as well as state and local government—everybody's doing it. And the reality is, a bunch that are saying they're doing it, aren't."

Finally, while there is an immediate benefit in getting people housed, the successes of chronic homelessness programs are short-term and not sustainable. As one advocate commented, "And so people start throwing up units and developers are like, 'Great, the money's out there, the capital's out there.' But there's no operating [funds] to sustain that." The case of chronic homelessness programs in one city attests to the limits of this strategy. In this city, agency advocates were able to obtain records from public hospitals and calculate the seventy-five "most expensive homeless people" in the area—specifically, those with the most frequent or longest visits to public hospitals. Program managers then conducted targeted outreach to locate these individuals and place them into housing. However, as a staff member of that program noted, as beds open up (as residents move on, or die) and "less expensive" people are brought in, the savings to the city will decrease. In other words, the relative cost of housing versus hospitalization will *increase,* perhaps until the chronic homelessness program actually becomes more expensive than leaving people unhoused and reliant on hospital systems. As business ventures, chronic homelessness programs have no loyalty to an ethic of housing people, despite the commitment of individuals working within those programs to just such an ethic.

Nonetheless, most advocates remain enthusiastic about the rise of Housing First as federal policy. They suggest that the economic argument—"it is more expensive to leave people unhoused"—is ultimately a politically efficacious means to reach a socially desirable end.

While it is hard to argue against the immediate provision of housing for vulnerable populations—or, for that matter, the provision of housing for all people at all times—I would suggest that the economic here is more than simply an argument. Rather than a contradiction in politics that results in a surprising socially desirable end, this can be understood as a reconstitution of the political in the form of a neoliberal biopolitics. The genius of Culhane, Kuhn, and their colleagues' research is that they were able to mobilize neoliberal discourse of cost and efficiency to successfully advocate what humanist or ethical discourses have failed to do—namely, that people in need of shelter should be housed as quickly as possible. In recasting housing insecurity in terms of financial cost, their research provides an economic justification for permanent, long-term housing. The danger of the research is of course the same thing—its synchronicity with a neoliberal reshaping of social justice imaginations. While others have pointed out the rise in neoliberal governance of managerial strategies derived from private business sectors, the strategies are not simply an external logic applied to a stable social field, but rather a transformative force reshaping the very conception of something like housing deprivation. The invention of chronic homelessness retrofits a social problem as an economic problem. Thus, while at a discursive level, chronic homelessness evokes addiction and hence individual behavior and personal attributes, in practice, it functions as a statistical model for assessing the economic costs of a subpopulation; chronic homelessness is at its heart an economic category.

Culhane and Kuhn's stratification of shelter use effected an important shift in how individual-level behaviors can be linked to the organization of shelter services. The focus of Culhane and Kuhn's argument is not on what is wrong with the chronically homeless and how to fix them. The characteristics they attribute to the chronically homeless—"being older, of black race, having a substance abuse or mental health problem, or having a physical disability"—remain at the aggregate level to identify a subpopulation.[37] The research acknowledges that inadequate " 'safety net' programs" force individuals to rely on emergency shelter systems.[38] It does not go as far as advocating structural changes that might slow or end the reproduction of housing insecurity—for example, challenging discriminatory renting practices or the racial wealth divide. But neither do the authors argue that service providers need to end drug and alcohol use among their clients. In fact, as noted above, the application of their research has deemphasized the importance of sobriety and other individual-level interventions. For Culhane and Kuhn and the federal policies that followed their research, the most important changes that must be made are in the allocation of resources at organizational levels. Thus, while the role of nonprofits in governance changes and nonprofit agencies again become renewed targets of governance, the existence of a nonprofit industrial complex that is free of accountability to social movements persists.

Given the shift to biopolitical concerns provoked by the invention of chronic homelessness, the end of mandatory social and psychiatric services is not so surprising after all. The biopoliticization of housing insecurity moves away from targeting individual behaviors as the point of intervention, as the population instead is taken up as the proper object of governance. In putting forth a biopolitical model that abstracts attributes and behaviors of individuals and organizes them as a statistical population, the invention of chronic homelessness undercuts the disciplinary technologies of the case management system. In other words, disciplinary mechanisms of individuated control, considered inadequate or ineffective, are being suppressed by population management techniques. In matching the profile of the chronically homeless, subjects are in effect biopoliticized, or absorbed into a governance that regulates a population's costs by economizing and securing its health and life chances. Concern with the apparently limited resources of municipalities, rather than with individual well-being, motivates this biopoliticization. The invention of chronic homelessness deemphasizes individual compliance with service requirements in favor of economic containment of population costs—in a move that unexpectedly benefits an abandoned and usually despised and degraded population. The shift to population level concerns legitimated the Housing First model not because the federal government accepted that mandatory services are paternalistic or offensive, but because it saw mandatory services as a deterrent it could no longer afford.

Thus, the invention of chronic homelessness points to the reconfiguration of disciplinary sites through biopolitical projects. As the persistence of pathologization attests, this is not an end to discipline. Chronic homelessness programs, like the HMIS database program discussed in the previous chapter, represent a rerouting of disciplinary technologies in a context of the biopoliticization of homelessness. If HMIS generates a homeless population as a mechanism for regulating service agencies, chronic homelessness initiatives form the population as a target of governance itself. Disciplinary case management puts in place the inter-subjective relationships that advocates use in outreach efforts to make contact with people on the street and engage them toward learning their health histories. Nonetheless, while the vulnerability index used by programs such as Project 50 engage at the individual level, its use is not toward developing a full, deep understanding of the individual as an individual. Rather, the index is used to glean specific points of data that connect that individual to a population defined in terms of health patterns and economic costs. That individual then becomes understood not so much as a case, but as a data match with a statistical profile. In this sense, the index translates between the individual and the population across a ground of economized health concerns.[39] As I argued in the case of HMIS, like any technology, the vulnerability index is not simply a tool, but must be recognized for its productive capacities. In translating back from the population, the index reproduces the homeless individual, not as pathological subject in need of mandatory case management, but rather, as a component part of a population that must be collectively managed through forms of housing that contain its economic impact.

Patricia Ticineto Clough helps characterize such "post-disciplinary" social programs, which she understands as indicating

> the increasing abandonment of support for socialization and education of the individual subject through interpellation to and through national and familial ideological apparatuses. The production of normalization is not only, or even primarily, a matter of socializing the subject; increasingly, it is a matter of directly bringing bodies and bodily affective capacities under an expanded grid of control, especially through the mar-ketization of affective capacity.[40]

For sure, the discourse of chronic homelessness continues to perform the disciplinary work of pathologizing residents of housing programs. In so doing, it may hold in place the imperative of reforming the individual, even if such an imperative is not mobilized as strongly in the present moment.[41] But in the meantime, a biopolitical model that addresses individuals as component parts of a population whose death and life chances are correlated with economics and managed through economic means, or what Clough refers to as "marketization," overrides the imperatives of socializing into responsible selves. Within this model, the immediate provision of housing becomes the most economically efficient means of managing this population. The biopoliticization of homelessness signals and produces the transformation of social programs into economic programs, a transformation that characterizes Jacques Donzelot's description of the transition from the social welfare state to the social investment state.[42] The economics do not end with the analysis that produces the category "chronic homelessness," but extend into and transform the programs to which that category gives rise.

The greatest danger in chronic homelessness programs is that they are part of neoliberal economies, and thus they enable and extend, rather than challenge, the very economic conditions that produce housing insecurity and deprivation in the first place. In our conversations, some advocates suggested to me that the fact that their programs benefit businesses by "cleaning up" city neighborhoods is not an irresolvable conflict. A staff person at one such program told me:

> I think we have the same interests. The business community in downtown, some of the leaders are a little bit . . . hard to swallow. But we have the same interests, right? I mean, I don't think they give a crap about homeless people, but they wanna see no one sleep on the street and we wanna see no one sleep on the street.

But we must ask if the interests of the neoliberal economy and populations living without shelter can ever be the same. As proponents of the programs note, 10-Year Plans come into being through the support of police and local business organizations, both of which eagerly support the effort to remove unsheltered individuals from public view. In this way, 10-Year Plans function as the second phase of a spatial-capital reorganization of the city that began with the destruction of skid rows. 10-Year Plans attempt to clean up the mess made by the evaporation of SROs and other forms of low-cost housing by removing the individuals left behind. 10-Year Plans do nothing to alter the structural conditions that reproduce and distribute housing insecurity and deprivation. In this sense, the plans preserve an earlier assumption of housing insecurity, as if removing "problem individuals" from "the streets" is an adequate solution. The fact remains that "the streets"—here we can substitute the racisms of labor markets, privatized housing, police/prison systems, and inadequate public assistance programs—will continue to produce unsheltered populations.[43]

Chronic homelessness initiatives are economic programs in that they (attempt to) remove obstructions to the smooth functioning of neoliberal consumer/tourist economies in urban centers, benefiting in the short term a small handful of clients who fit the profile of the chronically homeless. Chronic homelessness programs are furthermore economic in a second sense: the *management* of housing insecurity is itself an economic enterprise. The proliferation of chronic homelessness programs, the circulation of funding, the commissioning of studies and reports—all of this forms part of the nonprofit industrial complex, where the post-social state meets postindustrial service and knowledge industries. Contrary to rhetoric that associates "the homeless" with waste and cost, housing insecurity and deprivation prove to be sites of economic productivity in which individuals organized as "chronically homeless" become the raw material out of which studies and services are produced. While consumer/tourist economies may be served by removing unsightly reminders of poverty from view, the social service and knowledge industries that manage this removal are at odds with an end to housing insecurity. An actual elimination of housing insecurity and deprivation would also mean an end to the service and knowledge industries proliferating around managing and studying populations living without shelter. Hence, the complex of agencies and organizations produce new forms of industry that do not fundamentally challenge the social, political, and economic reproduction of housing insecurity and deprivation, even if they do reduce their immediate effects.

While some advocates argue that chronic homelessness initiatives contain something of an inherent contradiction in that they serve both the economic needs of neoliberal cities and the needs of a vulnerable population, there is no contradiction. Chronic homelessness programs serve the economy twice over: first by removing an economic obstacle and then by investing in a growing nonprofit industry of population management. The invention of chronic homelessness enacts the economizing of the social that characterizes neoliberalism, not simply by subjecting social programs to economic logics, but by transforming social programs into economic industries. The classic or Keynesian social welfare state organized the national population by stratifying it in terms of labor. Populations organized as potential or former workers, or as vital to the reproduction of labor, would be invested in through social programs; those subject to extraction but organized as outside labor would be socially abandoned. Under neoliberal biopolitics, the targets of social programs need not be addressed as labor. Rather, the clients of such programs are labored on by social service and knowledge industries—industries that sustain rather than challenge the neoliberal economies that produce housing insecurity and deprivation.

CONCLUSION

Surplus Life at the Limits of the Good

VISIT ANY MAJOR CITY IN THE UNITED STATES TODAY, AND YOU will be hard pressed to find immediate evidence of the 2008 housing bubble burst. At the peak of the crisis, in 2010, more than 2.9 million foreclosures were filed and over a million homes repossessed.[1] Given knowledge of the subprime mortgage crash and its aftermaths, the experience of the city today can be a dizzying and confusing one. This is not to say there are no remainders of that burst. In fact, while by 2013 the foreclosure rate was down to 1.04 percent from 2010's 2.23 percent, by the end of 2013, 19 percent of all homeowners owed at least 25 percent more than what their homes were worth.[2] "For sale" signs in "transitional neighborhoods," to use the social-Darwinist PR language of the real estate industry, offer some reminder of former occupants. But whatever evidence you might find is likely overshadowed by the more immediate visual evidence of a housing boom. Construction cranes hover over Seattle, D.C., San Francisco, Brooklyn, perched like alien invaders patiently considering our fate. No caution or modesty seems to curtail the construction efforts buzzing beneath these cranes. That a real estate development industry collapsed might be hard to fathom in the frenzy of steel, concrete, and glass all around us. That rental units in these buildings often start at over $2,000 a month for studio apartments, and that new condo construction in San Francisco is selling for cash at above asking price, would also puzzle observers who have been told we are in an extended "post"-recession stretch of stagnating wages and increasing wealth disparities.[3]

In 2008, when the mortgage loan bubble exploded, I was in the early stages of the research for this project, a project suddenly granted relevance as once again housing insecurity and deprivation become recognized and legitimated in their dispersal. A sense that "homelessness" was spreading and that "anyone could lose their home" assigned value to the abject affectable others who figured in homeless research. The homeless became the ghosts of possible futures, sent back in time to warn us. Of course, though, as *The Value of Homelessness* has shown, homelessness is anything but generalizable. Quite the contrary—nothing is more specific than "the homeless." The homeless are the techno-conceptual effects of policy frameworks, capital investment schemes, coconstructions of race and property, and the racial-subordinating effects of neoliberal political economic restructuring. It is not true that "anyone" could be homeless. Far from it, even if most of us live with increasing housing insecurity in a context Secretary of HUD Shaun Donovan described as "the worst rental affordability crisis that this country has ever known."[4] But some in fact are made to be homeless, constructed as unlikely to exit shelter systems, as most likely to be housing-deprived, organized as populations set to housing insecurity and the forms of illness and death that accompany life without shelter. While housing insecurity is the general condition of life in a capitalist context of privatized housing, homelessness is a very specific extraction from the housing system.

The danger of the affective generation of a "generalized homelessness" is that it obscures the cuts that sort populations for varying degrees of investment and insecuritizing. In fact, the 2008 mortgage crisis, far from having a leveling effect, intensified and retrenched existing cuts.[5] As evidenced in photographs accompanying two articles in the *New York Times,* how we make sense of this housing crisis reflects and obscures the racialized production of vulnerability to life without shelter. Published April 9, 2009, the first photograph accompanies an article headlined, "With Advocates' Help, Squatters Call Foreclosures Home."[6] The image depicted is a classic construction of the squalor and tragedy of poverty. Two adults and a toddler, presumably a family, lie together on an uncovered mattress. Silently, they face the same direction, as if watching television but in fact facing a fan barely visible in the frame as they attempt to cool off in the muggy Miami spring heat.

If you make your way to the caption below the photograph, it confirms they are a family and provides some context: "With their furniture in storage, Mia Dennis, Brandon Brown, and their daughter, Amelia, sleep on mattresses in their family's illegally reclaimed home." The empty room and undressed bed make sense when you know their possessions have been displaced or made inaccessible by foreclosure and eviction. But the visual evidence and terms of illegality do not generate sympathy. The designation as "squatters" by the headline gives no clue that the family inhabits what was already their home. The photograph confirms a story that blames those living in poverty for their experiences. What if the headline read "*families* call foreclosures home"? This is not to disavow a challenge to the criminalization of squatting. Far from it. The practice of housing takeovers presumes the immorality of private property and inverts legal logics to frame bank foreclosures as the moral wrong.[7] But in reading the headline and its image, we must recognize that a dominant discourse in defense of a private property regime is here mobilized against those who have suffered terribly within that regime.

A month later, on May 4, 2009, the *New York Times* published an article about the impact of the foreclosure crisis on renters. Rather than the criminalization of "squatters," the headline of this piece announces, "Once 'Very Good Rent Payers' Now Facing Eviction."[8] The two accompanying photographs immediately position their subjects as innocent and deserving of sympathy. The first photograph evokes some of the tragedy of the squatter photo, but with no sense of lazy resignation. In this image, two figures sit in a darkened room in the frame of a lit window. The lighting echoes the mystery and uncertainty of their lives in housing insecurity but does not position them as inevitable and resigned victims. The caption tells us, "After Kevin Brewster-Streeks, left, lost his job, he and his partner, Greg Armstrong, fell behind on rent and were forced to move." Note the passive language of lost jobs and falling behind, and the activeness of eviction—forced to move.

In the second photograph, a figure sits on a couch, peering at a stack of papers piled in her lap; beside her lies an intimidating stash of the bureaucratic detritus of modern financial life. Her upright position and furrowed brow represent the seriousness of her mission. She does not lie about all day, doing nothing about her challenges. Interestingly, the caption to her photograph echoes the one from the month before: "Since an eviction threat, Christine A. Lewis has had to borrow furniture and clothing. Her own things are stuck in storage."

That the figures in the second set of photographs are also black does not undermine an argument about the racialized subordination of housing insecurity and deprivation. The effects of the foreclosure crisis have been very racially specific. It does mean that in the "post-racial" context in which the racial-subordinating effects of housing insecurity are naturalized, the mobilization of sympathy for some subjects, coded as respectable and middle-class and hard-working, does not undermine but affirms the techno-conceptual linking of housing insecurity to race. The once good renters are the exception that proves the rule; they are the investable figures that allow for their affectable others.

This simultaneous exposing and obscuring of race repeats the techno-conceptual operations outlined in the preceding chapters. As neo-liberal housing insecurity settled into a form of racialized subordination, the raced nature of homelessness became highlighted in historical accounts of the new homeless, narrativized in ethnographic accounts like *Sidewalk,* and correlated with cost in statistical accounts and federal policy. Neutral, technocratic tools like HMIS are meant to abstractly develop solutions for problem populations marked by race but figured explicitly in terms of how many resources they consume and how effectively their mediating social service agencies contain and reduce those costs. Thus, social sciences and social services have prepped the social field for the circulation of these images of loss, despair, and abandonment. They have done so in two linked ways: first, through a techno-conceptual organization that naturalizes and obscures racialized insubordination, and second, through investing the production of these images and stories with moral worth derived from ethical necessity.

Regarding the first, we can return to the research undergirding federal chronic homelessness initiatives discussed in chapter 5. In their study of shelter use patterns, Dennis Culhane and Randall Kuhn describe those who are less likely to exit shelter systems as being "of black race." Here I want to dwell on the techno-conceptual work done by that deployment and the processes of racialization and economization it obscures. "Of black race": the awkward phrasing offers a clue to the statistical methods used in the study and also suggests other diagrams, or cuts we might make across that study and the material experiences it organizes. If we recall from chapter 5, using data collected in the New York City and Philadelphia shelter systems, Culhane and Kuhn employ a discrete-time logistic hazards regression. A logistic regression tests for the effects of whatever number of independent variables on a dependent variable. In other words, a logistic regression assesses a set of cause (independent variable) and effect (dependent variable) relationships. A logistic regression controls to cancel out the effect of other variables to test each independent variable's effect on the dependent variable, to figure out what is really causing a change. Culhane and Kuhn seek to understand what characteristics of an individual (or which independent variables composing the person) impact the likelihood of exiting shelter systems. Thus, the authors constructed a dependent variable to measure whether on any given day an individual stays or leaves the shelter system. Again, they wrote: "In general, being older, of black race, having a substance abuse or mental health problem, or having a physical disability, significantly reduces the likelihood of exiting shelter."[9] Thus, the independent variables they have concluded impact exiting shelter are age, race, substance use, and psychiatric and physical disability.

And so we get that "being of black race" reduces the likelihood of exiting shelter. But what goes into an independent variable? What is contained in that variable and obscured by it? What relationships are trying to express themselves through these statistics, speaking through the cuts of their categories? As Culhane and Kuhn note, "Given the social and economic barriers historically associated with race, it was not surprising that nonwhite clients would stay longer than white clients, although a 2.5-times-higher likelihood of exit for white males than nonwhite males in the Philadelphia shelter system was not anticipated."[10] They also write at the outset, "Black persons are expected to have a lower probability of exit due to restricted access to resources, as well as other barriers historically associated with black race."[11] Anti-black racism in the United States produces employment and wage discrimination, barriers to educational opportunity, exposure to environmental harms, and constant threat of arrest and imprisonment, to name just a few things. All of these have direct relationships to the ability to secure housing and also have relationships to the other independent variables, such as health. In his critique of regression models, Quincy Thomas Stewart argues they cannot account for "interactive processes," such as those named above.[12] Paul Holland argues that race cannot be a causal variable because "causes are experiences units undergo not attributes they possess."[13] Rather, Holland argues, as I am suggesting here, that racial discrimination is the proper independent variable to assess.

Tukufu Zuberi characterizes such statistical accounts as a form of racial reasoning, a case of white logic and white methods. Zuberi writes,

Conclusion

"Statistical models that present race as a cause are really statements of association between the racial classification and a predictor or explanatory variable across individuals in a population. To treat these models as causal or inferential is a form of racial reasoning."[14] If Kuhn and Culhane's study introduced measures of employment and education discrimination or exposure to environmental injustice, they would likely have found the same individuals "less likely to exit shelter" because of the effects of all those forms of racialized subordination. Despite the authors' acknowledgment of race/racisms, the variable here hides those experiences and interactive processes, making in statistical terms being black the cause of being homeless. But of course blackness does not cause homelessness. Rather, today antiblack racism produces extreme and intensified housing insecurity and deep vulnerability to living without shelter. The techno-conceptual organization of homelessness naturalizes relationships between racialized life and an experience of housing insecurity. The photographs discussed above affectively circulate those relations.

Such methodological commitments to measuring race bring with them ethical justification about the necessary and good work of social science inquiry. Chapter 2's discussion of ethnographic technologies of homeless management argued that the relationships of ethics and methods have been constructed in such a way that one inheres in the other; according to contemporary social science, sound and rigorous positivist methods secure ethical guarantees. Chapter 2 argued as well that the techno-conceptual organization of the homeless has a methodological dimension intrinsic to it. Social science produces the homeless as a research problem. It follows, then, that a certain ethical dilemma follows the homeless wherever they go as well. This is the melodrama animating the courtroom scene from Stephen Seager's *Street Crazy* discussed in chapter 3: What to do for those whose failed selves cannot do for themselves? I want to pause a bit on these ethical remains, at what we can think of as the limits of doing good.[15] If social sciences and social services have presumed to do good on behalf of housing deprived populations, this presumption has secured the techno-conceptual arrangements of capital, space, bodies, and populations that have obscured rather than challenged the race/property systems that organize and distribute sheltered and unsheltered experiences of life, health, illness, and death. To push at the limits of the good offers a way to traverse again the junctures of the social services and social sciences, and to think about how, in the context of a biopolitical neoliberalism, we might otherwise diagram politically challenging forms of knowledge.

The ethics of managing the failed selves of the homeless circulate and consolidate in a minor medical industry controversy from the 1990s. As reported in a 1996 article in the *Wall Street Journal,* for several decades, Phase I clinical trials conducted in Indianapolis by pharmaceutical giant Eli Lilly recruited heavily from populations living without shelter. Phase I trials test for toxicity, to determine whether new drugs are safe to test on actual patients in Phase II trials. Recruiting for Phase I trials is quite challenging, as they are potentially the most dangerous of any drug trial, and they offer participants no health benefits; subjects of Phase I trials are not being treated for anything, only monitored for reactions to a drug's harms. While in the 1990s the going rate for Phase I trials was as high as $250 a day, Indianapolis test subjects were paid $85. As Laurie P. Cohen wrote in her important exposé:

> Word of mouth about testing at Lilly—a company best known for the blockbuster drug Prozac—has gradually spread through soup kitchens, prisons and shelters from coast to coast. Today, so many homeless men come to Indianapolis seeking admittance to Lilly's research clinic that Matias Vega, medical director of the local Homeless Initiative Program, credits the clinic with creating a "shadow economy." One veteran nurse at the Lilly Clinic says that the majority of its subjects are homeless alcoholics.[16]

While some questioned the validity of these trials—the homeless participants are depicted as a binge-drinking lot who spend their payments primarily on booze—others wondered about the ethics of recruiting homeless populations, and whether or not the financial incentives, while measly, could nonetheless be seen as a form of economic coercion that took unfair advantage of destitution and desperation.

A 2002 article published in the *Journal of Medicine and Philosophy* addressed the use of homeless populations in clinical trials. Under the lead authorship of Tom L. Beauchamp, perhaps the most prominent figure in professional bioethics, the article approaches the issue from two angles. First, it asks if homeless populations should be grouped among other "vulnerable populations" who must be legally protected from participation in clinical trials, either because they are deemed to lack the mental faculties necessary to grant consent or because (as with prisoners) the potential for exploitation is so great. Beauchamp and his coauthors decide that, as a population, the homeless do not qualify as vulnerable and in need of protection. Second, the article asks if it is fair to exclude the homeless as a group from the opportunity to participate in trials. The authors decide that this would not be fair and that the right to participate should not be denied to people living without shelter. The authors argue that the way to avoid economic exploitation is to make sure the wage is *not so high as to be overwhelmingly persuasive:* "The key is to strike a balance between a rate of payment high enough that it does not exploit subjects by underpayment and low enough that it does not create an irresistible inducement."[17] Of course, a strict ban would not address the deep poverty that motivates participation. But in abstracting clinical trials from their political economic contexts, Beauchamp and his coauthors produce an ahistoric ethics that evacuates analysis of material economics and power.[18] Rendering participation a technical matter of rights removes from consideration the conditions of disease, starvation, and death temporarily forestalled through labor in this shadow economy.

Beauchamp's essay further presents the question as an abstract issue by not naming any specific corporations or instances. However, at the end of the article, in the first footnote, the following information appears:

> The authors were members of an external team of evaluators that examined current policies and procedures at the Lilly Laboratory for Clinical Research regarding the participation in drug studies of volunteers who may have no fixed or permanent residence ("the homeless"). The Advisory Panel, as it was called, was chaired by Tom L. Beauchamp. It was charged by Eli Lilly and Company to investigate the ethical issues in the participation of homeless persons and to make recommendations concerning its policies and procedures. This work was funded by Eli Lilly and Co.[19]

The conflict of interest is so blatant as not to require commentary. If that is what constitutes externality, perhaps someone should approach one of Eli Lilly's marketplace competitors and request funding to investigate the ethics of Beauchamp's advisory panel. But in the meantime, we can see the ways in which the ethical frame keeps in place the real material and social insecurity of unsheltered populations. The limits of doing good are that "the good" accepts and takes place within this uneven and unjust landscape. Cast from view and critical inquiry, the existence of housing insecurity is placed beyond question and granted de facto ethical status: that some must live without shelter is just a fact of life.

If professionalized bioethics has volunteered to adjudicate on behalf of a not-vulnerable but not fully agential homeless subject, for the social sciences, to do good has been, at the least, to document the other and its pain and, at the most, to suggest (for governance, when the other will not listen) what can be done about it. This good resides in the realm of research ethics. Institutional Review Boards (IRBs) have formalized a relationship between the ethical dimension of social scientific research and the methodologies those researches deploy. The assumption is that a completed project is an ethical project, as an unethical project would have been stopped at the gates by an IRB. But the ethical is inextricable from the methodological, and methodological choices do not just enact an ethical protocol, but continually open and close ethical possibilities. Ethics is an opaque zone of negotiation that most narratives of research mask over. Ethical dilemmas, like all political projects, are irresolvable—which is to say, they are contingent and mutable in their implications for challenging and reproducing power relations.[20]

During a visit to the City University of New York Graduate Center in 2007, architect and political theorist Eyal Weizman presented a public lecture about his work on the occupation of Palestine and the Israeli Defense Force (IDF).[21] In a conversation in a seminar hosted by the Center for Place, Culture, and Politics the following day, Weizman mentioned that video footage he had shared of IDF officers and other government officials was obtained under the false pretense of making a documentary. The political aims of the project and the uses to which it would be put were not revealed to the interview subjects. In response, one participant in the seminar joked that such a project would "never gain IRB approval" at a U.S. research university.

The conversation raised what should be a key question for all scholars: How do we conduct ethical research of unethical situations? A strictly instrumentalized ethics—such as that employed by Beauchamp's advisory panel—would argue that members of the Israeli government and military deserve the same application of research protocols as any other research subjects. While IRBs make special provisions for vulnerable populations deemed less powerful or powerless, they do not make special provisions for those deemed to be in positions of power. In other words, the appeal to universal principles sidesteps questions of power and force, eliding the IDF's disproportionate capacity to protect itself and its interests. It is easy to see the potential for collusion between institutions of great power (in this case, universities and the IDF), in which one regulates how the other can be studied, to its benefit, such that much cannot be revealed. But more subtly, we could ask: What do our ethical frames, like Beauchamp's, fail to capture? How might the unethical refuse to appear in such research? And what do we do with the fact that mechanisms developed to measure the ethics of research are embedded in the very institutional and governmental complexes we are trying to study? It seems that exactly the processes that concern much research, and certainly concern the present book—the violence and death produced by racial, economic, and social inequality—are processes that government and research institutions have played a key role in maintaining and reproducing.

This issue is not bad IRBs, or even bad research; the issue is what counts as "good" research in both senses of the word—methodologically and ethically sound. For decades, social science has circulated an accepted techno-conceptual organization of the homeless that supported and extended disciplinary governance regimes concerned to know and regulate individual homeless subjects. In the current moment, a biopolitical techno-conceptual organization of a homeless population amenable to economic regulation has joined this subject. Social science generates this biopoliticization but fails to recognize it does so, thus granting the population a "merely representational" status, positing the population as a stand-in for the individuals who supposedly compose it. This is the work of "of black race." But *The Value of Homelessness* has argued that in fact the reverse is true. The individual does not precede the population; rather, the individual homeless subject comes to be through the population that increasingly stands in for the individual. The life of the individual subject gives life to the population, and the subject is constituted in turn through that population. Thus, the homeless subject, revealed in critiques of medicalization, has not disappeared in these processes of biopoliticization. But the pathological homeless subject is being remade in the context of the neoliberal governance problem. Beauchamp's advisory panel accomplishes just such a task, as does *Sidewalk*'s methodological appendix. Such ethical work of the good produces the homeless subject of biopolitics in terms of a kind of flexible humanity that can be instrumentally applied and denied: a partial self capable of consenting to be researched upon, but incapable of knowing oneself and one's own needs. This is what I mean when I say social science preps the social for the circulation of those *New York Times* images of guilty and innocent, survivors and victims, doomed to be homeless and undeserving of such a fate.

Dwelling on these ethical and methodological remains is an effort to answer the question, What is this book for? While, of course, that is always a good question, normative imperatives lurk behind it. On the one hand is demand for a direct policy applicability of work on issues of social injustice. As I have shown, policy frameworks are not neutral; they are technical arrangements of the conceptual and material. A policy brings with it both explicit and implicit starting points. Policy appears practical only because its logics underwrite the construction of governance problems. To write outside the bounds of policy frames, as this project has attempted to do, is not impractical, even if its next steps are not immediately apparent. If this means we must rethink the good and the practical outside the limits of policy frames, we still are left with a deeper imperative behind the question of what a book like the present one is for. Here there is some argument against the utility of critical inquiry. I believe that the questions of how housing insecurity and deprivation are techno-conceptually organized have very real effects. Here I have mostly focused on the current arrangements and their consequences. The present project is limited in the ways it does not attend to contemporary forms of resistance and destabilization within the landscape of housing insecurity. But the preceding chapters evolved from a belief that the taken for grantedness of "homelessness" was both important and entrenched enough to require slow attention in its unpacking.

Sometimes, quick action is necessary. Evictions must be stopped, people must be housed. Sometimes those quick actions are full of the compromises that characterize modern political life. I remember one of my clearest introductions to that when I participated in a largely ad-hoc group called DASIS Watch in the fall of 2000. Local laws in New York City require that any person living with HIV/AIDS who requests emergency shelter must be housed that same day. DASIS, or the Division of AIDS Services and Income Support, suddenly and without explanation stopped complying with the law and began turning away clients. Brought together by the New York City AIDS Housing Network, those of us on DASIS Watch started to work in teams to stay with people in offices until they received housing placements. We would then accompany them to those placements to make sure they in fact existed.[22]

And how were people housed? Usually for one night, in crummy hotels, often many subway and bus stops from where they would need to return to the next day to begin the bureaucratic wrangling anew. We talked in our group about the ways in which we were greasing the wheels of a broken system, allowing these shitty placements to continue. Many of us were involved with anarchist models of organizing and activism, and we occupied this role of state proxy with some unease. We also recognized the immediate need, and the desire of people for the placements. Many of us and many of the clients were involved in longer term organizing projects around HIV/AIDS and housing and homelessness, and we saw this immediate work as a necessary and contradictory part of these larger movement projects.

The ground we walk is always as fraught, but our experiences do not always bring that so clearly to the surface. Urgency does not get us out of contradiction, and slowness, when that luxury can be afforded, does not keep us from acting. And slowness is a luxury we ought to demand and defend. This book is calling for the time and space for a necessary rethinking. The ethical value of our work on DASIS Watch was unresolved and unsatisfying. This seems a difficult but appropriate response to the kinds of vulnerability DASIS was producing. And this is what I aim to describe with the concept of "surplus life." If Giorgio Agamben's discussion of bare life helps describe a certain kind of internal abandonment that is productive of political and social order, it forgets, as Aihwa Ong and Ruth Wilson Gilmore help us see, to think about the political economy and administration of that abandonment. With the term "surplus life" I want to remember that social abandonment is an economic enterprise that is productive of a kind of surplus value. The management of surplus populations as surplus life (such as those housed by DASIS and those targeted by the programs the earlier chapters chronicled) keeps that life barely alive and in circulation within an economy. Surplus life circulates as numbers, such as costs to hospitals, or self-sufficiency improvement scores. Those numbers live through surplus life, and become the condition of possibility for it. The unsheltered populations subjected to Eli Lilly's drug testing seem a paradigmatic case of surplus life—and the ethical analysis of that testing seems a perfect illustration of how that life gets managed. That the bioethics panel hired by Eli Lilly concluded that the key to ethical involvement is paying subjects just enough to participate is a brutal example of how surplus life is governed and reproduced. That "just enough" is the condition of surplus life in neoliberal governance and economy—just enough to live, just enough to be economically productive, just enough not to cost too much in dying. Within such a terrain, we must move beyond the accepted terms of the good and its ethico-methodological attachments to maintaining the status quo.

My analysis of the homeless services industry as a neoliberal strategy for managing surplus life has been an occasion to rethink, through the contemporary context, one of the basic premises of Michel Foucault's thought. Whereas Foucault understood illness as counterposed to biopower, and death as the limit of biopower, the management of surplus populations through the homeless services industry points to the productive capacities of illness and dying, the value in what Achille Mbembe designates as "necropolitics." Foucault nonetheless also reminds us to think about what else is produced, what other excesses. What life is secured and grows through the near-death of surplus life? As the preceding chapters showed, the management of surplus life works toward securing the life of its management. In other words, surplus life is turned against itself, as it becomes a resource for strengthening neoliberal economic exploitation and the "good" governance technologies that make that exploitation possible.

The contradictory examples raised here suggest the surplus is also other diagrams, other political approaches that refuse the logics of exposure and obfuscation. And so this project has been an occasion to rethink not only homeless services, and the work of Foucault, but the work of social science as well. In its historical and current role as an arm of the state, social science has been central to the governance of populations living without shelter. Social science has set those populations into calculation with economics and, in defending its own good intentions, has granted ethical justification to projects of population management as well. By asking only limited questions—how to manage better homeless services, or how to get the homeless to best manage themselves—we perpetuate the conditions of surplus life, accepting those conditions as an inevitable, rather than a historical, arrangement. *The Value of Homelessness* has been my small effort to reframe housing insecurity and deprivation toward asking different questions. This moves us beyond the good, beyond homelessness. In so doing, I hope to contribute to a "bad" social science that might undermine, rather than underwrite, the technologies of neoliberal economy and governance that produce populations living always near death, as surplus life.

Notes

INTRODUCTION

1. *The Housing Monster* (Prole.info, 2012). www.prole.info.

2. The medical and pathological connotations of "homeless" are discussed in detail in chapter 3. I want to acknowledge that many people may self-identify with the term "homeless." Further, contesting the meaning of the term has been a productive political effort of activist groups; I am thinking of, for example, Picture the Homeless, an organization expressly committed to challenging political and media discourse about homelessness by self-generating alternative representations.

3. Ruth Wilson Gilmore, *Golden Gulag: Prisons, Surplus, Crisis, and Opposition in Globalizing California* (Berkeley: University of California Press, 2007), 28.

4. Essays in Dangerous Bedfellows, ed., *Policing Public Sex: Queer Politics and the Future of AIDS Activism* (Boston: South End Press, 1996) examine queer liberation struggles in the context of urban renewal and gentrification. Many of the authors in that collection participated in the activist groups I'm describing, and their analyses greatly informed my own. Samuel Delaney offers a sustained analysis of the effects of urban renewal on the public sex cultures of movie theaters in Samuel R. Delany, *Times Square Red, Times Square Blue* (New York: New York University Press, 2001). For a discussion of quality-of-life laws as a strategy for policing and arresting people living without shelter, see Alex S. Vitale, *City of Disorder: How the Quality of Life Campaign Transformed New York Politics* (New York: New York University Press, 2008).

5. William Armaline offers a critical perspective on the construction of youth subjectivity in residential programs. His descriptions of the practices and policies at his research site resonate with the program at which I worked and with the practices I myself engaged in. William T. Armaline, "'Kids Need Structure': Negotiating Rules, Power, and Social Control in an Emergency Youth Shelter," *American Behavioral Scientist* 48, no. 8 (2005): 1124–48.

6. A Center for American Progress study reports very high percentages of family rejection among homeless gay and transgender youth. The study also reports that homelessness is dramatically disproportionately experienced by gay and transgender youth of color. See Nico Sifra Quintana, Josh Rosenthal, and Jeff Krehely, *On the Streets: The Federal Response to Gay and Transgender Homeless*

Youth (Washington, D.C.: Center for American Progress, 2010), 7. However, the report does not investigate the structural reasons for this, or the ways in which the vulnerabilities produced by "family rejection" are mitigated by race and class. For an analysis of how sexual and gender marginalization intersect with racism and poverty, see Welfare Warriors Research Collaborative, *A Fabulous Attitude: Low-Income LGBTGNC People Surviving and Thriving on Love, Shelter, and Knowledge* (New York: Queers for Economic Justice, 2010).

7. This also represents a depoliticization of youth in the context of "service" on behalf of, rather than in terms of social mobilizing in solidarity with.

8. On "pushout" versus "dropout," see Michelle Fine, *Framing Dropouts: Notes on the Politics of an Urban High School* (Albany: State University of New York Press, 1991).

9. For an overview of how gender identity impacts experiences of state institutions, including shelters, prisons, and public benefits, see Paisley Currah and Dean Spade, "The State We're In: Locations of Coercion and Resistance in Trans Policy, Part 1," *Sexuality Research & Social Policy* 4, no. 4 (2007); Dean Spade and Paisley Currah, "The State We're In: Locations of Coercion and Resistance in Trans Policy, Part 2," *Sexuality Research & Social Policy* 5, no. 1 (2008).

10. For a discussion of the role of the proposition system in organizing California racial politics, see Daniel HoSang, *Racial Propositions: Ballot Initiatives and the Making of Postwar California* (Berkeley: University of California Press, 2010).

11. For example, see the work of Californians for Justice, http://caljustice .org/our-work/.

12. See Sylvia Rivera Law Project, *"It's War in Here": A Report on the Treatment of Transgender and Intersex People in New York State Men's Prisons* (New York: Sylvia Rivera Law Project, 2007) and Pascal Emmer, Adrian Lowe, and R. Barrett Marshall, *This Is a Prison, Glitter Is Not Allowed: Experiences of Trans and Gender Variant People in Pennsylvania's Prison Systems* (Philadelphia: Hearts on a Wire Collective, 2007).

13. In fact, it could be argued that gay marriage actually harms queer homeless youth, insofar as it invests in state enforcement of normative family arrangements and punishes people who live alone or with others in formations other than a sexual dyad. A number of queer scholars have taken on marriage from this angle. See for example Priya Kandaswamy, "State Austerity and the Racial Politics of Same-Sex Marriage in the US," *Sexualities* 11, no. 6 (2008): 706–25; Craig Willse and Dean Spade, "Freedom in a Regulatory State?: Lawrence, Marriage, and Biopolitics," *Widener Law Review* 11 (2005): 309–29.

14. For an influential early analysis of how white gay politics has failed to engage issues of racial and economic justice, and for suggestions about how it

might, see Cathy Cohen, "Punks, Bulldaggers, and Welfare Queens: The Radical Potential of Queer Politics?," *GLQ: A Journal of Lesbian and Gay Studies* 3, no. 4 (1997): 437–65.

15. For important organizing work on the criminalization of youth in California, see the Youth Justice Coalition, http://www.youth4justice.org/.

16. For a history of these political shifts and challenges to them, see Christina B. Hanhardt, *Safe Space: Gay Neighborhood History and the Politics of Violence* (Durham, N.C.: Duke University Press, 2013).

17. The work of this organization is discussed in Andy Merrifield, *Dialectical Urbanism: Social Struggles in the Capitalist City* (New York: Monthly Review Press, 2002).

18. As early as the late 1980s, advocates were noting the disappearance of SROs, an important form of housing for poor people, especially those without family safety nets. See part 3 of Sharon Marie Keigher, *Housing Risks and Homelessness among the Urban Elderly* (New York: Haworth Press, 1991). I consider the implications of the disappearance of SROs in chapter 3.

19. I share a brief report on this work in Craig Willse, "You Can't Go Home Again," *POZ Magazine*, no. 67, January 2001, 17.

20. Ward Harkavy, "Seduced and Abandoned," *Village Voice*, January 16, 2001, http://www.villagevoice.com/2001–01–16/news/seduced-and-abandoned/.

21. Avery F. Gordon, *Ghostly Matters: Haunting and the Sociological Imagination* (Minneapolis: University of Minnesota Press, 2008), 8.

22. I return to the contemporary context of housing insecurity in chapter 6.

23. See, for example, Jennifer Toth, *The Mole People: Life in the Tunnels beneath New York City* (Chicago: Chicago Review Press, 1995).

24. For a recent account, see Seth Holmes, *Fresh Fruit, Broken Bodies: Migrant Farmworkers in the United States* (Berkeley: University of California Press, 2013). For a historical account, see Richard J. Jensen and John C. Hammerback, eds., *The Words of César Chávez* (College Station: Texas A&M University Press, 2002).

25. See Karl Marx, *Capital, Volume 1: A Critique of Political Economy*, trans. Ben Fowkes (New York: Penguin, 1990), chap. 25.

26. This is distinct from a more common argument about prisoners as a cheap labor source. While prison labor is highly exploitative, from Gilmore's perspective, this is a secondary effect of a primary function of prisons in organizing the economy as a whole.

27. On Business Improvement Districts, see Kevin Ward, "'Policies in Motion,' Urban Management and State Restructuring: The Trans-Local Expansion of Business Improvement Districts," *International Journal of Urban and Regional Research* 30, no. 1 (2006): 54–75.

28. On file with author, received August 2010.
29. *Annual Report* (New York: The Doe Fund, 2011), 6.
30. *Annual Report* (New York: The Doe Fund, 2008), 2.
31. *Annual Report* (New York: The Doe Fund, 2012), 28.
32. *Annual Report* (New York: The Doe Fund, 2008), 2.
33. Manhattan Institute, http://www.manhattan-institute.org/.
34. Gilles Deleuze, *Foucault* (Minneapolis: University of Minnesota Press, 1988), 35.
35. Ibid.
36. Michel Foucault, *Discipline and Punish: The Birth of the Prison* (New York: Random House, 1977). Of course, this internalization of norms happens in addition to their caged confinement, a point that scholars who generalize eagerly sometimes forget.
37. Eugene Thacker, "Living Dead Networks," *Fibreculture Journal,* no. 4 (2005). http://four.fibreculturejournal.org/fcj-018-living-dead-networks/.

1. Surplus Life, or Race and Death in Neoliberal Times

1. In my summary of this and other studies, I am trying to keep the data bound to their technologies of measurement. In other words, the results, while telling us something general about the impact of housing insecurity and deprivation on health and life, should remain contextualized in relation to their sites and research methods. I also repeat the categories (of racial classification, for example) as used in each study.
2. B. Kerker et al., *The Health of Homeless Adults in New York City* (New York: New York City Departments of Health and Mental Hygiene and Homeless Services, 2005), 16.
3. Ibid., 19.
4. Whitney Hawke, Max Davis, and Bob Erienbusch, *Dying without Dignity: Homeless Death in Los Angeles County: 2000–2007* (Los Angeles: Los Angeles Coalition to End Hunger & Homelessness, 2007), 4.
5. Ibid., 5.
6. *Hate, Violence, and Death on Main Street USA: A Report on Hate Crimes and Violence Against People Experiencing Homelessness 2008* (Washington, D.C.: National Coalition for the Homeless, 2009), 10.
7. Ibid., 16.
8. Ibid., 35.
9. Michel Foucault, *The History of Sexuality: Vol. I, An Introduction* (New York: Vintage Books, 1990), 143.

10. Mariana Valverde, "Genealogies of European States: Foucauldian Reflections," *Economy and Society* 36, no. 1 (2007): 107.

11. Paul Rabinow and Nikolas Rose, "Biopower Today," *BioSocieties* 1, no. 2 (2006): 96–97.

12. Foucault, *The History of Sexuality*, 139.

13. "The homosexual" is Foucault's best known example of an abnormal disciplinary subject, demonstrating how subjectivity and embodiment get read through one another in a disciplinary model: "The nineteenth-century homosexual became a personage, a past, a case history, and a childhood, in addition to being a type of life, a life form, and a morphology, with an indiscreet anatomy and possibly a mysterious physiology." Ibid., 43.

14. Ibid., 139.

15. Michel Foucault, *Discipline and Punish: The Birth of the Prison* (New York: Random House, 1977), 136.

16. In Foucauldean scholarship, there is some inconsistency in how these terms are used, with some using "biopolitical" to describe any expression of biopower. In my reading I understand biopower as the general category, and use discipline (or anatomo-politics) and biopolitics to group together specific methods or technologies. My reading is shared by Paul Rabinow, "Artificiality and Enlightenment: From Sociobiology to Biosociality," in *The Science Studies Reader*, ed. Mario Biagioli (New York: Routledge, 1999), 407–17. The separation of the two modes or trajectories should be understood as heuristic rather than essential: it allows for an observation of varying emphases as well as identification of points of contact between vastly different technologies.

17. Michel Foucault, *"Society Must Be Defended": Lectures at the Collège De France, 1975–1976* (New York: Macmillan, 2003), 245.

18. Foucault, *The History of Sexuality*, 143.

19. Ibid.

20. Ibid., 136.

21. Foucault's acrimony toward Marxian theory should not distract us from the ways that the history of biopower is interimplicated with the history of capital's emergence. Like Marx, Foucault does not address the consequences of the connection of slavery to this joint history, which would suggest that as it is productivity (rather than its commodified form as labor) that is at the heart of capitalism and biopower, slavery is the originating condition of possibility. See discussion of Frank Wilderson in this chapter.

22. Foucault, *The History of Sexuality*, 138.

23. Foucault, *Society Must Be Defended*, 254.

24. Ibid.

25. Valverde, "Genealogies of European States," 175.

26. Foucault, *Society Must Be Defended,* 258.

27. Ibid.

28. Daniel J. Kevles, *In the Name of Eugenics: Genetics and the Uses of Human Heredity* (Cambridge, Mass.: Harvard University Press, 1985).

29. Patricia Ticineto Clough, "The Affective Turn: Political Economy, Biomedia and Bodies," *Theory, Culture & Society* 25, no. 1 (2008): 18.

30. Frank Wilderson, "Gramsci's Black Marx: Whither the Slave in Civil Society?," *Social Identities* 9, no. 2 (2003): 231.

31. Henry Wiencek, *Master of the Mountain: Thomas Jefferson and His Slaves* (New York: Macmillan, 2012).

32. Achille Mbembe, "Necropolitics," *Public Culture* 15, no. 1 (2003): 21.

33. Angela Y. Davis, *Are Prisons Obsolete?* (New York: Seven Stories Press, 2011).

34. Foucault, *Society Must Be Defended,* 253.

35. Clough, "The Affective Turn," 19. See also Patricia Ticineto Clough and Craig Willse, "Gendered Security/National Security: Political Branding and Population Racism," *Social Text 105* 28, no. 4 (2010): 45–63.

36. Ruth Wilson Gilmore, *Golden Gulag: Prisons, Surplus, Crisis, and Opposition in Globalizing California* (Berkeley: University of California Press, 2007).

37. Foucault, *Society Must Be Defended,* 251.

38. Cheryl Harris, "Whiteness as Property," *Harvard Law Review* 106, no. 8 (1993): 1714.

39. Ibid., 1716.

40. Ibid., 1718.

41. Ibid., 1727.

42. Andrea Smith, "Heteropatriarchy and the Three Pillars of White Supremacy: Rethinking Women of Color Organizing," in *Color of Violence: The INCITE! Anthology,* ed. Incite! Women of Color Against Violence (Boston: South End Press, 2006), 67–68. The third pillar described by Smith is Orientalism, which anchors war.

43. Harris, "Whiteness as Property," 1777.

44. George Lipsitz, "The Possessive Investment in Whiteness: Racialized Social Democracy and the 'White' Problem in American Studies," *American Quarterly* 47, no. 3 (1995): 369–87. I explore this history in greater detail in chapter 3.

45. Grace Kyungwon Hong, *The Ruptures of American Capital: Women of Color Feminism and the Culture of Immigrant Labor* (Minneapolis: University of Minnesota Press, 2006).

46. U.S. Department of Housing and Urban Development, Office of Community Planning and Development, *The Second Annual Homeless Assessment Report to Congress* (Washington, D.C., 2008), iv.

47. Martha R. Burt et al., *Strategies for Reducing Chronic Street Homelessness* (Sacramento: Walter R. McDonald & Associates, Inc. and The Urban Institute, 2004), 54.

48. New York City Department of Homeless Services, *Critical Activities Report, Fiscal Year 2011, Total DHS Services* (New York, 2011).

49. Randall Kuhn and Dennis Culhane, "Applying Cluster Analysis to Test a Typology of Homelessness by Pattern of Shelter Utilization: Results from the Analysis of Administrative Data," *American Journal of Community Psychology* 26, no. 2 (1998): 222.

50. Common Ground Insitute, *Project 50 One Year Progress Report* (Los Angeles, 2009).

51. Foucault writes, "The state is not a universal nor in itself an autonomous source of power. The state is nothing else but the effect, the profile, the mobile shape of a perpetual statification *(étatisation)* or statifications, in the sense of incessant transactions which modify, or move, or drastically change, or insidiously shift sources of finance, modes of investment, decision-making centers, forms and types of control, relationships between local powers, the central authority, and so on. . . . The state is nothing else but the mobile effect of a regime of multiple governmentalities." Michel Foucault, *The Birth of Biopolitics: Lectures at the Collège De France, 1978–1979* (New York: Picador, 2008), 77.

52. Daniel Guérin, *Anarchism: From Theory to Practice* (New York: Monthly Review Press, 1970).

53. David Theo Goldberg, *The Racial State* (Malden, Mass.: Blackwell Publishers, 2002), 6.

54. Cedric J. Robinson, *Black Marxism: The Making of the Black Radical Tradition* (Chapel Hill: University of North Carolina Press, 2000).

55. Mimi Abramovitz summarizes the contribution of socialist feminism to state theory thus: "Socialist feminists in particular argued that the welfare state arose not only to cushion the adverse impact of industrialization (liberal theory), to foster social solidarity (social citizenship theory), and to mediate the conflict between production for profit and production for need (Marxist theory), but also to underwrite the cost of social reproduction in the home. In other words, when the imperatives of profitable production—high profits, low wages, and a degree of unemployment—came into conflict with the requirements of social reproduction, the average family's need for adequate

resources to carry out its assigned caretaking and maintenance tasks forced the state to step in to shore it up economically." Mimi Abramovitz, *Under Attack, Fighting Back: Women and Welfare in the United States* (New York: Monthly Review Press, 2000), 94.

56. Foucault, *The History of Sexuality,* 140–41.

57. Ibid., 141.

58. Silvia Federici, *Caliban and the Witch: Women, the Body and Primitive Accumulation* (Brooklyn, N.Y.: Autonomedia, 2004); Kathi Weeks, *The Problem with Work: Feminism, Marxism, Antiwork Politics, and Postwork Imaginaries* (Durham, N.C.: Duke University Press, 2011). For an analysis of how the context of slavery changes questions of social reproduction, see Hortense J. Spillers, "Mama's Baby, Papa's Maybe: An American Grammar Book," *Diacritics* 17, no. 2 (1987): 64–82.

59. Of course, his use of the term "men" suggests that Foucault neglects those feminist accounts and the gendered organization of this labor.

60. Thomas Robert Malthus, *An Essay on the Principle of Population* (Cambridge: Cambridge University Press, 1992).

61. Valverde, "Genealogies of European States."

62. Robert Lieberman, "Race and the Limits of Solidarity: American Welfare State Development in Comparative Perspective," in *Race and the Politics of Welfare Reform,* ed. Sanford F. Schram, Joe Soss, and Richard C. Fording (Ann Arbor: University of Michigan Press, 2003), 30.

63. Ibid.

64. Ibid., 25.

65. Philip Sheldon Foner, *The Black Panthers Speak* (Cambridge, Mass.: Da Capo Press, 2002).

66. For an account of community and grassroots interventions, see Alyosha Goldstein, *Poverty in Common: The Politics of Community Action during the American Century* (Durham, N.C.: Duke University Press, 2012).

67. While Native peoples in the United States have been subject to racialization within white supremacist formations, their designation as "domestic dependent nations" within the United States means that the social and health needs of Native populations, when addressed by the federal government, have been managed through alternate tracks, including the Bureau of Indian Affairs.

68. Jeff Manza, "Political Sociological Models of the U.S. New Deal," *Annual Review of Sociology* 26 (2000): 304.

69. Ruth Wilson Gilmore, "Globalisation and US Prison Growth: From Military Keynesianism to Post-Keynesian Militarism," *Race & Class* 40, no. 2/3 (1998/1999): 176–77.

70. Martin Gilens, "How the Poor Became Black: The Racialization of Poverty in American Media," in *Race and the Politics of Welfare Reform,* ed. Sanford F. Schram, Joe Soss, and Richard C. Fording (Ann Arbor: University of Michigan Press, 2003), 101–130.

71. Kenneth J. Neubeck and Noel A. Cazenave, *Welfare Racism: Playing the Race Card Against America's Poor* (New York: Routledge, 2004), 145–76.

72. Foucault, *Society Must Be Defended,* 258.

73. Ibid., 254.

74. Dean Spade has argued that any project of redistribution is a biopolitical project, and thus necessarily engages in state racism. Comment at "The U.S. Non-Profit Industrial Complex and Its Discontents" panel discussion, Annual Meeting of the American Studies Association, Washington D.C., November 2009.

75. For notable exceptions, see Jasbir K. Puar, *Terrorist Assemblages: Homonationalism in Queer Times* (Durham, N.C.: Duke University Press, 2007); Melinda Cooper, *Life as Surplus: Biotechnology and Capitalism in the Neoliberal Era* (Seattle: University of Washington Press, 2008).

76. Emile Durkheim, *The Division of Labor in Society* (New York: Simon and Schuster, 1997).

77. Luciana Parisi and Tiziana Terranova, "Heat Death: Emergence and Control in Genetic Engineering and Artifical Life," *CTHEORY* (2000). http://www .ctheory.net/articles.aspx?id=127.

78. Foucault, *Society Must Be Defended,* 249.

79. Ibid., 246.

80. David Harvey, *The Condition of Postmodernity: An Enquiry into the Origins of Cultural Change* (Oxford: Blackwell Publishers, 1989), 129.

81. Ibid.

82. Ibid., 141–42.

83. Patricia Ticineto Clough, "Future Matters: Technoscience, Global Politics, and Cultural Criticism," *Social Text 80* 22, no. 3 (2004): 11.

84. Jacques Donzelot, "Michel Foucault and Liberal Intelligence," *Economy & Society* 37, no. 1 (2008): 131.

85. Gilmore, "Globalisation and US Prison Growth," 179. This socialization has occurred through the family, as family structures are meant to pick up the slack of the social welfare state that once saw itself as stabilizing the family. One way to frame today's unsheltered population—understood to be largely single adult men—is as impoverished people with no family network to absorb them. This simultaneous reliance upon and abandonment of the family might help explain the hysterical paranoia around family values that characterizes the recent neoliberal era in the United States.

86. On the current status of the racialized wealth gap, see Signe-Mary McKernan et al., *Less than Equal: Racial Disparities in Wealth Accumulation* (New York: Urban Institute, 2013).

87. Karl Marx, *Capital, Vol. 1* (New York: Penguin, 1990).

88. Gilmore, "Globalisation and US Prison Growth," 182.

89. Abigail R. Moncrieff, "Cost-Benefit Federalism: Reconciling Collective Action Federalism and Libertarian Federalism in the Obamacare Litigation and Beyond," *American Journal of Law & Medicine* 38 (2012): 288–325.

90. Ruth Wilson Gilmore, "In the Shadow of the Shadow State," in *The Revolution Will Not Be Funded: Beyond the Non-Profit Industrial Complex,* ed. INCITE! Women of Color Against Violence (Cambridge, Mass: South End Press, 2007), 44–45.

91. INCITE! Women of Color Against Violence, ed., *The Revolution Will Not Be Funded: Beyond the Non-Profit Industrial Complex* (Cambridge, Mass.: South End Press, 2007); Michael Edwards, *Just Another Emperor? The Myths and Realities of Philathrocapitalism* (New York: Demos, 2008).

92. "Media Justice and the Crime of Poverty: An Interview with Tiny from POOR Magazine," *Angola 3 News,* March 25, 2010, http://angola3news.blog spot.com/2010/03/media-justice-and-crime-of-poverty.html.

93. Dylan Rodriguez, "The Political Logic of the Non-Profit Industrial Complex," in *The Revolution Will Not Be Funded: Beyond the Non-Profit Industrial Complex, ed.* INCITE! Women of Color Against Violence (Cambridge, Mass: South End Press, 2007), 37.

94. Ibid., 29.

95. Foucault, *The Birth of Biopolitics,* 121.

96. Ibid., 116.

97. Harvey, *The Condition of Postmodernity,* 286. It has also meant a rise of risk, driving what Randy Martin describes as the financialization of everyday life, in which individuals bear those risks and take on speculative roles of finance capital. Similarly, we see the increased importance of things like carbon futures, in which we bet against security and wager on disaster. Kaushik Sunder Rajan suggests that the post-Fordist shift drives a move to more and more speculative forms of investment in risky life. Randy Martin, *Financialization of Daily Life* (Philadelphia: Temple University Press, 2002); Kaushik Sunder Rajan, *Biocapital: The Constitution of Postgenomic Life* (Durham N.C.: Duke University Press, 2006).

98. Gilmore, "In the Shadow of the Shadow State," 45.

99. Giorgio Agamben, *Homo Sacer: Sovereign Power and Bare Life* (Stanford, Calif.: Stanford University Press, 1998).

100. Leonard C. Feldman, *Citizens without Shelter: Homelessness, Democracy, and Political Exclusion* (Ithaca, N.Y.: Cornell University Press, 2006), 60–62.

101. Aihwa Ong, *Neoliberalism as Exception: Mutations in Citizenship and Sovereignty* (Durham, N.C.: Duke University Press, 2006), 7.

102. Mbembe, "Necropolitics," 39.

2. HOMELESSNESS AS METHOD

1. James D. Wright and Beth A. Rubin, "Is Homelessness a Housing Problem?," in *Understanding Homelessness: New Policy and Research Perspectives* (Washington, D.C.: Fannie Mae Foundation, 1997), 205–24.

2. Jill Quadagno, *The Color of Welfare: How Racism Undermined the War on Poverty* (New York: Oxford University Press, 1994).

3. U.S. Department of Housing and Urban Development, Office of Community Planning and Development, *The 2013 Homeless Assessment Report (AHAR) to Congress, Part 1: Point-in-Time Estimates of Homelessness* (Washington, D.C., 2013).

4. On the possessive individual, see Grace Kyungwon Hong, *The Ruptures of American Capital: Women of Color Feminism and the Culture of Immigrant Labor* (Minneapolis: University of Minnesota Press, 2006).

5. Nels Anderson, *The Hobo: The Sociology of the Homeless Man* (Chicago: University of Chicago Press, 1961). I first found this definition in the work of Kenneth Kusmer, which directed me to Anderson's text.

6. Kenneth L. Kusmer, *Down and Out, on the Road: The Homeless in American History* (New York: Oxford University Press, 2003), 4.

7. Peter H. Rossi, *Down and Out in America: The Origins of Homelessness* (Chicago: University of Chicago Press, 1989), 47–48.

8. Ibid., 48.

9. George Steinmetz, "The Genealogy of a Positivist Haunting: Comparing Prewar and Postwar U.S. Sociology," *Boundary 2* 32, no. 2 (2005): 109–35.

10. Patricia Ticineto Clough, "The New Empiricism: Affect and Sociological Methods," *European Journal of Social Theory* 12, no. 1 (2009): 45.

11. Douglas A. Harper, *Good Company: A Tramp Life* (New York: Paradigm Publishers, 2006).

12. Raewyn Connell, *Southern Theory: The Global Dynamics of Knowledge in Social Science* (Sydney: Allen & Unwin, 2007).

13. Eric J. Hobsbawm, *The Age of Revolution: 1789–1848* (New York: Vintage Books, 1996); Cedric J. Robinson, *Black Marxism: The Making of the Black Radical Tradition* (Chapel Hill: University of North Carolina Press, 2000).

14. Roderick A. Ferguson, *Aberrations in Black: Toward a Queer of Color Critique* (Minneapolis: University of Minnesota Press, 2004), 16.

15. Ibid., 17.

16. Ibid., 76.

17. See also Stephen Steinberg, *Race Relations: A Critique* (Stanford, Calif.: Stanford Social Sciences, 2007).

18. Ferguson, *Aberrations in Black,* 26.

19. Connell, *Southern Theory.*

20. Denise Ferreira da Silva, *Toward a Global Idea of Race* (Minneapolis: University of Minnesota Press, 2007), 35.

21. "Unhoused" is Duneier's term.

22. Duneier compares the text as presented by Wacquant and the original full text from which quotes are gleaned on pages 1553–60 of his response. Mitchell Duneier, "What Kind of Combat Sport Is Sociology?," *American Journal of Sociology* 107, no. 6 (2002): 1551–76.

23. Loïc Wacquant, "Scrutinizing the Street: Poverty, Morality, and the Pitfalls of Urban Ethnography," *American Journal of Sociology* 107, no. 6 (2002): 1521.

24. Mitchell Duneier, *Sidewalk* (New York: Farrar, Straus and Giroux, 1999), 122–32.

25. Lisa Duggan, *The Twilight of Equality?: Neoliberalism, Cultural Politics, and the Attack on Democracy* (New York: Beacon Press, 2003), xvi.

26. The culture of poverty thesis was advanced by Daniel Patrick Moynihan in what has become known as the Moynihan Report. See Daniel Patrick Moynihan, *The Negro Family: The Case for National Action* (Washington, D.C.: Office of Planning and Research, United States Department of Labor, 1965). For feminist academic and activist responses to the Moynihan Report, see Patricia Hill Collins, *Black Feminist Thought: Knowledge, Consciousness, and the Politics of Empowerment* (New York: Routledge, 1991); Joyce Ladner, *Tomorrow's Tomorrow* (Garden City, N.Y.: Doubleday, 1972); Premilla Nadasen, *Welfare Warriors: The Welfare Rights Movement in the United States* (New York: Routledge, 2005); Hortense J. Spillers, "Mama's Baby, Papa's Maybe: An American Grammar Book," *Diacritics* 17, no. 2 (1987): 64–82; Kimberle Crenshaw, "Demarginalizing the Intersection of Race and Sex: A Black Feminist Critique of Antidiscrimination Doctrine, Feminist Theory and Antiracist Politics," *University of Chicago Legal Forum* 1989 (1989): 139–67.

27. Duneier, "What Kind of Combat Sport Is Sociology?," 1551.

28. Duneier, *Sidewalk,* 170.

29. On workfare states, see Jamie Peck, *Workfare States* (New York: Guilford Press, 2001). On the valorization of work ethics in liberal thought, see Kathi

Weeks, *The Problem with Work: Feminism, Marxism, Antiwork Politics, and Postwork Imaginaries* (Durham, N.C.: Duke University Press, 2011).

30. Duneier, "What Kind of Combat Sport Is Sociology?," 1565.

31. On new technologies of the self as empowered entrepreneur, see Mitchell Dean, *Governmentality: Power and Rule in Modern Society* (London: SAGE, 1999); Barbara Cruikshank, *The Will to Empower: Democratic Citizens and Other Subjects* (Ithaca, N.Y.: Cornell University Press, 1999).

32. Duneier, *Sidewalk,* 317.

33. Max Weber, *The Protestant Ethic and the Spirit of Capitalism and Other Writings* (New York: Penguin, 2002).

34. Craig Willse, "Life beyond Work," review of *The Problem with Work: Feminism, Marxism, Antiwork Politics and Postwork Imaginaries,* by Kathi Weeks, *ephemera* 14, no. 3 (2014): 545–52.

35. Jane Jacobs, *The Death and Life of Great American Cities* (New York: Random House, 1961).

36. Duneier, *Sidewalk,* 28.

37. Ibid., 36.

38. Ibid., 55.

39. Ibid., 62.

40. Ibid., 75.

41. Ibid.

42. Ibid., 72.

43. Ibid., 78.

44. Patricia Ticineto Clough, *The End(s) of Ethnography: From Realism to Social Criticism* (New York: Peter Lang, 1998), 24.

45. Duneier, *Sidewalk,* 201.

46. Ibid., 190.

47. Ibid., 37.

48. Duneier, "What Kind of Combat Sport Is Sociology?," 1574.

49. Ibid., 1575.

50. Ibid., 1573.

51. See, for example, Sylvia Wynter, "Unsettling the Coloniality of Being/Power/Truth/Freedom: Towards the Human, after Man, Its Overrepresentation—An Argument," *CR: The New Centennial Review* 3, no. 3 (2003): 257–337.

52. Andrea Smith, "Queer Theory and Native Studies: The Heteronormativity of Settler Colonialism," *GLQ: A Journal of Lesbian and Gay Studies* 16, nos. 1–2 (2010): 42. On the relationship of "affectability" to racial subordination, Smith is drawing from Denise Ferreira da Silva, *Toward a Global Idea of Race* (Minneapolis: University of Minnesota Press, 2007).

53. Duneier, "What Kind of Combat Sport Is Sociology?," 1563.

54. Duneier, *Sidewalk*, 353.

55. Ibid., 187.

56. Jacobs, *The Death and Life of Great American Cities*. Cited in Duneier, *Sidewalk*, 192.

57. See INCITE! Women of Color Against Violence, ed., *Color of Violence: The INCITE! Anthology* (Boston: South End Press, 2006); Christina B. Hanhardt, *Safe Space: Gay Neighborhood History and the Politics of Violence* (Durham, N.C.: Duke University Press, 2013).

58. Duneier, *Sidewalk*, 313.

59. Pheng Cheah, "Violent Light: The Idea of Publicness in Modern Philosophy and in Global Neocolonialism," *Social Text* 43 (1995): 163–90.

60. Clough, *The End(s) of Ethnography*, 17.

61. Duneier, *Sidewalk*, 348.

62. Gayatri Chakravorty Spivak, "Can the Subaltern Speak?," in *Marxism and the Interpretation of Culture*, ed. Cary Nelson and Lawrence Grossberg (Champaign: University of Illinois Press, 1998), 90.

63. Tukufu Zuberi and Eduardo Bonilla-Silva, "Toward a Definition of White Logic and White Methods," in *White Logic, White Methods: Racism and Methodology*, ed. Tukufu Zuberi and Eduardo Bonilla-Silva (Lanham, Md.: Rowman & Littlefield Publishers, 2008), 17–18.

64. Denise Ferreira da Silva, *Toward a Global Idea of Race* (Minneapolis: University of Minnesota Press, 2007), 35.

3. FROM PATHOLOGY TO POPULATION

1. Kenneth L. Kusmer, *Down and Out, on the Road: The Homeless in American History* (New York: Oxford University Press, 2003), 3.

2. Ibid., 74.

3. Ibid., 74–75.

4. Peter H. Rossi, *Down and Out in America: The Origins of Homelessness* (Chicago: University of Chicago Press, 1989), 18.

5. Ibid., 184.

6. For accounts of the New Deal, see Edwin Amenta, *Bold Relief: Institutional Politics and the Origins of Modern American Social Policy* (Princeton, N.J.: Princeton University Press, 1998); Jill Quadagno, *The Color of Welfare: How Racism Undermined the War on Poverty* (New York: Oxford University Press, 1994); Theda Skocpol, *Protecting Soldiers and Mothers: The Political Origins of Social Policy in United States* (Cambridge, Mass.: Harvard University Press, 1992).

7. Kusmer, *Down and Out*, 232.

8. This is another example, of course, of the ways that inclusion into state apparatuses is always a process of both homogenization and differentiation/exclusion. Stuart Banner, *How the Indians Lost Their Land: Law and Power on the Frontier* (Cambridge, Mass.: Harvard University Press, 2005).

9. Kusmer, *Down and Out,* 210. Not until 1969 did the United States Supreme Court put an end to settlement issues regarding social welfare programs.

10. Rossi, *Down and Out in America,* 25.

11. Kusmer, *Down and Out,* 218.

12. Rossi, *Down and Out in America,* 25.

13. Ibid., 21.

14. Ibid., 27.

15. Kim Hopper, "Homelessness Old and New: The Matter of Definition," in *Understanding Homelessness: New Policy and Research Perspectives,* ed. Dennis P. Culhane and Steven P. Hornburg (Washington, D.C.: Fannie Mae Foundation, 1997), 17.

16. James D. Wright and Beth A. Rubin, "Is Homelessness a Housing Problem?," in *Understanding Homelessness: New Policy and Research Perspectives,* ed. Dennis P. Culhane and Steven P. Hornburg (Washington, D.C.: Fannie Mae Foundation, 1997), 212.

17. Cited in Kusmer, *Down and Out,* 230.

18. Hopper, "Homelessness Old and New"; Rossi, *Down and Out in America*; Kusmer, *Down and Out.*

19. Rossi, *Down and Out in America,* 38–39.

20. Ibid., 28–29.

21. Kusmer, *Down and Out,* 236.

22. Wright and Rubin, "Is Homelessness a Housing Problem?," 211.

23. Angela P. Harris, "From Stonewall to the Suburbs?: Toward a Political Economy of Sexuality," *William & Mary Bill of Rights Journal* 14 (2006): 1539–82; George Lipsitz, "The Possessive Investment in Whiteness: Racialized Social Democracy and the 'White' Problem in American Studies," *American Quarterly* 47, no. 3 (1995): 369–87.

24. Neil Smith, *The New Urban Frontier: Gentrification and the Revanchist City* (New York: Routledge, 1996).

25. Ibid., 6–7.

26. Kusmer, *Down and Out,* 239. See also Hopper, "Homelessness Old and New," 23.

27. Kusmer, *Down and Out,* 242.

28. Skocpol, *Protecting Soldiers and Mothers.* See also *Color of Violence: The INCITE! Anthology,* ed. Incite! Women of Color Against Violence (Boston: South End Press, 2006); Kusmer, *Down and Out.*

29. The massive expansion of the prison system from the 1970s on, as well as the extremely disproportionate targeting of racially subordinated populations for imprisonment, is well documented. See Ruth Wilson Gilmore, *Golden Gulag: Prisons, Surplus, Crisis, and Opposition in Globalizing California* (Berkeley: University of California Press, 2007); Loïc Wacquant, *Punishing the Poor: The Neoliberal Government of Social Insecurity* (Durham, N.C.: Duke University Press, 2009).

30. Kusmer, *Down and Out*, 239.

31. Martha R. Burt et al., *Strategies for Reducing Chronic Street Homelessness* (Sacramento Calif.: Walter R. McDonald & Associates, Inc. and The Urban Institute, 2004).

32. Cited in Hopper, "Homelessness Old and New," 47.

33. Eva Cherniavsky, "Neocitizenship and Critique," *Social Text 99* 27, no. 2 (2009): 4.

34. There is very little documented history of HUD available. Lawrence L. Thompson, who worked in the department for over twenty-five years, self-published a history following his retirement. His account has helped form my own, which is based as well on congressional records and HUD's own documentation. Lawrence L. Thompson, "A History of HUD" (self-published manuscript, 2006).

35. United States Code, Title 42, Chapter 119, Subchapter I, §11301. The mention of Native Americans in the act is notable, especially considering the lack of homeless programming targeting these populations, as well as the lack of other groups being named, especially African Americans. The federal government winds up developing a separate "Indian housing" program in supposed response to Native housing insecurity.

36. United States Interagency Council on Homelessness, *Federal Strategic Plan to Prevent and End Homelessness* (Washington, D.C., 2009), 4.

37. The present book will go on to investigate in detail two of HUD's recent programs. Chapter 4 looks at the development of databases, protocols, and reporting requirements for agencies receiving HUD funding. Chapter 5 explores HUD's chronic homelessness programs.

38. United States Department of Housing and Urban Development, *Programs of HUD: Major Mortgage, Grant, Assistance, and Regulatory Programs* (Washington, D.C., 2011).

39. See the act at https://www.onecpd.info/resources/documents/Homeless AssistanceActAmendedbyHEARTH.pdf.

40. *NCH Policy Recommendations: HUD McKinney-Vento Reauthorization* (Washington, D.C.: National Coalition for the Homeless, 2009).

41. United States Department of Housing and Urban Development, *Overview of FY2014 President's Budget* (Washington, D.C., 2014), 23.

42. Bob Jessop, *State Power: A Strategic-Relational Approach* (Malden, Mass.: Polity Press, 2007).

43. For this model of neoliberalism, I am drawing from work in political sociology and geography, including Jessop, *State Power*; Neil Brenner, *New State Spaces: Urban Governance and the Rescaling of Statehood* (New York: Oxford University Press, 2004); Neil Brenner and Nik Theodore, *Spaces of Neoliberalism: Urban Restructuring in North America and Western Europe* (Malden, Mass.: Wiley-Blackwell, 2003); Jamie Peck, "Political Economies of Scale: Fast Policy, Interscalar Relations, and Neoliberal Workfare," *Economic Geography* 78, no. 3 (2002): 331–60.

44. Wendy Brown, *States of Injury* (Princeton, N.J.: Princeton University Press, 1995).

45. Brenner and Theodore, *Spaces of Neoliberalism*.

46. Robert R. Desjarlais, *Shelter Blues: Sanity and Selfhood among the Homeless* (Philadelphia: University of Pennsylvania Press, 1997), 2.

47. Stephen B. Seager, *Street Crazy: America's Mental Health Tragedy* (Redondo Beach, Calif.: Westcom, 2000), x.

48. Ibid., xi.

49. Irving Kenneth Zola, "Medicine as an Institution of Social Control," *Sociological Review* 4 (1972): 487–504.

50. David M. Cress and David A. Snow, "The Outcomes of Homeless Mobilization: The Influence of Organization, Disruption, Political Mediation, and Framing," *American Journal of Sociology* 105, no. 4 (2000): 1063–1104; Vincent Lyon-Callo, *Inequality, Poverty, and Neoliberal Governance: Activist Ethnography in the Homeless Sheltering Industry* (Toronto: University of Toronto Press, 2008).

51. Nancy Tomes, *The Art of Asylum-Keeping: Thomas Story Kirkbride and the Origins of American Psychiatry* (Philadelphia: University of Pennsylvania Press, 1994).

52. Andrew T. Scull, *Madhouses, Mad Doctors and Madmen: Social History of Psychiatry in the Victorian Era* (London: Athlone Press, 1981).

53. Kenneth J. Neubeck and Noel A. Cazenave, *Welfare Racism: Playing the Race Card against America's Poor* (New York: Routledge, 2001).

54. On race suicide panics, see Donna Haraway, "Teddy Bear Patriarchy: Taxidermy in the Garden of Eden, New York City, 1908–1936," in *Culture/Power/History: A Reader in Contemporary Social Theory,* ed. Nicholas B. Dirks, Geoff Eley, and Sherry B. Ortner (Princeton, N.J.: Princeton University Press, 1994), 49–95.

55. Ian Robert Dowbiggin, *Keeping America Sane: Psychiatry and Eugenics in the United States and Canada, 1880–1940* (Ithaca, N.Y.: Cornell University Press, 2003). For an important analysis of how categories and diagnoses of mental illness are racialized and emerge in the context of imperialism and post-colonialism, see Suman Fernando, David Ndegwa, and Melba Wilson, *Forensic Psychiatry, Race and Culture* (New York: Routledge, 1998).

56. This movement found its strongest sociological expression in the work of Thomas Szasz, which has been connected to Foucault's work and that of Erving Goffman to constitute something of an academic antipsychiatry movement. Thomas Szasz, *The Myth of Mental Illness* (New York: Harper & Row, 1974); Michel Foucault, *Madness and Civilization* (London: Tavistock, 1961); Erving Goffman, *Asylums* (New York: Anchor Books, 1961).

57. Desjarlais, *Shelter Blues*, 30.

58. Thomas G. Blomberg and Karol Lucken, *American Penology: A History of Control* (New Brunswick, N.J.: Transaction Publishers, 2010), 221–22.

59. Alexander R. Thomas, "Ronald Reagan and the Commitment of the Mentally Ill: Capital, Interest Groups, and the Eclipse of Social Policy," *Electronic Journal of Sociology* 3, no. 4 (1998).

60. Pushing further, Liat Ben-Moshe argues for starting with a conception of incarceration that includes institutions confining people with disabilities alongside prisons and jails. Liat Ben-Moshe, "Disabling Incarceration: Connecting Disability to Divergent Confinements in the USA," *Critical Sociology* 39, no. 3 (2013): 385–403. For a summary of research on the prevalence of psychiatric disabilities among imprisoned populations, see Rich Daly, "Prison Mental Health Crisis Continues to Grow," *Psychiatric News*, October 20, 2006.

61. Mimi M. Kim and Julian D. Ford, "Trauma and Post-Traumatic Stress among Homeless Men," *Journal of Aggression, Maltreatment & Trauma* 13, no. 2 (2006): 1–22.

62. See, for example, Nancy Summers, *Fundamentals of Case Management Practice: Skills for the Human Services* (Belmont, Calif.: Cengage Learning, 2011).

63. Theresa Funiciello, *Tyranny of Kindness: Dismantling the Welfare System to End Poverty in America* (New York: Atlantic Monthly Press, 1993).

64. Jamie Peck and Adam Tickell, "Neoliberalizing Space," *Antipode* 34, no. 3 (2002): 384.

65. Manfred B. Steger and Ravi K. Roy, *Neoliberalism: A Very Short Introduction* (New York: Oxford University Press, 2010).

66. Peck and Tickell, "Neoliberalizing Space," 384.

67. Jamie Peck, *Workfare States* (New York: Guilford Press, 2001).

68. Wacquant, *Punishing the Poor.*

69. Neubeck and Cazenave, *Welfare Racism.*

70. Aihwa Ong, *Neoliberalism as Exception: Mutations in Citizenship and Sovereignty* (Durham, N.C.: Duke University Press, 2006), 3.

71. Grace Kyungwon Hong, *The Ruptures of American Capital: Women of Color Feminism and the Culture of Immigrant Labor* (Minneapolis: University of Minnesota Press, 2006), 6.

72. Ibid., 3.

73. Ibid., 20.

74. Grace Kyungwon Hong, "Existentially Surplus: Women of Color Feminism and the New Crises of Capitalism," *GLQ: A Journal of Lesbian and Gay Studies* 18, no. 1 (2012): 87–106.

75. Ibid., 91.

76. Harris, "From Stonewall to the Suburbs?," 1543.

4. GOVERNING THROUGH NUMBERS

1. Office of the Federal Register, "Department of Housing and Urban Development: Homeless Management Information Systems (HMIS) Data and Technical Standards Notice," *Federal Register* 68, no. 140 (2003): 43431.

2. United States Department of Housing and Urban Development, *Homeless Management Information (HMIS) Fact Sheet* (Washington, D.C., 2006), 1.

3. Paul Michael Garrett, "Social Work's 'Electronic Turn': Notes on the Deployment of Information and Communication Technologies in Social Work with Children and Family," *Critical Social Policy* 25, no. 4 (2005): 531.

4. Lev Manovich, *The Language of New Media* (Cambridge, Mass.: MIT Press, 2001).

5. Geoffrey C. Bowker and Susan Leigh Star, *Sorting Things Out: Classification and Its Consequences* (Cambridge, Mass.: MIT Press, 1999).

6. Eugene Thacker, *The Global Genome: Biotechnology, Politics, and Culture* (Cambridge, Mass.: MIT Press, 2005), 105–6.

7. Ibid.

8. James C. Scott, *Seeing like a State: How Certain Schemes to Improve the Human Condition Have Failed* (New Haven, Conn.: Yale University Press, 1999); Patricia Cline Cohen, *A Calculating People: The Spread of Numeracy in Early America* (New York: Routledge, 1999); Theodore M. Porter, *Trust in Numbers: The Pursuit of Objectivity in Science and Public Life* (Princeton, N.J.: Princeton University Press, 1996); Ian Hacking, *The Taming of Chance* (Cambridge: Cambridge University Press, 1990).

9. Porter, *Trust in Numbers.*

10. Ian Hacking, "Biopolitics and the Avalanche of Printed Numbers," *Humanities in Society 5*, nos. 3–4 (1982): 279–95.

11. HUD provides links to forty-seven vendors that sell McKinney-Vento compliant HMIS software packages. See http://www.hmis.info/Software/.

12. United States Department of Housing and Urban Development, Office of Community Planning and Development, *Homeless Management Information System (HMIS) Data Standards, Revised Notice*, 2010, 40. HUD additionally requires what it calls "program-specific data elements" for some streams of McKinney-Vento funding, such as its Housing Opportunities for People with AIDS (HOPWA) program.

13. Ibid., 49–50.

14. Office of the Federal Register, "Department of Housing and Urban Development: Homeless Management Information Systems (HMIS) Data and Technical Standards Final Notice," *Federal Register 69*, no. 146 (2004): 45890.

15. The reports can be accessed at https://www.onecpd.info/hdx/guides/ahar/.

16. United States Department of Housing and Urban Development, Office of Community Planning and Development, *The Annual Homeless Assessment Report (AHAR) to Congress* (Washington, D.C., 2007); United States Department of Housing and Urban Development, Office of Community Planning and Development, *The 2012 Annual Homeless Assessment Report (AHAR) to Congress* (Washington, D.C., 2013).

17. Office of the Federal Register, "Department of Housing and Urban Development: Homeless Management Information Systems (HMIS) Data and Technical Standards Final Notice," (Washington, D.C., 2010): 45897.

18. Adele E. Clarke et al., "Biomedicalization: Technoscientific Transformations of Health, Illness, and U.S. Biomedicine," *American Sociological Review 68*, no. 2 (2003): 161–94; Sharon E. Straus and Finlay A. McAlister, "Evidence-Based Medicine: A Commentary on Common Criticisms," *CMAJ: Canadian Medical Association Journal 163*, no. 7 (2000): 837–41.

19. Office of the Federal Register, "Department of Housing and Urban Development: Homeless Management Information Systems (HMIS) Data and Technical Standards Notice" (Washington, D.C., 2010).

20. United States Department of Housing and Urban Development, *Homeless Management Information (HMIS) Fact Sheet*.

21. Abt Associates, "Introduction to Homeless Management Information Systems (HMIS)," a presentation prepared for the U.S. Department of Housing and Urban Development.

22. Stephen Webb, *Social Work in a Risk Society: Social and Cultural Perspectives* (New York: Palgrave Macmillan, 2005), 121–25.

23. Ian Robert Dowbiggin, *Keeping America Sane: Psychiatry and Eugenics in the United States and Canada, 1880–1940* (Ithaca, N.Y.: Cornell University Press, 2003); Edward Shorter, *A History of Psychiatry: From the Era of the Asylum to the Age of Prozac* (New York: Wiley, 1998).

24. Bob Sapey, "Social Work Tomorrow: Towards a Critical Understanding of Technology in Social Work," *British Journal of Social Work* 27, no. 6 (1997): 810.

25. Nigel Parton, "Changes in the Form of Knowledge in Social Work: From the 'Social' to the 'Informational'?," *British Journal of Social Work* 38, no. 2 (2008): 11.

26. Katja Franko Aas, "From Narrative to Database: Technological Change and Penal Culture," *Punishment & Society* 6, no. 4 (2004): 379–93.

27. The one-night count has not disappeared. Major cities around the United States annually recruit volunteers to participate in one-night counts, and HUD has attempted to systemize this with point-in-time estimates.

28. See for example, Elijah Adiv Edelman, "'This Area Has Been Declared a Prostitution Free Zone': Discursive Formations of Space, the State, and Trans 'Sex Worker' Bodies," *Journal of Homosexuality* 58, nos. 6–7 (2011): 848–64.

29. Parton, "Changes in the Form of Knowledge in Social Work," 6.

30. Ibid.

31. Patricia Ticineto Clough, *Autoaffection: Unconscious Thought in the Age of Technology* (Minneapolis: University of Minnesota Press, 2000).

32. For an important and incisive account of disciplining mechanisms and subject-production in a homeless shelter, see Vincent Lyon-Callo, *Inequality, Poverty, and Neoliberal Governance: Activist Ethnography in the Homeless Sheltering Industry* (Toronto: University of Toronto Press, 2008).

33. Torin Monahan, ed., *Surveillance and Security: Technological Politics and Power in Everyday Life* (New York: Routledge, 2006); Kevin D. Haggerty and Richard V. Ericson, "The Surveillant Assemblage," *British Journal of Sociology* 51, no. 4 (2000): 605–22.

34. Haggerty and Ericson, "The Surveillant Assemblage," 613. (Poster 1990: 97).

35. Ibid., 614.

36. On the actuarial turn, see Porter, *Trust in Numbers*.

37. United States Department of Housing and Urban Development, *Demonstrating the Uses of Homeless Data at the Local Level: Case Studies from Nine Communities* (Washington, D.C., 2007), 28.

38. In pointing to the regulation of homeless service agencies, I do not mean to endorse their activities, or suggest they should not be regulated. I mean only

to point to how the productive capacities of universal data elements are used for many purposes well beyond the counting or even tracking of homeless individuals. The professionalization of social services, the use of social services to extend state power, and the role of social services in maintaining inequality all remain to be explored in this context. Such issues are taken on in relation to homelessness by Lyon-Callo, *Inequality, Poverty, and Neoliberal Governance;* Theresa Funiciello, *Tyranny of Kindness: Dismantling the Welfare System to End Poverty in America* (New York: Atlantic Monthly Press, 1993). Broader critiques of welfare systems and the role of nonprofits in governance are provided by Frances Fox Piven and Richard Cloward, *Regulating the Poor: The Functions of Public Welfare* (New York: Vintage, 1993); INCITE! Women of Color Against Violence, ed., *The Revolution Will Not Be Funded: Beyond the Non-Profit Industrial Complex* (Cambridge, Mass.: South End Press, 2007).

39. United States Department of Housing and Urban Development, *Fifth Annual Progress Report on HUD's Strategy for Improving Homeless Data Collection, Reporting and Analysis* (Washington, D.C., 2006), 22.

40. Abt Associates, "Arizona Homeless Evaluation Project," 2006.

41. United States Department of Housing and Urban Development, *Fifth Annual Progress Report on HUD's Strategy for Improving Homeless Data Collection, Reporting and Analysis,* 22.

42. *NCH Policy Recommendations: HUD McKinney-Vento Reauthorization* (Washington, D.C.: National Coalition for the Homeless, 2009).

43. Ian Hacking, "Making Up People," *London Review of Books,* August 17, 2006.

5. The Invention of Chronic Homelessness

1. United States Department of Housing and Urban Development, Office of Community Planning and Development, *The Second Annual Homeless Assessment Report to Congress* (Washington, D.C., 2008), iii.

2. James J. O'Connell, *Premature Mortality in Homeless Populations: A Review of the Literature* (Nashville, Tenn.: National Health Care for the Homeless Council, 2005), 1.

3. For an important account of resistance to police violence and gentrification in skid row, see Jordan T. Camp and Christina Heatherton, eds., *Freedom Now! Struggles for the Human Right to Housing in LA and Beyond* (Los Angeles: Freedom Now Books, 2013).

4. Neil Smith, *The New Urban Frontier: Gentrification and the Revanchist City* (New York: Routledge, 1996).

5. Gary Blasi and Forrest Stuart, *Has the Safe Cities Initiative in Skid Row Reduced Serious Crime?*, self-published report (Los Angeles, 2008).

6. *Vulnerability Index: Prioritizing the Street Homeless Population by Mortality Risk* (Los Angeles: Common Ground Institute, n.d.).

7. Ben Bergman, "L.A. to Offer Housing to 50 'Most Vulnerable' People," National Public Radio, December 19, 2007. http://www.npr.org/templates/story /story.php?storyId=17401929.

8. Jamie Peck, *Workfare States* (New York: Guilford Press, 2001).

9. The association of "chronic homelessness" with racial status and substance use was developed by Dennis P. Culhane and Randall Kuhn, to be discussed later in this chapter. Dennis P. Culhane and Randall Kuhn, "Patterns and Determinants of Public Shelter Utilization among Homeless Adults in New York City and Philadelphia," *Journal of Policy Analysis and Management* 17, no. 1 (1998): 23–43.

10. Among others, Löic Wacquant has connected the erosion of social safety nets with the expansion of punishment systems. Löic Wacquant, *Punishing the Poor: The Neoliberal Government of Social Insecurity* (Durham, N.C.: Duke University Press, 2009).

11. Sam Tsemberis and Ronda F. Eisenberg, "Pathways to Housing: Supported Housing for Street-Dwelling Homeless Individuals with Psychiatric Disabilities," *Psychiatric Services* 51, no. 4 (2000): 487–93.

12. "Feds Push Efforts to House the Homeless," *American City & Country,* August 2006.

13. *Housing First Principles* (Seattle, Wash.: Downtown Emergency Services Center, n.d.).

14. See the work of the Harm Reduction Coaltion, http://harmreduction .org/.

15. "Safe Haven" is the designated category for HUD-funded housing programs targeting persons with psychiatric disabilities.

16. Tsemberis and Eisenberg, "Pathways to Housing."

17. Using newspaper databases, I conducted Boolean searches for "chronic* homeless*" for thirty years, from 1980 to 2009, in the *New York Times, Los Angeles Times,* and *San Francisco Chronicle,* and reviewed all articles in which those terms appeared. My discussion of news coverage and terminology is based on that research.

18. Randall Kuhn and Dennis Culhane, "Applying Cluster Analysis to Test a Typology of Homelessness by Pattern of Shelter Utilization: Results from the Analysis of Administrative Data," *American Journal of Community Psychology* 26, no. 2 (1998): 211.

19. Dennis P. Culhane and Randall Kuhn, "Patterns and Determinants of Public Shelter Utilization among Homeless Adults in Philadelphia and New York City," *Journal of Policy Analysis and Management* 17, no. 1 (1998): 23.

20. Dennis P Culhane, Stephen Metreaux, and Trevor Hadley, "Supportive Housing for Homeless People with Severe Mental Illness," *Leonard Davis Institute of Health Economics Issue Brief 7*, no. 5 (2002): 1–4.

21. Malcolm Gladwell, "Million-Dollar Murray," *New Yorker,* February 13, 2006.

22. Martha R. Burt et al., *Strategies for Reducing Chronic Street Homelessness* (Sacramento, Calif.: Walter R. McDonald & Associates, Inc. and The Urban Institute, 2004), xiii.

23. See the National Alliance to End Homelessness, http://www.endhome lessness.org/pages/community-plans.

24. Burt et al., *Strategies for Reducing Chronic Street Homelessness,* xxi.

25. Tsemberis and Eisenberg, "Pathways to Housing." See also William T. Armaline, "'Kids Need Structure': Negotiating Rules, Power, and Social Control in an Emergency Youth Shelter," *American Behavioral Scientist* 48, no. 8 (2005): 1124–48.

26. Burt et al., *Strategies for Reducing Chronic Street Homelessness,* xxi.

27. Ibid.

28. Ibid., 10.

29. National Archives and Records Administration, "Notice of Funding Available (NOFA) for the Continuum of Care Homeless Assistance Program," *Federal Register* 73, no. 133 (July 10, 2008): 39844.

30. United States Interagency Council on Homelessness, *The 10-Year Planning Process to End Chronic Homelessness in Your Community: A Step-by-Step Guide* (Washington, D.C., n.d.), 3.

31. Ibid., 4.

32. Kuhn and Culhane, "Applying Cluster Analysis to Test a Typology of Homelessness," 219.

33. United States Interagency Council on Homelessness, *From Good . . . to Better . . . to Great: Innovations in 10-Year Plans to End Chronic Homelessness* (Washington, D.C., n.d.).

34. Ibid.

35. National Coalition for the Homeless, *Poverty versus Pathology: What's "Chronic" about Homelessness?* (Washington, D.C., 2002).

36. Michel Foucault, "Nietzsche, Genealogy, History," in *The Foucault Reader,* ed. Paul Rabinow (New York: Pantheon, 1984), 88.

37. Culhane and Kuhn, "Patterns and Determinants of Public Shelter Utilization," 23.

38. Ibid., 41.

39. Koray Çalışkan and Michel Callon, "Economization, Part 1: Shifting Attention from the Economy towards Processes of Economization," *Economy and Society* 38, no. 3 (2009): 369–98.

40. Patricia Ticineto Clough, "Future Matters: Technoscience, Global Politics, and Cultural Criticism," *Social Text 80* 22, no. 3 (2004): 14–15.

41. The imperative of "self-work" is certainly being mobilized in other contexts—drug courts, for example. See Rebecca Tiger, *Judging Addicts: Drug Courts and Coercion in the Justice System* (New York: New York University Press, 2012).

42. Jacques Donzelot, "Michel Foucault and Liberal Intelligence," *Economy & Society* 37, no. 1 (2008): 115–34.

43. *A Plan, Not a Dream: How to End Homelessness in Ten Years* (Washington, D.C.: National Alliance to End Homelessness, 2000).

CONCLUSION

1. Les Christie, "1 Million Homes Repossessed in 2010," *CNN Money,* January 13, 2011, http://money.cnn.com/2011/01/13/real_estate/foreclosures_2010/index.htm?iid=EL.

2. Les Christie, "Foreclosures Hit Six-Year Low in 2013," *CNN Money,* January 16, 2014, http://money.cnn.com/2014/01/16/real_estate/foreclosure-crisis/.

3. Andrew Fieldhouse, "5 Years after the Great Recession, Our Economy Still Far from Recovered," *Huffington Post,* June 26, 2014, http://www.huffingtonpost.com/andrew-fieldhouse/five-years-after-the-grea_b_5530597.html.

4. Shaila Dewan, "In Many Cities, Rent Is Rising Out of Reach of Middle Class," *New York Times,* April 14, 2014.

5. Paula Chakravartty and Denise Ferreira da Silva, eds., "Race, Empire, and the Crisis of the Subprime," Special issue, *American Quarterly* 64, no. 3 (2012).

6. John Leland, "With Advocates' Help, Squatters Call Foreclosures Home," *New York Times,* April 10, 2009.

7. *Gentrification Is Dead: A Proposition* (Center for Pan-African Development, n.d.).

8. Manny Fernandez, "Once 'Very Good Rent Payers' Now Facing Eviction," *New York Times,* May 4, 2009.

9. Dennis P. Culhane and Randall Kuhn, "Patterns and Determinants of Public Shelter Utilization among Homeless Adults in Philadelphia and New York City," *Journal of Policy Analysis and Management* 17, no. 1 (1998): 23.

10. Ibid., 39–40.

11. Ibid., 26.

12. Quincy Thomas Stewart, "Swimming Upstream: Theory and Methodology in Race Research," in *White Logic, White Methods: Racism and Methodology*, ed. Tukufu Zuberi and Eduardo Bonilla-Silva (Lanham, Md.: Rowman & Littlefield Publishers, 2008), 114.

13. Paul W. Holland, "Causation and Race," in *White Logic, White Methods: Racism and Methodology*, ed. Tukufu Zuberi and Eduardo Bonilla-Silva (Lanham, Md.: Rowman & Littlefield Publishers, 2008), 100.

14. Tukufu Zuberi, "Deracializing Social Statistics: Problems in the Quantification of Race," in *White Logic, White Methods: Racism and Methodology*, ed. Tukufu Zuberi and Eduardo Bonilla-Silva (Lanham, Md.: Rowman & Littlefield Publishers, 2008), 132.

15. This chapter's title was inspired by the name of the 2009 conference of the Researchers and Academics of Colour for Equality (R.A.C.E.) Network, "Compassion, Complicity, and Conciliation: The Politics, Cultures, and Economies of 'Doing Good.'"

16. Laurie P. Cohen, "Lilly's 'Quick Cash' to Habitues of Shelters Vanishes Quickly," *Wall Street Journal*, November 14, 1996.

17. Tom L. Beauchamp et al., "Pharmaceutical Research Involving the Homeless," *Journal of Medicine and Philosophy* 27, no. 5 (2002): 555.

18. For a political economic analysis of the clinical trials industry, see Jill A. Fisher, *Medical Research for Hire: The Political Economy of Pharmaceutical Clinical Trials* (New Brunswick, N.J.: Rutgers University Press, 2008).

19. Beauchamp et al., "Pharmaceutical Research Involving the Homeless," 560.

20. I am thinking, for example, of Chela Sandoval, *Methodology of the Oppressed* (Minneapolis: University of Minnesota Press, 2000); INCITE! Women of Color Against Violence, ed., *The Revolution Will Not Be Funded: Beyond the Non-Profit Industrial Complex* (Cambridge, Mass.: South End Press, 2007).

21. See, for example, Eyal Weizman, *Hollow Land: Israel's Architecture of Occupation* (New York: Verso, 2012).

22. Craig Willse, "You Can't Go Home Again," *POZ Magazine*, January 2001.

Index

Agamben, Giorgio, 48–49, 180
anatomopolitics. *See* disciplinary power
Anderson, Nels, 56, 59
Arizona: homelessness and programs, 131–32, 135
Armaline, William, 183n5
asylums: history of, 98–99, 119; homelessness and, 99–100

bare life, 48–49, 180
Beauchamp, Tom L., 175–77
biopolitics, 26–27, 107, 179; HMIS and, 118, 125–26, 134–36; homeostatic model, 42–43; and neoliberalism, 41, 48, 50–51, 106, 163, 168; race and, 30–32, 31, 42, 82, 134, 164; state form, 35–36; state racism, 28–32; welfare state and, 37–38. *See also* biopower; Foucault, Michel
biopower, 12, 19, 25, 35, 36, 41, 181, 187n16; capitalism and, 36–37; race and, 29–31; state racism and, 28–29, 32, 40–41; versus classical power, 27. *See also* biopolitics; disciplinary power; Foucault, Michel
Bush, George W.: administration, 92, 141, 153

California Proposition 21 (Juvenile Crime Initiative), 7

California Proposition 22 (Knight Initiative), 7
capitalism and biopower, 36–37
case management, 118–17, 122–23; compliance requirements, 143, 149, 154, 183n5; compulsory services, 146–47, 150; as disciplinary power, 101–2; electronic turn, 119–20; HUD's impact on, 110–11, 159, 164; as technology of control, 140–41
chronic homelessness, 21; definitions, 52–53, 139, 160–61; economic discourse, 152–53, 156–58, 162–63, 165–68; history of term, 151–52, 160–61; HUD initiatives, 139, 153–54, 156–58; impact on service provision, 154–55; media discourse, 153; race and, 152, 163–64, 172–73, 205n9; in research, 152–53
Clough, Patricia Ticineto, 29, 31, 44, 59, 71–72, 78, 165–66
Columbus, Ohio: homelessness and programs, 133
Community Mental Health Act of 1963, 98–99
Connell, Raewyn, 60, 62, 64
Continuum of Care, 103, 116, 121, 129–30, 132, 135, 143, 206
Culhane, Dennis, 152–53, 157, 160, 163–64, 172–73
culture of poverty discourse, 66, 68, 73, 194n26

CRAIG WILLSE is assistant professor of cultural studies at George Mason University.